THE GAME CHANGER

How Harry Reid Remade the Rules and Showed Democrats How to Fight

JON RALSTON

SIMON & SCHUSTER
New York Amsterdam/Antwerp London
Toronto Sydney/Melbourne New Delhi

Simon & Schuster
1230 Avenue of the Americas
New York, NY 10020

First Simon & Schuster hardcover edition January 2026

Interior design by Wendy Blum

Manufactured in the United States of America

10 9 8 7 6 5 4 3 2 1

Library of Congress Cataloging-in-Publication data is available.

ISBN 978-1-9821-9441-3
ISBN 978-1-9821-9443-7 (ebook)

To Sara,
who makes everything better,
and Jordana,
who lights up every day.

CONTENTS

CONTENTS

THE GAME CHANGER

PROLOGUE

Harry Reid was despondent.

It was 1979, and the chairman of the Nevada Gaming Commission had just learned that Kansas City mobsters caught on FBI wiretaps had referred to someone they controlled as "Cleanface." Reid knew—as did many others—they meant him. It was an ironic reference to the thirty-nine-year-old's pristine image. The implication of the wiretaps to the feds was that Reid was unclean: the state's top casino regulator could be—and had been—compromised.

After the wiretaps surfaced, raising questions about his integrity, Reid reported a death threat to the FBI, with the caller saying he would be "going out on a table." Armed guards were stationed at his home. For Reid, it had become too much to bear.

The chairman went to visit the man who had appointed him, former governor Mike O'Callaghan, who had left office a few months earlier. Reid believed he owed it to O'Callaghan, his mentor since high school, to tell him to his face that he was leaving the job that the governor had given him to resurrect his public career after two devastating campaign losses for US Senate (1974) and Las Vegas mayor (1975). He could not credibly regulate the state's most important industry while this cloud hung over him.

O'Callaghan was having none of it. The gruff, blunt veteran of the Korean

War, who had only one leg after being wounded in combat, knew that if Reid stepped down, he would always be seen as a tool of the mob.

"If you resign it'll be the biggest mistake you ever make in your life," Reid recalled the governor saying.

Reid remained on the gaming regulatory panel for two more years and eventually was cleared of any wrongdoing. He never looked back.

This was the pivotal moment in the political life of a man who would go on to become the most powerful elected official in Nevada history and one of the most consequential national leaders of the twenty-first century. Reid would use the gaming commission as a springboard to run for a newly created congressional seat in 1982, which eventually led to the US Senate, where he would serve for thirty years and become the Democratic leader for the last third of his tenure.

Reid's career can be seen like the fifteen marathons he ran—an endurance test where he worked harder and stayed longer than anyone else, always playing the long game. He came from nothing and nowhere—Searchlight, Nevada, a hopelessly poor hamlet not far from Las Vegas that gave him a will to succeed despite an alcoholic father and what could barely be called a home. Reid would survive taking on the mob, being investigated by the state and the FBI, barely winning reelection to the Senate in 1998, and getting elected to a fifth term in 2010 in a race few thought he could win.

Reid's indomitability after that moment of doubt in 1979 became the signature feature of a remarkable career in which he became one of the most accomplished and polarizing figures of his time. His willingness to join any fight he believed was worthwhile—even if others did not think it was worth the risk—and his ability to rally his troops to the cause changed the culture of Washington, for good and ill. From that day forward, Reid showed no fear, becoming almost as ruthless as the mob bosses whom he helped drive from the state, a political godfather whose blessing would be sought by hundreds of Nevada elected officials and candidates. Like a Mafia chieftain, Reid put family above all else—and he was occasionally faulted for doing so. He somehow found a way to compartmentalize, or perhaps rationalize, in a way *The Godfather*'s Michael Corleone would understand: not personal, just business.

"I did what no one else would do," Reid often said, which he meant as a simple statement of fact, but it also revealed how little self-reflection he did in the pursuit of his goals. He hectored bankers to save a casino company and perhaps the Las Vegas Strip during the Great Recession; he intimidated hedge fund managers to kill coal plants planned by Nevada's electric monopoly; and he legally bought senators' votes with lucre for their states to ensure the Affordable Care Act became the law of the land. There were few lines he would not cross or rules he would not bend.

But Reid also performed private deeds of kindness. As a former Capitol policeman, he treated his security detail with respect, insisting they eat dinner inside the same restaurants where he dined and picking up the tab. He had a genuine relationship with Astrid Silva, an undocumented Dreamer who came to the United States as a four-year-old and became a pen pal and friend. When a staffer kept botching phone numbers of people for him to call back, Reid called her aside, discovered she was dyslexic, and comforted her, marveling at how difficult it must have been for her to achieve what she had.

"Harry was tough as nails, a fighter to his core, but one of the most compassionate individuals you could ever imagine," said his friend New York senator Chuck Schumer, who succeeded him as Democratic leader.

Reid altered the course of history for his state and for the country on more than one occasion. It wasn't just the health care law named for President Barack Obama that would not have passed without his persistence. He persuaded Jim Jeffords, a Vermont Republican, to caucus with the Democrats as the millennium dawned, which drastically changed the Senate dynamic. Reid, in partnership with Nancy Pelosi, the woman he lionized as the greatest Speaker in history, also fought off President George W. Bush's efforts to privatize Social Security. Reid upended Senate tradition and created a historical hinge in 2013, changing the filibuster rules to ensure President Obama's judicial nominees could be considered, but he also opened the door to Republicans' turning the tables when they regained control of the Senate, invoking the precedent to push through President Trump's Supreme Court nominees.

Closer to home, Reid created an unmatched environmental legacy while also relishing being the protector of the mining industry—a needle few others could have threaded. He also changed a virtually all-white Nevada judiciary into a rainbow, brushing aside accusations of identity politics over qualifications. It is not a stretch to say that every Nevada politician of the last half century in both parties has a Harry Reid story to tell—tales of kindness or nastiness, elevation or defenestration. He made or broke more careers than any Nevada politician in history—including indisputable giants such as the execrable senator Pat McCarran, a McCarthy-era anti-Semite and nativist whose name was erased from the Las Vegas airport and replaced with Reid's shortly before his death in 2021.

Reid left an indelible mark on the national scene, too, the pro-life Mormon who came to lead a pro-choice party, a restrictionist on immigration for the first half of his career who advocated for the DREAM Act, a Democratic darling of the National Rifle Association who later became an advocate for gun control, and a man who once thought being gay was a choice before he spoke at a gay staffer's wedding and later supported same-sex marriage.

That last switch he explained in typical Reid style:

"I came to the conclusion: An individual will not go through the hell they have had to go through during that time, being gay. It would not be a choice. They did it because they couldn't help themselves."

The protean Reid, born on the cusp of World War II in an oft-ridiculed small state, changed as Nevada's population became larger and more diverse, his positions flipping as his stature grew. Reid insisted he evolved, arguing that remaining intellectually static was the mark of a narrow thinker.

It's hard to miss the essential duality of a man who wrote thousands of handwritten notes throughout his life to colleagues, many of them heartfelt, often signing off with "your forever friend," while he also brusquely and dismissively talked about his political foes, calling a sitting Republican president a "liar" and "loser" and a Republican presidential candidate a tax dodger sans evidence. When he ended some of his scrawled thank-you missives "I have a long memory," that, too, had a double meaning. Reid, who had close to photographic recall, remembered who had been true to him but also who had wronged him. "Don't worry," he once told a staffer, "vengeance is in my soul."

Through his half century in public life, Reid remained a man of striking contradictions. He was a devout Mormon, who regularly attended church and read scripture every night, but who would not hesitate to go biblical against political enemies. He was against abortion as a matter of religion, but he became a favorite of women's groups because he did not stifle pro-choice advocates in his caucus. He was as grounded a person as you could ever meet, but he also believed in UFOs—so much so that he helped secretly funnel a fortune to a Pentagon program to study sightings.

Despite his often awkward interactions with the media, Reid also cultivated close friendships with those who ran journalism outlets in Nevada, including Hank and Brian Greenspun of the *Las Vegas Sun* (Reid helped Brian Greenspun get on the board of Barrick Gold, a huge mining company). For a politician who eked out victories, every little bit helped.

Reid lived his public life in prose but his private life in poetry, including a sixty-two-year love affair with his wife, Landra, his closest friend and counselor, who helped protect him and the family. Reid accomplished all he did by combining his work ethic with his transactional instincts, by hiring the best people he could find, promoting remarkable women into his inner circle on Capitol Hill and Nevada, by making connections with his colleagues and private sector people who could help him retain power, and by encouraging the kind of loyalty that is enduring and priceless. No one ever spent more time on the Senate floor finding out what his colleagues needed—displaying a disarming style and wry humor behind the scenes that contrasted with his awkward, occasionally gaffe-prone public appearances. (Once, when Reid arrived at what he did not realize was a toga-themed fundraiser in a suit, the greeter asked whether he could take the senator's clothes. "How many of you are there?" the former boxer deadpanned.)

"He was very secure in who he was in a town with very insecure people," said Kristen Orthman, his former spokeswoman. Echoed Kai Anderson, his erstwhile legislative director who went on to run lobbying behemoth Cassidy & Associates: "Much of what he got done, he got done because he didn't worry about what people thought of him."

What Reid cared about was the acquisition of power and using it to the ends he saw were justified—for his country, his state, his family, his friends. While he was a long-distance runner, he also sprinted through most of his days, hanging up on people to save time and meet his packed schedule.

Not having a rearview mirror is dangerous, though, and the senator had a few crashes. His Reidisms became legendary and infamous, from declaring the Iraq War lost to publicly wondering what could ameliorate the smell of tourists in the Capitol to musing that a Black man from Illinois—one who spoke with a "Negro dialect" if he needed to—could be elected president. Often, as with his unsubstantiated claims about Republican presidential hopeful Mitt Romney's taxes, there was a method to his madness, but Reid also acknowledged that he was impulsive and counted on his stellar staff to clean up after him. ("I can't believe him sometimes," one staffer wrote in a 2014 internal email after he spoke to the Asian Chamber of Commerce in Las Vegas and said: "I don't think you're smarter than anybody else, but you've convinced a lot of us you are," and "One problem that I've had today is keeping my Wongs straight." He later apologized.)

All of this had benefits and drawbacks, with his duality reflected in the polar responses to him. Reid was beloved by his staff, by progressives (some of the time), by many of his colleagues, by President Obama. But this product of a small town became so reviled in rural Nevada that a man once told one of Reid's opponents, "There are only two people I hate—the man who shot my dog and Harry Reid."

Reid, the Senate maestro who also was part of the dysfunctional mess the

Senate became, was a survivor against the odds, just like the town where he grew up. Reid wrote a book about Searchlight in 1998 called *The Camp That Didn't Fail*, a turgid historical tome but one he treasured. Without understanding the place of his birth and how it began to shape him, Harry Reid himself could not comprehend where he came from and, more important, where he was going.

Reid might not have looked back, but he always had Searchlight on his mind.

CHAPTER ONE

THE BOY WHO WOULDN'T FAIL

Harry Mason Reid was born shortly after World War II began on December 2, 1939, in a speck in the Nevada desert that was as far from his future home in the Washington, DC, Ritz-Carlton as anyone could have imagined.

A once-thriving mining camp before the turn of the century, about fifty-five miles south of Las Vegas and twenty miles east of the California border, Searchlight had very little of anything when Reid was born. About two hundred people. No paved roads. No churches. No radio station or newspaper. No economy to speak of, outside of a few brothels. And no hospitals—Reid was born in his grandmother's two-room shack, attended to by one of the few physicians who occasionally lived in the little burgh.

The origin of the town's name is unknown. Though there are several stories, the most accepted is attributed to George Frederick Colton, a Utah prospector who first discovered a lucrative gold vein in 1897 and exclaimed, "There is something here, boys, but it would take a searchlight to find it."

The Reid family arrived in Searchlight in 1902 when mining claims were proliferating at strikes with names such as Blossom, Quartette, Duplex, and Crown King. John Reid, the future senator's paternal grandfather, and his wife, Harriet, moved there from California. John, who had many jobs in his itinerant life, came for the prospect of gold, as did many others.

John failed to strike gold and returned to California in 1910, and his wife gave birth to a son, Harry Vincent Reid, in 1913 at Cajon Pass. For reasons the future senator never knew, the Reids returned to Searchlight in 1927.

Despite many setbacks, the town was still there, presaging the life of its favorite son, the ultimate political survivor. In 1927, only fifty people lived there. By the time Harry Reid Jr. was born twelve years later, the town had declined, the mines had run dry, the railroad had been abandoned, and only prostitution and Searchlight's proximity to California and military bases kept it alive.

Reid's first home was built out of vestigial railroad ties, doused in creosote to repel termites and held together by chicken wire. A plaster coating was later applied by his father. Harry was the third of four children—Don was twelve years older, Dale was nine years his senior, and twenty-two months after Harry came into the world, Larry was born.

The house, like many in Searchlight in those days, had no running water, no toilet. Young Harry had to trudge to an outhouse, often in the freezing desert cold. He slept in an eight-by-eleven-foot room with Larry. There was one other bedroom and a front room, slightly larger than the tiny bedrooms, with linoleum floors that Reid remembered as always being icy. Six people crammed into a shack that, despite Harry Sr.'s efforts, looked as if it could collapse with a huff and a puff. The yard was just rocks.

Inez Orena and Harry Reid Sr. met when she moved to Searchlight from Sandy, Utah, with her husband and two boys, but her marriage didn't last. She was twenty-eight and Harry Sr. was twenty-six when Harry Jr. was born. Harry Sr. already was raising Don and Dale as if they were his own, and the boys never thought of themselves as half brothers.

"We were very protective of each other," Reid recalled.

What Reid did not know—and would only learn decades later in his early thirties while going through his father's papers—was that his parents were not yet married when he and Larry were born. They did so when Reid was five. He rarely talked about it, and when he discovered they were born out of wedlock, Reid called his younger brother, and his salutation was simple and emblematic of the deadpan humor that would become one of his hallmarks: "Hey, you little bastard!"

NINE DAYS AFTER Harry Jr. was born, his father nearly died.

Being a hard rock miner was strenuous and dangerous work, going underground, navigating treacherous shafts, sometimes hundreds of feet deep, and setting explosive devices in hopes of finding treasure. On December 11, 1939, Reid's father was in an eighty-five-foot-deep shaft inside a mine owned by Bi-Metals Mining Company near Kingman, Arizona. He was planting dynamite in holes up and down the shaft, with the bottom one designed to set off the rest. He had finished eleven of them and was starting to climb back up when the first fuse malfunctioned. A stick of dynamite exploded and Reid's father was catapulted into the air, separating the sole from one of his shoes. He lay in darkness, as his carbide lamp had been blown to smithereens, badly injured with three hundred shards in his body. The ladder, damaged in the blast, was barely usable.

A courageous coworker, Carl Myers, who had been working twenty-five feet above him, climbed down to pick up the six-foot, 180-pound Harry Sr., carefully navigating the shattered ladder and carrying him out of the mine. The ten other sticks of dynamite exploded just as Myers and Harry Sr. escaped.

"Searchlight Miner Rescues Pal in Face of Death by Dynamite," read one headline. Mason Reid, Harry Sr.'s brother and from whence Harry Jr. got his middle name, had died a few years earlier at the age of twenty-six in a similar explosion, his skull "fearfully crushed," as a local newspaper reported.

For some time after the close call, Harry Sr. would lie on the couch as Inez picked out remnants of embedded rocks that would rise to the surface of his flesh while the young child watched. Despite the risks, Reid's father had a strange affinity for the work in the mines, overseen by sometimes unscrupulous owners whose checks occasionally bounced. Harry Sr. struggled to find employment in the declining industry in and around Searchlight. In the first year of Harry Jr.'s life, his father reported working twenty-one weeks, making only $432, equivalent to about $9,500 today.

Harry Reid Sr. was extraordinarily strong, with an upper body like a weight lifter, easily able to lift a fifty-gallon water barrel and put it on a truck or carry a couple of unwieldy, heavy railroad ties, one under each arm. He was so athletic and burly that he could walk on his hands, his son would tell his children. That strength was an undeniable asset underground, where Harry Sr. eschewed precautions taken by other miners to help stay balanced in those narrow, dark shafts.

But it was more than his physical prowess that made Harry Reid Sr. a skilled miner. Although he never made it to high school, he was quite intelligent, and his memory was remarkable.

"He could go down underground, take a compass with him, and he could come up with a piece of graph paper and he could draw what the mine was like underneath," Reid recalled.

Harry Sr. was a self-taught miner, just as he schooled himself to become a gifted carpenter, blacksmith, and welder. The son soon came to realize the only time his father was really happy was when he was belowground, so he would tag along, with his own lunchbox and mining tools, and spend time with his dad. Young Harry changed the carbide in his father's light, lit cigarettes for him; as he got older, he helped his father shovel and later even worked by himself in the mines as a teen. They would return home to the shack, filthy from the day's work. His taciturn father didn't impart much to his son, but he would often tell him to never do anything "half-assed. You either do it or don't do it." That lesson, it would become clear later, took.

HARRY REID SR. was withdrawn and cold much of the time, and the laconic son said he often felt he was like his father in that way, once saying "if quiet is a heritable trait, we got quiet from my father."

In contrast to her husband, Inez Orena Reid was gregarious and loved being around people. She would later cheer for her son at his football and baseball games, so loudly that he could hear her cries of support. His father was never there, but young Harry didn't resent it. "I just knew that's who he was," he remembered. His mother tried her best to fill the gaps.

Inez, he would learn, had been raised in the Mormon Church, never finished high school, and had little formal education. She was a redhead who liked to sing despite bad or missing teeth, mostly because she was smashed in the face with a softball during a game in Utah and could not afford proper dental care. (Later, after he got some money from working at a gas station, Harry Reid would buy his mother a set of teeth for $250.) Inez helped the family income by becoming the town laundress, often taking in the wash from the brothels in Searchlight. She kept her supplies in a cubbyhole in the house, pulling them out whenever a dealer in the casino or prostitute in the brothel needed something washed.

There were no stores in Searchlight, so when the children needed clothes, Inez ordered from a catalog. When they needed groceries, they would make the long drive in a borrowed un-air-conditioned car to Henderson or Las Vegas.

When Inez wasn't wrapped up in the latest Zane Grey adventure novel, she and Harry Sr. would go out to drink. Often, they would both come home drunk, and sometimes Harry Sr. would become violent. The brothers occasionally would have to break up the fights.

Inez would eventually become the rock her son needed, encouraging him at every turn, the mooring to steady him during his childhood. Decades later, in 2005, he would pen a handwritten note to Republican senator Trent Lott after the Mississippian's mother died, writing, among other things: "I wish you could have known my mom, she was the best."

EVERYONE IN SEARCHLIGHT, it seemed, had a sobriquet. Big Nose Pete. Cripple Jack. Big John. They called young Harry Reid "Pinky" because of his reddish complexion and strawberry-blond hair. Years later, some of his relatives would call him a shortened version, "Uncle Pink."

The school in Searchlight had two rooms, one for elementary and one for middle school. There was no high school. Often when he spoke of those days, Reid told the same joke. "My eighth-grade class graduated six," Reid said. "I graduated in the top third of my class."

Having a December birthday, Reid was always the youngest among his schoolmates. Some of the kids were a year or more older than him, and often much bigger, so he had to try harder to succeed in academics and sports.

Reid never went hungry, but he had friends who did. One day, at a friend's house, he opened the refrigerator, which had only a plastic bottle of syrup. His friend drank from the bottle because he was famished.

It didn't hit home until decades later, when Reid's niece sent him pictures of the place he called home, just how Dickensian a childhood he had lived. "I could not believe I was raised that way," he said.

There wasn't much to do in Searchlight, so Reid did what he could to stay occupied. He carved out ditches for power lines. He dug graves with his dad at the cemetery. And he (illegally) drove a water truck for some men drilling a well.

He spent a fair amount of time with his paternal grandmother, Harriet, the only grandparent he knew. When he was a preteen, she told him that if he could kill a rabbit, she would cook it for him. Reid found one of his older brother's .22 caliber rifles and off he went. He saw a rabbit, shot, and missed. He then fired a second bullet and nicked the rabbit. Showing the doggedness that would serve him well later, he chased the rabbit until he caught it, then brought it home and skinned it, and his grandmother cooked it. It was a rabbit stew he would always remember.

In a town that offered little hope for escape, young Harry Reid found his at a brothel-casino owned by the man he called "the biggest whoremonger in town," Willie Martello. Martello was an outsized character, a pre–Las Vegas Strip visionary who saw an opportunity to pick up patrons from Los Angeles from the military bases across the state line. After the war, Martello purchased an existing hotel, renamed it after his favorite beer, and the El Rey Club was born. It was a pretty drab place, but Martello added many amenities, including Searchlight's first in-ground swimming pool. While kids across the country were learning to swim in YMCA and community pools, Reid was schooled at Martello's brothel.

The El Rey also was a refuge for Reid, as Martello let him into the club when there were shows, beginning what would become a lifelong love of music. The boy would listen to what he called "good Western music," such as Ernest Tubb, aka the Texas Troubadour, a country music pioneer.

Martello also became something of a mentor, even a father figure for a boy with an often absent one. Once, as Reid recalled, "my friend and I came on the El Rey property and we saw cases of empty bottles. You could return them and get some money, so we loaded up our vehicle as far as it would go and traded in the bottles. Next time [Martello] saw me, he told me, 'I know you stole those bottles from me . . . If you wanted something, all you had to do was ask me. You've got a future ahead of you. Always be honest in everything you do.'"

He got a lecture on honesty from a brothel owner. "My childhood was not one where I had lessons in morality around the dinner table at night or Sunday school or church," he said. Instead, he learned from whoever was willing to dispense wisdom. And Martello was willing.

The young boy also retreated into books. His sullen father read a lot, although never to his son. But Harry Jr. found books in the school library that would transport him out of Searchlight, especially those by Jack London. He fell in love with *The Call of the Wild* and *White Fang*. It sparked a lifetime love of reading for a man who became a senator and would much rather stay at home and read a book than go to dinner at the Capital Grille.

Reid had one other way to escape the quotidian drudgery of small-town America, a way to connect to the outside world he knew so little about: his little 1940s radio.

It was frustrating at times because holding the signal in middle-of-nowhere Searchlight was not easy. Reid learned what evil lurks in the hearts of men by listening to *The Shadow*. *Gunsmoke* and *Dragnet* were two of his favorites. And once in a while, Reid would listen to a man he would encounter in a very different role many years later, a broadcaster named Ronald Reagan.

What really captivated the young boy, though, was listening to baseball, beginning a lifelong passion for the sport. An eight-year-old Reid fell in love with the Cleveland Indians when they won the World Series in 1948. He could name the entire starting lineup decades later. Reid, who had never seen a Black person in Searchlight, also became aware of the man who had broken the sport's color barrier, Jackie Robinson.

"As I look back on my childhood in Searchlight, Jackie Robinson's impact on me went beyond what he did in any Major League Baseball stadium," Reid said at a March 2, 2005, ceremony to present the Congressional Gold Medal to Robinson's widow, Rachel. "Because along with giving me something to dream about on summer afternoons in the Nevada desert, Jackie Robinson brought the civil rights movement to my hometown—not with speeches or demonstration but by example. While he was playing second base twenty-five hundred miles away in Brooklyn, he was also opening minds and reshaping attitudes in rural Searchlight and towns just like it across America."

GROWING UP IN Searchlight, Harry Reid had no politics, no religion, and no health care.

The Reids didn't need to adhere to the old dictum about never discussing politics or religion at the dinner table. Neither subject arose very often. It's not that his parents didn't believe in God; they just didn't believe in talking about it, and they were not part of any organized religion.

The only thing approximating religion in his home, he said, was Franklin Roosevelt, whom his mother loved. Inez hung on the wall a navy-blue stitched pillowcase with a fringe and it had that famous FDR wartime quote embroidered into it in bright yellow: "We can. We will. We must."

The resoluteness of the sentiment stuck with Reid, whose entire career would be infused with that mantra, one he would repeat in many a speech.

Young Harry was a hearty boy who rarely got sick, which was lucky because health care was nonexistent. There were no doctors or dentists in town. (The kids often helped their parents pull teeth with pliers.) In those days, the state of Nevada had a tuberculosis wagon that tested people for the disease, and once Inez tested positive. But with no doctors nearby, the family just waited. It turned out to be a false positive.

Reid's younger brother, Larry, was not so lucky. He broke his leg in a bicycle mishap and lay in bed for weeks. Even if there had been a doctor to see, there was no money for one. Harry remembered that he couldn't even touch Larry's bed because he was in so much pain. Larry's leg never healed correctly, and he developed a slight bend.

The only time Reid could remember the family seeing a doctor was when he was about ten years old and he was deathly ill. "Could you take Pinky to the hospital?" his mother asked some friends who had a car. They went to Henderson and a doctor immediately operated on the boy to remove a growth on his large intestine. "I would have died if they hadn't taken me there," he said. "But health care should not be a crapshoot. You should be able to go to the doctor when you're sick."

What did not kill him gave him a strong belief that no one should be deprived of health care, no matter their financial circumstances.

REID LOVED HIS hometown for the crucible that forged his character, but he hated how insular it was. "In my youthful mind, I knew one thing, that I wanted to get the hell out of Searchlight," he said a few months before he died. But while he wanted to escape, Reid had a paradoxical reverence and affection for the place. Besides writing a book about Searchlight, Reid would have his campaign teams create ads about it, he named his political action committee (Searchlight Leadership Fund) after it, an elementary school there would bear his name, and he built a home there and stayed until 2014. He hated the isolation and the narrow-mindedness, but he loved the toughness, the relentlessness, the determination it instilled in him. The fabric of Searchlight was stitched into Reid's character and eventually, he would embrace it.

Reid came to be proud of his provenance, boasting about it, telling stories to anyone who would listen, even taking a C-SPAN crew for a tour in 1998. And he would defend it, too. In 1986, after an AP reporter described Searchlight as a "one-street hellhole," petitions of protests were drafted, Reid got involved, and the managing editor of the news service would pen an apology to the townsfolk for the "unfortunate characterization," copying Reid on his missive.

In his Capitol office, Reid kept a picture of the house where he was raised because, he would say in a speech on the Senate floor commemorating the 110th anniversary of the town in 2008, "it serves as a reminder of how my hometown has shaped my work on behalf of Nevada throughout my career in Congress."

Reid's will to survive, whether it was rebounding from political setbacks or pancreatic cancer, came from a place that would create and then test his character. He would continuously strive to be, as his father would have said, "a real man," willing to do whatever needed to be done.

Reid relished being underestimated, knowing that he had to keep moving forward, without fear and often with humor, to escape his hometown and yet never forget what he learned there. Searchlight became a place after he ascended to the pinnacle of power that governors, senators, and many others visited to pay homage, to talk to Pinky in his home.

The Searchlight years clearly affected Reid much later when he arrived in DC. It's hard not to trace his standing up for—some would say shilling for—the mining industry at every turn to thoughts of his father. When he turned thirteen, Reid would leave Searchlight, at least for most of his weeks. But there would always be no place like home. You could take the boy out of Searchlight, but you would never take Searchlight out of the man.

The teen was more concerned with athletics early in his high school life than anything else, including religion or academics. “I was not a good student,” Reid remembered. “I didn’t care, didn’t try, it didn’t mean anything to me. I was a baseball and football player.”

Only later in his high school life, with a girlfriend and teacher as motivators, would Reid apply himself to his studies. As Vincent memorably said of his friend: “He fell in love with being smart.” Or as another high school pal, J. J. Balk, put it: “He was not a naturally smart guy. And he would admit that. But he would overwhelm himself with knowledge. His entire life. And that’s how he became who he was.”

But for now, sports came first.

His older brothers, Dale and Don, had been excellent athletes, but Harry had none of his half sibling’s natural abilities. He played baseball and football at Basic, but he was never a star.

His high school friends remembered that Reid was as hard a worker as anyone on the team. “Whatever he did in real life was the way he approached athletics,” his lifelong friend Don Wilson recalled. “He was a hustler. He had a dog in him. He would not quit on anything. And he just kept getting better.”

He took on the position of batting practice catcher, a thankless, invisible role. On the football team, because he now weighed about 190, he was put on the offensive line as a left guard. He would stay after practice and run twenty laps because he was slow and wanted to get in better shape.

“To be a good athlete, you have to have speed,” Reid said. “I never had speed. And so I made up for it with vigor and tenacity.”

Reid’s dogged approach paid off: after his sophomore year, he started every game as an offensive lineman.

Many years later, when he ran for lieutenant governor, Reid would change his high school position in his campaign biography to right guard, fearful that his opponents would make hay out of him being to the left. Wasn’t he afraid that someone would check the yearbook, where number 65 is pictured and labeled as “left guard”? He scoffed. “No one’s gonna go check the yearbook,” Reid said.

Reid also found another sport in high school that he could do well in. That was politics.

Reid won his first student council race as a sophomore, running for treasurer of the junior class. Reid would call it "the most important election I was ever involved in."

The man who would later win two congressional and five Senate races said that victory changed his trajectory at Basic High School. "It doesn't sound like much, junior class treasurer," Reid recalled. "But when I was elected junior class treasurer, I finally felt I had been accepted by my peers."

LANDRA

IF REID TOLD the story once, he told it a thousand times. It became known among his friends and his staff as the "short shorts" story.

Landra Joy Gould, then a sophomore at Basic High School, lived on a busy street in Henderson. Reid, then a junior, was in a car driving by one day and: "There she is, out in the yard, washing the family car," Reid recalled. Gould was five feet tall, with dark brown eyes and raven hair. But what Reid remembered was: "She was in short shorts." He was smitten at first sight, the beginning of what would become a long, long story.

Landra Gould was born in Los Angeles on June 19, 1940, the only child of Ukrainian Jewish immigrants, Earl and Ruth, who had separately come to the United States to escape anti-Semitism and get an education. Her parents met in Los Angeles, where he had an office near a boxing ring and was a physician to many of the famous fighters of the day.

Doc Gould, as everyone called him, moved his family to Las Vegas when Landra was ten. In an earlier sojourn there with relatives, she had learned to swim in the Flamingo Hotel pool—the place built by the mobster Bugsy Siegel.

The Gould family bounced around from Las Vegas to Henderson for a few years before settling in the latter city, where Doc Gould was the only chiropractor. Soon after that first sighting, Reid asked Landra on a date.

He took her to a movie at the Victory Theater in Henderson, but they had a little trouble getting there. Reid, of course, did not have a car, so he borrowed one from a friend. But the starter didn't work, so they had to get the car rolling down a hill, and he popped the clutch into gear. They hit it off and began dating, but soon there would be trouble.

Doc Gould, who had become one of Henderson's most prominent citizens, wanted his daughter to marry the proverbial nice Jewish boy. They were fine if she was having fun with the boy without religion, but that would not last.

Landra, though, was smitten. "He was funny," she remembered thinking after that first date. "He was quick and witty and had a dry sense of humor."

She remembered something else, too. "He was very kind. He didn't have a lot of friends. But he always reached out to people who didn't have friends."

Perhaps this was the soul of an elected official in waiting, always trying to expand his network.

The relationship that began with the short shorts sighting lasted a lifetime, Landra's presence evident in everything Reid did. She was in key strategy meetings, often influencing his decisions from personnel moves to Supreme Court nominees. He would go home to be with her rather than spend time at events. His personal email for many, many years was landrajoy@aol.com. And whenever she was in distress—as when she'd fallen ill, or was in a terrible car accident (she was in a couple)—those around him said he was inconsolable, almost unable to function, unrecognizable from his relentlessly focused persona. Whatever artifice or deception Reid would later be accused of, this love affair was real, a sixty-two-year marriage that defied all the odds, especially in the political world.

"It's the purest love I've ever seen," said Rebecca Kirszner Katz, a longtime staffer, shortly before he died. "They are just soulmates in a way that a lot of politicians pretend to be. They thoroughly love being in each other's presence. He still watches her in a room when she walks in, after all these years."

BY HIS SENIOR year, Reid had a girlfriend, he was a starter on the football team, and he was a big man on campus. He was urged by classmates to run against the class president, Russell Williams, and he tabbed his good friend Rey Martinez to run his race. Landra helped him write a speech to get votes. He simply outworked a more popular kid who was considered a shoo-in, and with Martinez's help, he won.

Reid's senior year was one of glory days, and not just because he led the class. In perhaps another hint of his career to come, Reid tested his acting chops, playing fourth-billed Dr. John Sully in the senior play, *Double Door.* It was a mystery thriller set in New York about the machinations of a prominent family that lead to a murder plot. Reid's wry self-review years later: "I dazzled as Dr. John Sully."

BIG MIKE

THE MOST SIGNIFICANT event of Reid's senior year, though, and one that would change the course of his life, came when a man named Donal Neil "Mike" O'Callaghan arrived to teach history at Basic High. Neither of them knew it then, but a partnership was about to form that would last for a half century. Not only would O'Callaghan set him on the road to Capitol Hill, but without him, Reid may never have ascended to the pinnacle of his career. It was a personal and political symbiosis that endured until his mentor's death in 2004. O'Callaghan helped mold him in his early years, later saved him from political oblivion, then guided him throughout his career.

A native of Wisconsin, O'Callaghan moved to Nevada in 1956. He had lost his left leg when a mortar exploded during the Korean War—he received Bronze and Silver Stars for his bravery. O'Callaghan recovered from his wounds, obtained a wooden leg he would wear for the rest of his life, and managed to finish his studies at the University of Idaho, receiving a bachelor's degree in education. He arrived at Basic High to teach history and government, and his life would soon become entwined with the new student body president.

Reid and his cronies didn't think much of the new teacher when they first set eyes on him, just a guy with a limp and a comb-over. But that would change a couple of days later.

A classmate had just clobbered a smaller kid when O'Callaghan walked up to him and said, as Reid remembered it: "I think you're chickenshit. You beat up on somebody smaller than you. I bet you're afraid to come down to the Boys Club after school and get into the ring with me."

The bully couldn't say no, so he and many of O'Callaghan's students trudged to the Boys Club gym. "They get into the ring with their boxing gloves on," Reid began, "and if the fight lasted thirty seconds, I'm exaggerating. He hit [that bully] so hard that he hit his head on the [floor of the] ring. O'Callaghan thought he had killed him."

Suddenly, Reid was interested in boxing and his new teacher.

They had daily contact because O'Callaghan was an adviser to the student council. Reid looked up to the war hero, and O'Callaghan saw something in the young man who was not the best athlete but, O'Callaghan would later write, "displayed grit, eagerness, and a fierce competitive spirit that more than made up for his physical limitations."

In the foreword to Reid's book about Searchlight, O'Callaghan wrote: "There was always something different about Harry, and I think, now, that it must have been the spirit of the mines in Searchlight, something raw and untamed and confident. He had no fear."

O'Callaghan trained his boxing corps by having them run down the road toward Railroad Pass, about seven and a half miles from Henderson. The teacher would drive a car behind his boys, honking if they were going too slow, pushing them to go faster.

Reid's weight made him a heavyweight, but O'Callaghan knew what might happen if he went against actual fighters in that class, so he became very protective of his young protégé—an instinct that would be evident for decades to follow.

"The Golden Gloves came up, and Mike was teaching us and he knew who Harry's opponent was going to be," high school pal J. J. Balk remembered. "And he chose to keep Harry out of the fight because he knew he was going to get hurt."

Serious boxing would have to wait. (Later, Reid would fight in the Golden Gloves, losing in a title fight after cutting his foe, who wanted to win more, as Reid saw it. He called it a "great lesson to me and I tried to never let it happen again in life, that anyone would want to win more than I.") For now, the senior class president was content to improve in football and baseball. He dreamed of being a professional athlete, and he was not ready to give that up just yet.

By the end of his senior year, Reid had quite the list of accomplishments, the Class of '57 yearbook overflowing with pictures of the class leader. He made the honor roll, attended Boys State (he would be elected mayor, an irony that would become apparent a couple of decades later), received an Elks Leadership award, was in Spanish Club, and was a finalist for an award at the Sun Youth Forum put on by the Las Vegas newspaper. Reid, even though he never talked about it later, also ran track and played basketball and was a member of the Lettermen's Club for the best athletes. He was also proud of the honor his classmates bestowed on him when they voted him "Most Humorous," which may well surprise people (except those who really knew him). His student body presidency featured the inaugural Student Council Conventions, with Basic taking the lead in assembling student body officers from around the county.

Reid won a scholarship to the College of Southern Utah in Cedar City, a two-and-a-half-hour drive from Southern Nevada, to play football and baseball. Before he could go, though, he had to find money for tuition. Even with the scholarship, he needed to cover what the athletic grant did not. That's where O'Callaghan came in—he rounded up some local businessmen to pool their resources to bridge the gap.

Reid wanted Landra to come with him—and she wanted to go—but Doc Gould put his foot down once he realized this was not a mere high school romance. She would stay home and attend UNLV on an academic scholarship, but the relationship did not abate. "My dad kind of went crazy and did some foolish, foolish things," Landra said. "He caused all kinds of trouble—tear up letters, hang up the phone while I was talking to [Reid]."

Doc Gould went so far as to tell his daughter that if she planned to marry Reid, he would have a traditional Jewish funeral for her. She would be dead to him.

Indeed, Doc Gould was so determined to squelch the romance that once while Reid was home from school and arrived at the house for a date, they came to blows.

As another couple waited in the car, Gould, who had a flair for the theatrical, accosted Reid and told him he could not take out his daughter. The two began shoving and eventually, either from a blow or a slip, the doctor was on the ground.

DURING THIS TIME, Reid was undergoing some rude awakenings of his own. When he arrived on campus at the College of Southern Utah in 1957, the seventeen-year-old felt out of place.

"I went up to Utah and all these Mormon men had been away on Mormon missions, and they had beards and families," as he put it. "It was like putting a kid in with a bunch of adults."

As if that weren't disorienting enough, Reid's athletic career—or his idea of one to come—evaporated. He almost immediately injured his foot in football, sustaining nerve damage, and had to start wearing a brace. He was depressed, and then he had an epiphany.

"I was sitting on my bed in the dorm room there," he said. "My three dormmates were at the football game. I was sulking because I wasn't on the field. And as I sat there on the bed, I thought: 'What am I going to do now? I'm not going to be the athlete I wanted to be' . . . I said to myself, you know, I've never gotten good grades. I've been in class now a month or so and things hadn't been very hard. I bet if I tried, I could make good grades. And that was a transition for me."

Reid was still able to box despite his bum foot. He lost thirty pounds and eventually had about three dozen amateur fights. Once, when his pals came to watch him fight, Reid lost. He was, as his pal Richie Vincent remembered, disconsolate. "We bought a case of Regal Pale beer, longnecks," Vincent recalled. "That's the only time I saw Harry drinking in my whole life."

(Vincent believed that Reid was influenced as much by his father's alcoholism as his Mormon faith in his decision to become a teetotaler. Even though he thought his father was tough, Reid also saw what damage alcohol wrought.)

He continued to box for a couple of years, but he soon realized "I wasn't as tough as I thought I was." Reid fought a few exhibitions with professionals, got pummeled a time or two along the way, then gave it up.

HE BOOSTED HIS grades by his second year, and after he earned an associate arts degree, Reid decided to go to Utah State in Logan, seven and a half hours from Las Vegas. Traveling a couple of hours back and forth from Cedar City so that he and Landra could see each other was one thing. But Logan was far from Las Vegas, and that distance combined with the Goulds making life miserable for Landra helped the couple decide it was time. She was willing to give up her collegiate career for her future husband—a sacrifice Reid would later mention in many speeches.

Reid never actually proposed; the couple just had a matter-of-fact discussion. They planned to elope until some of Reid's friends went to Reverend Walker, asking him to intervene. By now, Walker was a bishop, and he offered to marry the couple—they were both nineteen—in the Mormon chapel so that they could have someone they both knew well perform the ceremony, rather than a justice of the peace, a stranger.

They worried Gould's father would find out and try to stop the ceremony. The Goulds were already suspicious. Landra told them on a Friday that she was going to spend the weekend with a friend in Las Vegas. Her mother, though, saw she had cleaned out the closet, and Doc Gould began calling around town to see what anyone might know.

Walker had sworn Reid's friends to secrecy. On Saturday, September 12, 1959, Reid's friend Ron McAllister, at a strapping six-five, stood guard, on the lookout for Dr. Gould. "We knew, to use the vernacular of the day, if Doc Gould came, all hell would break loose," Walker recalled.

It was a small group, a handful of friends and Reid's mother. Harry Sr. did not attend.

At the ceremony, Walker said, he gave "one of my better discourses on marriage, the sanctity of marriage. So I gave it my best shot, even gave them a certificate and sent them on their way. And I never in all my years had an experience I appreciated more. I had a hard time, emotionally, without crying, getting through that marriage."

That was the only marriage he ever presided over with non–church members, a measure of his affection for both of his students.

After the ceremony, Landra called her parents and told them about the marriage. Then the couple left for Logan in a '54 Chevy to begin the next chapter. They honeymooned in Mesquite, just outside Las Vegas, before continuing up to Cedar City. When they arrived, there was a letter waiting from Doc Gould. He told his daughter that as her father, he had every right to do whatever he had to do to prevent a marriage outside of the faith. But, he added, now that they were married, that part was over.

The Goulds visited the Reids for Thanksgiving that first year. "I'm sure they wanted to see if their only child was okay," Landra said. "And things were okay. And from that point on, it was completely different."

The Goulds had accepted their new son-in-law.

THE REIDS ARRIVED in Logan that summer as newlyweds and needed a place to live. So they checked the newspaper and found a basement apartment for let, and they called the owner.

The first question the proprietor, Matthew Bird, asked was a simple one: "Are you LDS?"

Even though they were not of the faith—and Bird had been on three church missions—he rented the apartment to the Reids. It was dark and small, but it was the couple's first home.

Landra secured a job at the library of the Thiokol Chemical plant in Brigham City, an hour outside of Logan, taking the bus to and from work while her husband tended to his studies.

Reid was busy, too, accelerating his political activism by setting up the first Young Democrats chapter in school history. (He later received a letter from President Kennedy congratulating him for the feat.) He also had decided to go to law school.

In Reid's last year, Professor Leonard Arrington, an author who would later become known as the dean of Mormon history, took Reid under his wing and made him his assistant. Reid graded papers for the economist, whose *Great Basin Kingdom* would be published the following year. Arrington opened new veins of knowledge for the young college student, taking him to conferences around the country and developing an enduring friendship with Reid.

As his political education continued, Reid was also undergoing a religious transformation. One day, he walked upstairs to borrow something from his landlord, a devout Mormon. Through a window, he saw the family gathered around the dinner table, praying. It profoundly affected him. "He saw the guy, his wife, and their children, doing what normal people do, having dinner and he said, 'I've never had anything like that in my life,'" said his high school friend Don Wilson.

After their problems with the Goulds over religion, Reid and Landra did not want "a divided family," as she put it. "If we were going to belong to any kind of church, we wanted to be on the same page. That was kind of the beginning principle."

While Reid was gazing at the Birds' idyllic LDS family life, Landra discovered her driver on the bus to the chemical plant was a missionary. He invited her to learn more about the church.

The lessons took. In February 1960, the Reids became members of the Church of Jesus Christ of Latter-day Saints.

Reid rarely talked about his faith, but what little was known was that he was devout. He attended church regularly with Landra and he occasionally taught Sunday school. While Reid was a committed Mormon, he also would come to know the political benefits of harnessing the growing LDS vote in Las Vegas. Despite Salt Lake City admonitions that the faithful were not to intertwine the church and politics, Reid would have people in the Mormon community work with him as organizers, which became more and more divided as his career progressed and he became more partisan. His religion also was something he had to navigate once he began to ascend in the Senate, because as a pro-life Mormon, he was an unlikely leader of a pro-choice party.

REID WAS AN A student at Utah State, eventually graduating Phi Kappa Phi with degrees in political science and history. He also minored in economics at the Jon M. Huntsman School of Business, an ironic foreshadowing, as the school's namesake would play a role in one of the more controversial chapters of his career.

In Reid's senior year, he was awarded a Fulbright scholarship to study in Israel. But he had no money, and his first child, Lana, had been born in March, so he decided to go directly to law school instead. He was accepted at the George Washington University in DC, but Reid knew he had to work to pay his way. So he approached his mentor, Mike O'Callaghan, who by then was starting to get enmeshed in Democratic politics in the state. O'Callaghan wrote to Nevada's lone congressman, Democrat Walter Baring, and asked him to provide his protégé with a patronage job. By happenstance, Reid was at O'Callaghan's house when the letter arrived saying Baring could not help the young Mr. "Reed."

O'Callaghan, incensed, immediately called Baring.

Reid heard the exchange. "He said, 'My favorite student, one of my prized students. I wrote to you asking to give him a patronage job. You wrote back to me. You didn't even have the decency to spell his name right. It's spelled R-e-i-d. You need to understand that he's going to get a patronage job from you, or I will work as hard as I can to make sure you don't win the next election.'"

Baring relented, and the young family of three moved to the nation's capital, where Reid began his studies and a job as a Capitol policeman earning $5,500 annually. The first year was as difficult as any they would have in their marriage.

Reid was working from three in the afternoon to eleven at night as a Capitol policeman, so he'd leave the apartment at six thirty in the morning and not return until eleven thirty at night. The Reids also were unprepared for the higher cost of living. Landra initially took a job at a drugstore but had to quit when she became pregnant with their second child, Rory. Around that time, Reid's mother, Inez, left his father because of his alcoholism and bouts of violence and moved in with the young couple.

The nadir came when the transmission went out on the family's Buick. A desperate Reid went to the associate dean of the law school, Ed Potts, and asked whether he could get financial help. Potts's response, Reid recalled decades later: "Young man, I think you should drop out of law school."

Reid refused to succumb. The car repair was covered by the church after a local Mormon bishop interceded. But Reid held a grudge for decades against the school, rejecting entreaties to speak after he was in Senate leadership. He finally agreed to give an address in 2005, when he also received an honorary degree. He did not hold back. "I told them how terrible George Washington had been to me."

Meanwhile, his job as a night shift Capitol cop was not as taxing as his law school work. "Sometimes there was nothing going on," he recalled, "nothing, just quiet. These great, big empty halls. I knew these buildings better than anybody."

Reid would hide in a cubbyhole and tackle his schoolwork on a small, portable typewriter. But he also felt the vibe of the buildings, the import of what was going on there, day after day.

Reid occasionally visited his patron, Baring. He vividly remembered a conversation with the congressman right after John F. Kennedy had been assassinated in November 1963. Baring, who tacked to the right after an early liberal career, had been critical of Kennedy. But Reid was shocked by the congressman's reaction to the president's death. "He said it was good they got rid of him," Reid recalled. (Reid also recounted a slightly different version of this story in his autobiography, but Baring's son has insisted that his father never would have said such a thing.)

Reid applied himself and finished law school in a little more than two years. There was never any doubt that the family, now four, would return to Las Vegas, where their relatives lived. But they needed money, and Reid could not wait to take the bar, which in those days in Nevada was only given once a year in September. So he petitioned the state supreme court to be allowed to take the exam before he graduated.

The justices granted his request and Reid came home to take the bar exam. O'Callaghan met him at the Reno airport. Reid remembered his mentor pressing a fifty-dollar bill into his hands, a denomination Reid had never seen before. "He didn't have that kind of money, living on his disability pension and teaching school," Reid said of his mentor. "But he always took care of me."

He took the bar exam in September 1963 inside the Masonic Hall in Reno with about a hundred other prospective lawyers, including another Las Vegan named Richard Bryan. Reid and Bryan briefly chatted in the hall with about a dozen banquet tables set up for the test takers, eight to ten at each table. They didn't know it then, but their lives would soon become closely intertwined in the Nevada political world for half a century.

Two months later, on November 19, 1963, the list of those admitted to the bar was released. Harry Reid's name, along with a handful of others, was listed at the bottom as "admitted at a later date."

Three months later, Reid graduated from George Washington and on February 24, 1964, he was admitted to the Nevada bar.

As he and Landra returned to Las Vegas so that he could begin his career as a trial lawyer, they were relieved to be out of DC.

"Those were hard, really hard years," Landra said. "We couldn't wait to get out of Washington. And we thought we would never, ever come back."

CHAPTER THREE

LIFE BEFORE THE ARENA BECKONED

When Harry and Landra Reid returned to Las Vegas in 1964 with two toddlers, the newly minted lawyer had to find a job. Again, Mike O'Callaghan would be helpful. Reid's well-connected mentor introduced him to some of the best lawyers in Las Vegas, then a city of about a hundred thousand people.

Eventually, one of the city's prominent firms, Singleton, DeLanoy and Jemison, hired the budding attorney, who would soon become one of the top trial lawyers in the state. By the time he stopped practicing nearly two decades later, Reid estimated he had more than a hundred jury trials under his belt.

The young lawyer loved going to court and defending his clients, whether they were insurance companies, as many were in his first year, or down-and-outers who seemingly had hopeless cases, ones that affectionately became known around the courthouse as "Harry Reid specials."

Rex Jemison, a brilliant appellate attorney who rarely appeared in court, took Reid under his wing. He would concoct the courtroom strategies, and Reid would execute them.

Early in his career, that synergy paid off in an unusual case. Clayton Sampson was a former paratrooper who had been charged with burglary after parachuting from the top of a coin company warehouse. A private detective had been waiting for him on the ground and shot him, grazing his stomach. Sampson was arrested and put on trial, with Reid acting as his court-appointed attorney.

The deputy district attorney in what should have been a slam-dunk case was Richard Bryan, whom Reid had met at the bar exam in Reno a few months earlier. "Harry got him off," Bryan ruefully recalled decades later, insisting it was a strategy crafted by Jemison along with favorable jury instructions.

The defense? Entrapment. Reid argued Sampson had been set up, talked into the burglary attempt. The jury took only twenty minutes to acquit him.

According to his tax return, Reid reported making just under $11,000 that first year as a lawyer—about $100,000 in today's dollars. Not a bad start, even after he tithed $1,200 to the Mormon Church. He was driving a new Plymouth and was garnering a reputation for winning unwinnable cases.

Reid also helped a high school classmate named Larry Bolden—or as Reid put it later, "I saved his career." He was not exaggerating.

Bolden had been a star athlete at Basic High and one of the first Black deputies hired by the Clark County sheriff's department. Bolden told Reid that he had been denied promotion from sergeant to lieutenant, accused of cheating because he was sweating heavily during the exam. "Well, you always sweat," Reid replied to his high school friend.

Reid took the case to court and won, and eventually Bolden became the first African American deputy chief in Las Vegas police history. He died in 2000 after a distinguished career.

"Harry took that case and brilliantly exposed the racial discrimination within the police department during a time when such arguments were not welcomed or encouraged," O'Callaghan later wrote.

But there was more to it than that. At the time, the police department was overseen by Sheriff Ralph Lamb, a legendary lawman who was more king than cop, "John Wayne, Wyatt Earp, and Dirty Harry all rolled into one," as Nevada Congresswoman Dina Titus once described him.

"[Reid] taking Ralph Lamb to court and suing him over the non-promotion of Larry was a big, big deal," Bill Marion, a longtime Reid aide, recalled. "Nobody took on Ralph in those days."

Bolden never forgot it. He held barbecues for Reid during campaigns, and that saga helped solidify Reid's support in the African American community.

"He really felt sorry for people who were injured," recalled Bruce Alverson, who practiced law with Reid for years. "And he could never say no to anybody. It could have been the deadest case in the world, and he would take the case. He always thought he could win every case, and he took some terrible, terrible cases to trial."

Despite his immersion in the law and his eagerness to go to court, Reid refused to participate in the standard social niceties of the day—a harbinger of what was to come.

"This was when businesspeople, lawyers joined the Chamber of Commerce, got involved in the Lions Club and all of that," Bryan recalled. "I joined many of these organizations. Harry joined none."

Bryan was already plotting his own political course that would take him to Carson City, but Reid had no such ideas. He was focused on his family and building his law practice.

ALTHOUGH HE WAS doing well at the law firm, Reid would soon take on another position. In the summer of 1965, the city attorney's job in Henderson became vacant, and Reid's father-in-law suggested the part-time job would be good experience. Doc Gould was still a formidable figure in Henderson, and he went to the council members on his son-in-law's behalf. On August 25, 1965, by a unanimous vote, Reid was appointed Henderson city attorney. He beat out five other attorneys who sought the job. The *Las Vegas Review-Journal* reported that Reid was "believed to have the inside track," presumably because of Doc Gould's intervention. He was twenty-five years old.

There really wasn't much to being city attorney—Henderson was a city of only about fifteen thousand people in 1965. Reid had plenty of time to continue working for the private firm, where he was clearly on a partnership track just a few years out of law school. He did not expect that the door was about to open the following year for his first foray into electoral politics.

Through his experience in insurance defense cases, Reid had developed relationships with many doctors in the community. He also did some administrative law at the local hospitals, including Southern Nevada Memorial Hospital, the county facility that specialized in indigent care.

Some of the doctors at the hospital believed the executive suite was rife with corruption, especially because the administrator, Jack Staggs, was a pharmacist who had a drugstore on the premises.

A group of doctors approached Reid and suggested he run to be a trustee of the hospital, then an elected position. It wasn't all altruism, though. Reid had an unpleasant experience before the board when he was representing a doctor, recalling even decades later that the chairman, an orthopedic surgeon named George Madsen, was arrogant and rude to him and his client. "I decided I was going to get even and run against him," Reid said.

He had no campaign experience, but the young lawyer gathered his high school friends, the "Henderson mafia," as some called it. They helped make yard signs, and he had cards printed to pass out at events.

Reid would first have to make it through the primary—the top four contenders would move on and two would be elected in the general—and the competition was stiff. Two incumbent trustees were running—William Pursel, an insurance agent, and Madsen.

The *Las Vegas Sun* endorsed the outsider for the job. "We think conditions require a change in the administration of the hospital and we can wholeheartedly recommend candidate Harry Reid," the paper gushed.

The two incumbents finished on top in the primary, but Reid showed respectably, with 11,801 votes, trailing Madsen (14,434) and Pursel (13,616). A pharmacist named Murray Kachad was well behind, garnering 4,429 votes.

Soon after the primary, Reid heard from Kachad.

"He told me, 'Look, I can't beat the bastards, but with my help, you can,'" Reid recalled. "'I'll raise money for you, and you can run ads in newspapers and that kind of stuff.' And sure enough, he came through."

In those days, print ads were very important, so Reid bought several with his outsider slogan on top: A BOLD STEP FORWARD.

The ads emphasized his experience as city attorney and his work with the state bar and Clark County Legal Aid, which helped poor people.

The money, Kachad told Reid, was coming from the "Jewish mafia," and the candidate did not learn until later what his new friend meant: they were pawnbrokers.

"They were really good to me, and this isn't in any way meant to be politically incorrect, but it was also my political entry into Jewish politics," he said. "I won that election because of the pawnbrokers."

One week before the election, Kachad publicly pulled out of the contest and endorsed Reid. That same day, November 1, 1966, the *Sun* published a large Reid ad: "Your doctor agrees Harry Reid will make a fine hospital trustee." Below were the names of forty-two doctors.

The *Sun* also endorsed his candidacy, declaring: "In our judgment, it is essential that a new face come on the board because of possible implications of things going on."

When the results were tallied on November 8, 1966, it wasn't close: Reid had 30,926 votes, well ahead of Pursel, who trailed with 22,943 votes and barely defeated Madsen (22,604) for the second spot on the hospital board.

Reid later would repay the pawnbrokers when he became a state legislator, pushing through a bill to allow them to charge higher interest rates. Many years later, he remained both amazed and proud that he was able to pull that off.

"Can you imagine me?" he asked. "First of all, trying to help pawnbrokers, and secondly, making it so glaringly wrong by asking that they could charge more in terms of interest."

At the time, Reid rationalized that Las Vegas is a place where unlucky gamblers would pawn a ring or watch to get out of town and that the pawnbrokers "can earn a living."

The pawnbrokers would be Reid's friends for life.

AS 1967 DAWNED, Reid was working long hours as a rainmaker for the law firm, as city attorney for Henderson, and as a newly elected member of the hospital board. Something had to give, and it eventually did.

On March 13, the firm rewarded Reid for his work by making him a partner, albeit a minor one. (Reid's name would be added to the firm on January 1, 1969.)

The partnership agreement stipulated that if the firm made a $200,000 profit, Reid would get $28,000—about a quarter million in current dollars; if it was more, then Reid would get $7,500 of the next $50,000. Anything above $250,000 and Reid would get 3 percent. He was also given the option of buying more points from the other partners to become a bigger shareholder. He had been doing well. Now Harry Reid was about to become a rich man.

Newly elected to the hospital board and knowing that the law firm would consume much of his time, Reid resigned as city attorney. Henderson was growing and the part-time job was becoming more of a full-time responsibility.

With more time to focus on his duties as a hospital trustee, Reid and his doctor friends had one goal and that was to oust Staggs, the hospital administrator. Because the hospital was charged with taking indigent patients, its finances were constantly in flux and occasionally in the red. Someone had to be the scapegoat. But Reid, who would eventually become a legislative master, had to learn the first rule: count to a majority of votes.

By the end of his first year on the board, Reid had emerged as Staggs's fiercest critic. By December, Reid was ready to make his move—but he had not yet honed his vote-counting skills. He had, however, set the table quite well, and he knew how to work the media.

"County Hospital Broke," blared the headline on December 6 in the

Las Vegas Review-Journal. A week later, Reid confirmed to the media that doctors at the hospital had given Staggs a vote of no confidence in a landslide of 50–6. In a *Review-Journal* story, Reid praised the doctors for their courage and said the matter would be discussed at the upcoming board meeting. On December 17, Reid publicly excoriated the board chairman and the hospital's public relations team for crafting a statement that hurt the hospital's image, criticizing him and the doctors who had asked for Staggs's ouster.

At the December 19 board meeting, showing perhaps the first evidence of the unvarnished public fire that would characterize his career, Reid unleashed what the newspaper called a "blistering attack" on Staggs. Reid accused Staggs of hardly ever being at the hospital, being seen drunk at an administrator's meeting, and owning land near the hospital. Staggs said he would consult an attorney about Reid's statements, implying he had been defamed.

When Reid made a motion that Staggs "be dismissed immediately," only one doctor on the board, Quincy Fortier, voted with him.

But Reid did not relent, criticizing Staggs every chance he could. As the new year turned, Staggs had had enough. Reid, elected chairman of the board, claimed—or feigned—surprise on January 3 when Staggs resigned, along with two of his backers on the board. Reid was hardly a graceful winner, telling the *Sun* they "resigned like two kids in a tag match they said they didn't want to play anymore." The *Sun*'s hospital beat reporter, Judy Edsall, wrote about how "brash young Harry, threatening the establishment, refusing to treat each oration like a message from Olympus . . . a baby-faced gadfly," had bested Staggs and veteran board members.

By April, under a new administrator, the hospital was back in the black. Reid had another reason to celebrate that month, too, as his third child, Leif, was born. Then, one day over lunch, Reid got some life-changing advice that would pave the way for his secure financial future, even if he didn't realize it at the time.

Reid and other attorneys were in downtown Las Vegas, taking an afternoon break from court. Lou Wiener, a veteran lawyer and raconteur, had some counsel for the young lawyer with the growing family.

"Young man, I have made millions, I have lost millions, and today I am broke," he said. "Take my advice: Don't buy stock, businesses, boats, or big cars. Invest only in undeveloped real estate. No one can damage it. They can find bodies on it, piss on it, and the value still goes up."

Reid, who admired Wiener, would take those words to heart. As he wrote four decades later to Wiener's law partner, Jim Rogers, a TV station chain owner who became his close friend and ally, "I followed that advice and have done pretty well—even my Searchlight land is now valuable." (Reid would sell that property in 2014 for $1.75 million.)

"Pretty well" is an understatement. Dozens of land purchases and sales (including some of Landra's family holdings), some which would become fodder for controversy as his career progressed, would eventually make Reid a multimillionaire. But before he embarked on a lifetime of real estate investing, he had more pressing business.

Columnists began to float his name for higher office, and by mid-1968, Reid had decided to run for the Nevada Assembly, ostensibly so he could change laws governing the local hospital board.

CHAPTER FOUR

A CAPITAL IDEA

Las Vegas legislative elections in 1968 were a free-for-all.

In Clark County, where Las Vegas is located, there were nine assembly seats available in District 4. At that time, the population of the metro area was about two hundred thousand, less than half of the state. Only about eighty-six thousand of those living in Clark County were registered to vote.

When Reid announced his candidacy on June 5, he had his work cut out for him. He was one of nineteen candidates on the Democratic side vying for nine tickets to the general election, and five of the contenders were incumbents. His position on the hospital board helped his profile, as did his stint as city attorney, both of which he invoked during his announcement speech. But he also ran as being tough on crime, favoring the use of isotope machines for officers in the field to detect narcotics on suspects and allowing police to "make arrests and searches by radio and telephonic warrants." It was not a liberal platform.

Reid also came forward with a proposal to reduce summer vacation for schools from twelve weeks to six weeks, arguing that the three-month break was an anachronism from the days when children had to help their parents on farms. Reid also seized on a consumer advocacy platform with two attention-grabbing planks designed to use two unpopular groups as foils: collection agencies and the local phone company.

Reid's friend and fellow lawyer Bryan, who was then thirty-one and also running for the assembly, recalled that the twenty-eight-year-old Reid was a much better fundraiser than he was, even though he was a much more vanilla personality on the stump. Reid raised a lot of money in 1968—more than $10,000, according to his self-accounting, or a little more than $80,000 in today's dollars.

There were no disclosure requirements at the time; they weren't instituted until the post-Watergate era. But Reid kept meticulous records, using the yellow legal pads that would become his signature note-taking method throughout his life. At the top of his primary sheet was his largest donor, at $2,500, and his first one: "SDJ&R," his law firm's initials.

He also received plenty of casino money, according to his legal pad, including the Stardust ($500), then owned by a group that included Moe Dalitz, a Vegas Man of the Year who had left behind his bootlegging enterprises for Nevada's land of second chances; and "HH" ($1,500), the reclusive billionaire Howard Hughes, who was then trying to add the Stardust to his gaming empire. Campaign donations also came from the Sahara ($500); the Tropicana ($300); the Flamingo ($200); Horseshoe ($100), owned by Benny Binion, a convicted murderer in Texas but a pillar of the community in Las Vegas whom Reid later unsuccessfully tried to get pardoned; Dunes ($200), then owned by the attorney Morris Shenker, who represented mobsters and Teamsters boss Jimmy Hoffa; and Caesars Palace ($200). The money gave Reid the ability to run print ads during the primary, right before the September 3 balloting. The series of tepid ads, which began in late August, pictured him in a law library and emphasized "Harry Reid Is Qualified" and "Harry Reid Is Capable."

They played up his hospital board experience and accomplishments ("Installation of an Intensive Care Unit"), his service on boards such as the American Cancer Society, and his tenure as a boxing judge for the state Athletic Commission.

The campaign paid off. Not only did Reid make it through the primary as one of the nine top vote getters, he finished first with 12,439 votes, ahead of five incumbents and his friend Bryan, who finished third. Reid had only received 9 percent of the ballots cast, but he had three hundred more votes than anyone else, including the second-place finisher, Keith Ashworth, a respected incumbent.

The general election promised to be a tougher challenge because turnout would be much higher—it was a presidential year, after all, and the Richard Nixon–Hubert Humphrey contest would boost the numbers. Also adding to the challenge: all the Democrats and Republicans running for District 4, eighteen people competing for nine seats, and eight incumbents were in the mix. If those assembly members were reelected, that left just one slot for a newcomer such as Reid or Bryan.

The money kept coming in—$1,500 from the law firm, another $1,000 from Hughes, and the gaming companies contributed again. Reid's list of possible donors included Willie Martello, the brothel owner from Searchlight.

Reid raised enough campaign cash to run not just print ads but also a TV spot. His crusade against collection agency practices on behalf of "Mr. Wage-earner," as he put it, was effective. But even more so was his opportune evisceration of the Central Telephone Company, or Centel, which was roundly being criticized for its service. Reid could not believe his luck when the company engaged with him.

Reid's assault on the utility was three-pronged: he accused it of having subpar service, of requiring exorbitant deposits, and of underpaying employees. He clearly struck a chord with voters, who responded to his consumer watchdog profile.

As the election neared, the battle became more intense as the utility fought back. In a "BULLETIN" sent to employees shortly before the election, Centel insisted it would respond through press releases to Reid's "insinuations" in his TV ad. "His appraisal of the quality of our service is basically an attack on all of us as employees of the company," the internal document said.

"Mr. Reid's attack of [*sic*] us is completely uncalled for and totally unjustified."

The last few days before the election, Reid had full coverage of his crusade. On November 2, he declared the company "a privately owned monopoly with a profit structure that can easily support a system of better service for Southern Nevada."

The next day, the *Sun* published a story headlined "Central Telephone Reps Deny Accusations by Harry Reid." This is called, in the parlance of campaigns, free media.

"Battle Warms: Reid Back Again, Insists Phone Executives Missing the Issues," read a *Sun* headline the day before the November 5 balloting. On Election Day, the company ran a quarter-page ad with an all-caps "NOTICE" at the top, which characterized Reid's "offensive statements" as an attack on the employees. The ad also suggested Reid "is not the type of individual who should be entrusted with a public office. If he speaks rashly and irresponsibly, he may act that way if elected to public office."

The ad ended with a simple request: "We urge you not to vote for Harry Reid."

Despite the phone monopoly's efforts, 28,349 voters cast ballots for Reid, propelling him to a first-place finish. He had less than 8 percent of the vote but he beat incumbent Ashworth by fourteen hundred votes. One incumbent failed to make the top nine, leaving room for Bryan to finish seventh.

REID ARRIVED IN Carson City in 1969 for the fifty-fifth session of the biennial Nevada legislature in the minority, the first time the Democrats had not controlled the assembly since 1931. Partisanship was not as acute in those days in the capital, and Speaker Howard McKissick gave the young attorney from Las Vegas plenty of latitude, which he eagerly seized.

Reid became enmeshed in his first debates over issues that would affect him for the rest of his public life and show his contradictory nature, from abortion to gun control.

It was an eventful session for the rookie, who sponsored many bills with Bryan, and they were eventually dubbed the "Gold Dust Twins" by McKissick, an echo of the same nickname conferred on the Speaker and Harry Swanson, a fellow lawyer from Washoe County, ten years earlier.

Reid laid out his priorities for the session in a "To Whom It May Concern" memo that included some controversial proposals, including a gun-control bill to "make a three-day waiting period mandatory," a law lowering the voting age to nineteen, a conflict of interest law to prevent any elected official from "self gain," and a law requiring more than just signing a marriage register to be married. In his memo on the last one, Reid wrote that the status quo "reminds me of Revolutionary Russia in the early 1990's [*sic*], when the same method was used for becoming married . . . I think a ceremony or other procedure is absolutely necessary." Reid also wanted a package of collection agency reform bills (fulfilling a campaign promise), a law to make it a felony for failing to "support his children," and a law allowing the media to be present at all legal proceedings.

He had an ambitious agenda—sometimes too ambitious. He and Bryan sponsored a measure to outlaw firebombs, arguing that there had been some notable incidents in Southern Nevada. The bill sailed through the assembly, got out of a Senate committee, and was set for a vote on the upper house floor. That was when Bill Farr, a Sparks senator, began to speak. Bryan described him as positively rhapsodic about the bill, and the two young assemblymen could not believe their luck. And then, as Bryan put it, "He dropped the nickel on us."

As Bryan remembered it, Farr said, "I commend the two assemblymen from Las Vegas on their excellent legislation. It is timely and necessary. It's so good, we passed it last session."

The Gold Dust Twins were red-faced but undaunted, sponsoring a slew of measures, many of which made it into law. Those included reforms to the collection agency statutes and eviction laws. But some of their do-gooder bills, to force lobbyists to register, or for liberal causes, such as reforming utility regulation as Reid continued his crusade against the phone company, died in the Republican-controlled legislature. Reid failed in his attempt to change laws on how the hospital board he had left was constituted, but his payback to the pawnbrokers who had helped elect him to that board passed. Reid argued that they had not had an increase in their minimum charge since 1951, that their rate of return was "very small," and he pushed through an increase from two to three dollars per transaction.

Reid also took a high-profile stand against giving lawmakers a $300 monthly expense account, condemning the eleventh-hour attempt to increase pay when "we haven't even come close to solving the problems of teachers." It eventually died after public protests, and Reid, as he did several times during the session, was praised for his opposition by the *Las Vegas Sun* owner, Hank Greenspun, in a front-page column. Greenspun would go on to refer to Reid as "one of the bright young men of Nevada politics." Early in the session, Reid was the main sponsor, and one of only three backers, of that mandatory three-day waiting period for handgun purchases, with a misdemeanor penalty attached for violating the law. This was almost unheard of in Nevada (although Republican governor Paul Laxalt had surprisingly suggested a waiting period the previous year), a state where gun rights were sacrosanct.

Reid was willing to go to great lengths to push the bill through, even accepting Assemblyman William Swackhamer's invitation to travel to rural Battle Mountain and speak to the Rod and Reel Club. Bryan also was invited, but as he would remember later, "I wasn't the sharpest knife in the drawer, but I knew that would not be fun, so I said, 'You go ahead and go, Harry.'"

The intrepid young assemblyman trekked to Battle Mountain in tiny Lander County, later relating the story to Greenspun in vivid detail. He told the gathering that no one had a constitutional right to "be armed to the teeth" and that the bill would save lives. He was lustily booed and called a Communist.

"Can you imagine I was dumb enough to do that?" Reid recalled decades later.

The bill went nowhere.

Much more celebrated that session was the legislature's grappling with an attempt to liberalize the state's abortion law, which was put in place in 1911 and allowed the procedure only when the life of the mother was threatened. A similar measure had passed the assembly in the previous session but died in the Senate.

The original measure was still fairly restrictive. A woman could only have an abortion if three physicians attested that her life was in danger or the baby would be born with significant defects. She could also seek an abortion in cases of rape or incest, but only if she provided police with the offender's name.

The measure went through the Judiciary Committee, and the pro-life Reid was active in the discussions. The freshman assemblyman pushed for the permissive period to be reduced from sixteen weeks to eight and was rebuffed. Reid successfully amended the bill to change a mandatory Nevada residency requirement down from six months to twelve weeks. Reid also argued for language that mandated the husband's consent, saying in committee, "If my wife suddenly got really peeved at me, I would like to be able to prevent her from getting an abortion to get even with me."

After a series of amendments, Reid seconded the motion to approve the bill and added, "The bill as it now stands is pretty good, but I am not promising to vote for it on the floor."

He did, though, and the measure failed when a rural Republican assemblyman changed his vote at the last moment. Other Mormons in the assembly voted against the measure, and Reid would later write that he "helped fashion an abortion law" because he was worried that the Supreme Court would impose its will on states—this was four years before *Roe v. Wade* was decided in 1973—and he wanted to make the procedure safe in the first trimester. Whether or not that was his true motivation, Reid would spend the next few decades trying to thread the needle on abortion between his religion and critical Democratic special interests, trying not to alienate either side or the women he served and worked with.

BEYOND ABORTION AND gun control, the issue that fixated Reid and caused him the most heartache was a parochial proposal to bring dog racing to his adopted hometown of Henderson. The idea was embraced by the entire city elite, from the mayor and city council to business leaders. Jim Gibson, a Democratic state senator from Henderson who would become one of the most powerful lawmakers in Nevada history, helped get the bill out of the Senate.

The opposition was fierce, led by the gaming industry and especially its most celebrated member, Howard Hughes. Hughes and the casinos considered dog racing a threat to their tourist base, a way to siphon visitors from the Strip to a location well south of where their action was. So the lobbying was intense, with Hughes front man Tom Bell, who had made political contributions to Reid and others, recruiting the likes of the legendary oddsmaker Jimmy "the Greek" Snyder to help persuade lawmakers to kill the legislation.

The *Henderson Home News*, though, was positively ecstatic about the potential infusion into the local economy, a boon for a city that was known as that smelly place south of Vegas with all those World War II–era industrial plants. As the vote loomed, the newspaper printed "TODAY IS THE DAY!" at the top of the page and urged readers to send telegrams to a list of key votes, including Reid. The paper's lead columnist and co-owner, Morry Zenoff, even wrote front-page pieces calling it a battle "of good vs. evil."

Reid had a Hobson's choice. He could vote with the interests of the place he had called home for so much of his life or he could do what his contributors wanted—Hughes had helped propel him into the assembly, and many of the casinos had backed him as well. The night before the measure was scheduled to come to the floor, he met with his good friend Bryan to try to invent a way to get out of voting.

"I said, 'Landra's parents own twenty-five acres of land in Henderson. And ultimately she will inherit that so if I vote for that or against it, it's a conflict of interest. So I'll just say I have a conflict of interest. I can't vote.' So that's what I did."

Later, he would smile when asked how that comported with the fearless image he would later cultivate, and simply say: "I think it's pretty clever what I did, myself."

On April 17, 1969, Reid rose to speak before the vote and delivered a remarkable bit of thespianism surely better than his dazzling turn as John Sully in high school. "I can truthfully say to you and the other members of the Legislature that this is the hardest vote I have been called upon to cast this session," he began. He went on to address rumors of pressure and even bribes, of how important this was to Henderson, where despite his Las Vegas residence he was considered an assemblyman from Henderson. Reid then mentioned the twenty-five acres owned by his mother-in-law and claimed she had called him about the land appreciating during the dog-racing debate. Reid, who had just manufactured this conflict less than twenty-four hours earlier, ended with a dramatic flourish: "Now, this has been a very difficult thing for me and I have thought much about it and slept very little last night . . . It is an obvious conflict of interest and I can vote no other way."

The vote was not close—the bill lost in a landslide, 23–11. The recriminations in Henderson were immediate. Zenoff published a box at the top of page one: "Here is 'Black List' of those from this area who killed dog bill," highlighting those he blamed for the measure's loss, including Reid, and insisting he would remind voters every month so they "can repay them in kind when any or all of them run for future office."

DESPITE THE POST-SESSION pummeling in Henderson, by most measures the 1969 legislature was a success for Reid. He had his name on a fifth of the bills introduced and became known as a true workhorse in Carson City. He also clearly loved the job, and if there were any doubts that he was looking ahead to the next race, they would soon be dispelled.

The Gold Dust Twins were often mentioned together in the media as two young lawmakers to watch. They were name-checked during the session as possible state senate candidates in 1970, although Bryan arguably had a higher profile and was making all the right moves. Unlike Reid, who rarely made the social rounds, Bryan was a bon vivant, often at the capital bars having drinks or dinner with colleagues of both parties. That's partly why, Bryan would say later, he was voted outstanding freshman by his colleagues even though Reid had sponsored and passed more bills. "They liked me better because they got to know me," Bryan said.

Instead, Reid spent the session ensconced at the Frontier Motel not far from the capital complex. His law firm partner, Drake DeLanoy, had offered Reid his house at Lake Tahoe for the few months of the legislative session. But, as Reid remembered it, he stayed for one night, the house made strange noises, and the snow was unbearable and terrifying to drive in.

However, Reid was not averse to a kind of frivolity other than hitting the bars, and he and Bryan developed a reputation as capital practical jokers, albeit with an occasional mean streak. Once, when they heard a lobbyist had lost his wallet, they sent a telegram to his wife: "Left your wallet at my place. See you next time you are up. Love, Barbara." Another time, during a legislative tour of a brothel, they passed out the business cards of a colleague to all the women. This was what passed for Gold Dust Twin humor.

For months, Reid had equivocated publicly about his next step, saying he might seek a state senate seat. Pundits floated his name for several offices, including governor. "Don't dismiss the young man lightly," the *Sun* columnist Paul Price wrote of a possible Reid gubernatorial candidacy. "He has qualifications; a staunch Mormon, aggressive and ambitious attorney, personable, handsome and a formidable politician."

Governor Laxalt had announced in September that he would not, as President Richard Nixon had hoped, run for the Senate against the incumbent Howard Cannon and instead decided to retire from politics. Lt. Gov. Ed Fike, also a Republican, announced he would seek the governorship, leaving the second slot open. In Nevada, there is no formal governor–lieutenant governor ticket—they run separately—but the pair would be inextricably linked in the media. The Democrats had no obvious candidate for governor, and with Laxalt promising to help Fike, it was presumed to be a Republican year in Nevada, albeit at Nixon's midterm.

By spring, though, Reid's high school guiding light, Mike O'Callaghan, declared he was going to seek the state's highest office. O'Callaghan had run the health and welfare division in the previous administration, but he had never held elective office. A former Clark County Democratic Party chair now living in Carson City, O'Callaghan ran for lieutenant governor and lost in 1966. Fike was a prohibitive favorite.

Reid said his decision to run for lieutenant governor was impulsive, but the prospect of being on a pseudo ticket with O'Callaghan surely proved irresistible. The Republicans also had no formidable contender in the race when Reid formally announced his candidacy on May 13, 1970. He was only thirty years old, and, if elected, he would be the youngest lieutenant governor in the state annals.

During his announcement speech, a coy Reid distanced himself from whoever the Democratic candidate for governor might be and insisted he could work with Fike should he win. On a platform that every Democrat could embrace, Reid said he was committed to fight for higher teacher pay and smaller class sizes and railed against corporate interests who killed his pollution regulation bills in the legislature. He touted consumer protection legislation—his war with the phone company had worked so well during his assembly race—and he vowed to end "a wasteful and appalling policy of benign neglect toward [Nevada's] aged and its truly needy citizens." Despite predictions of a Republican wave, Bob List, then a Republican candidate for attorney general, said he realized O'Callaghan and Reid might pull off an upset when "Fike was holding hundred-dollar-a-plate luncheons and dinners, and O'Callaghan and Reid held a one-dollar hot dog cookout in the park in Reno. And the place was packed."

State Democratic Party powers were not so sure about Reid's candidacy. He was a first-term legislator, not well-known at all in Southern Nevada, much less statewide. Soon, another name began to float in columns: Bill "Wildcat" Morris, a well-heeled attorney who had been involved in Democratic Party politics for years and had run unsuccessfully for attorney general four years earlier.

Morris, who had appropriated his nickname from Las Vegas High School, where he was a football star, went to see Reid to persuade him to drop out of the race. He opened a briefcase filled with hundred-dollar bills, offering to pay off Reid's campaign debt. Reid declined.

Reid wasn't exactly a novice when it came to fundraising, as he had shown in his assembly race, and he had a few friends, too. When he went to visit the Lady Luck casino owner, Andy Tompkins, who would become a lifetime friend, Reid was surprised by how much he was willing to donate. Indeed, it was the largest contribution he had ever received, $10,000, which he gave to Reid in one hundred $100 bills.

"I didn't know what to do with it," he said. "I had a suit on, so I stuffed it in all the pockets I could find." Harry Reid walked out of the casino in the spring of 1970 with the equivalent of $75,000 today.

Reid campaigned hard even though his competition for the September primary was not stiff and the Republicans had yet to coalesce around a candidate. He continued to rail against the phone company. He declared that young drivers caught with pot should have their licenses revoked for a year, and he presciently argued that a burdened state supreme court needed an appeals court to lighten its load—something that would happen forty-four years later.

The Republicans finally had their candidate in July when Bob Broadbent, a Clark County commissioner and the first mayor of Boulder City, a Las Vegas suburb, announced for lieutenant governor.

Broadbent, who was fifteen years older than Reid, told reporters that he was running to continue unified government, as had existed with Laxalt and Fike. By any measure, he was a formidable candidate, a pharmacist by trade who had never lost an election and the first Republican elected to the Clark County Commission in twenty years. During his tenure, Broadbent developed a reputation for being outspoken and fearless, speaking out against hidden mob ownership of casinos.

Broadbent adopted a standard Republican line against Reid: "My opponent, who is a fine young man, happens to have compiled an extremely liberal record during his brief tenure in public office," Broadbent said in a speech shortly after the primary. The commissioner then made his case, highlighting Reid's gun waiting period bill, the measure allowing pawnbrokers to charge more interest, and, of course, the proposal to liberalize Nevada's abortion law. Broadbent said Reid's initiatives would cost millions of dollars, saying by contrast that he would "not make immature and irresponsible promises I cannot keep."

Reid embraced his record, suggested he was helping the children and the poor, and he even went biblical: "For what shall it profit us if we shall have a surplus in our treasury and we shall lose a whole generation of children?"

But it was not all sweetness and light. Reid called Broadbent an "uninformed, manufactured candidate" who was to the right of Nixon and Laxalt and declared, "It would be tragic to have such an uninformed man a heartbeat away from the governor's chair . . . Bob is out of touch with the 20th Century."

Reid was also keenly aware that he was seen as O'Callaghan's handmaiden, so he had a three-by-five card on which he scribbled "Agreement with O'Callaghan" and followed it with lines to repeat, such as: "Lt. Gov. cannot be a rubber stamp" and "No one told me to run" and "I traveled the state personally and independently of anyone else."

Shortly before the election, the *Las Vegas Review-Journal* endorsed Broadbent, gushing that he "probably knows more about the nuts and bolts of government than any candidate in Nevada history seeking top office." But the newspaper, which would become Reid's chief media antagonist (mostly on and sometimes off) for the next nearly half century, couldn't leave it at that, arguing the comparison with Reid was unfavorable to the assemblyman: "The office of lieutenant governor requires a man who has the maturity, good judgment and experience to serve as acting governor in an emergency."

On the Sunday before the election, Reid paid for an ad featuring a picture of Landra and his three young children with endorsements from "prominent Nevadans," including two well-known Republican community figures and Rep. Walter Baring, whose "good riddance" comments after JFK was killed apparently were now forgotten by the ambitious assemblyman.

On November 3, 1970, the Nevada conventional wisdom was set on its ear as Democrats swept most major offices. O'Callaghan upset Fike, who had been accused in a national Jack Anderson column of a conflict of interest; Sen. Howard Cannon had won reelection; and Reid handily dispatched Broadbent, becoming the youngest lieutenant governor in Nevada history. Reid won by nearly fourteen thousand votes, garnering 58 percent to Broadbent's 42 percent. It wasn't close and Broadbent attributed the loss to Reid's hard work and six months' head start. Reid also was helped by a growing Democratic voter registration advantage in Clark County, which would become a pivotal factor in coming elections for Reid and others as Southern Nevada became the population center of the state. (Broadbent would go on to a distinguished career as an assistant Interior secretary and director of what is now Harry Reid International Airport.)

It did not escape many that the top two state offices were now held by products of the Henderson school system, one a teacher and the other his prized pupil. In a fawning column shortly after the election, the *Sun*'s Hank Greenspun suggested the result must have "exceeded their most imaginative dreams . . .

"In the lives of these men, it has been obvious that both do have goals far beyond mere self-interest. There has been a dedication to the best interests of their community and there will be a two-man team in Carson City which has progress in mind for all of Nevada."

CHAPTER FIVE

CHASING HUGHES AND CLIMBING THE NEXT RUNG

Three weeks after Reid won his race for lieutenant governor in November 1970, the largest player on the Las Vegas Strip left town literally under the cover of darkness.

Howard Hughes, the biggest financial force in Nevada and owner of six casinos, traveled by van to Nellis Air Force Base, where he was whisked on a private plane to the Bahamas. He had rarely been seen in Las Vegas since he arrived four years earlier, and he would never return before his death in 1976.

Despite his virtual invisibility, Hughes had changed the face of the Strip, buying a passel of properties, some of which had been mob-owned. The perception was beginning to take hold—although the reality would lag behind by a decade or so—that Hughes had heralded a new era of corporate rather than mob domination of casinos in Nevada.

Thus, the question of what would become of his gaming holdings, as a power struggle erupted among Hughes executives, was the biggest challenge confronting the incipient O'Callaghan-Reid administration. Nothing less than the future of the state was at stake, as Hughes controlled one-third of the revenue generated on the Las Vegas Strip.

During his campaign, O'Callaghan had made it clear that he disagreed with Gov. Paul Laxalt's laissez-faire attitude toward Hughes. Laxalt had argued that he allowed Hughes to circumvent normal procedures and not appear before state gaming regulators because the mysterious mogul brought such instant credibility.

However, unlike Laxalt, O'Callaghan wanted a face-to-face sit-down with Hughes, especially after he left the state, to ensure he was not on his deathbed, as rumored, and he turned to his trusted lieutenant for help. The new governor did not have time to do the necessary detective work involved to get Hughes to agree to a meeting. But he understood the minimal demands of the lieutenant governor's job and knew Reid could take it on with discretion and doggedness.

Reid also had accepted money from Hughes—the billionaire had been a major donor to both of his campaigns. It's also possible O'Callaghan assigned Mormon church member Reid the job of inducing Hughes to meet with him because the billionaire had surrounded himself with a palace guard, five of whom were known as "the Mormon Mafia."

In late spring 1971, Reid began reaching out to various Hughes intimates to try to ascertain the mogul's state of mind and physical well-being, as well as to get them to persuade the billionaire to sit down with O'Callaghan or jeopardize his Nevada holdings. But this was not just about Hughes; it was about the evolution of a state that had been suffused with mob influence since Bugsy Siegel famously built the Flamingo in 1946. This was about Nevada becoming respectable, symbolized by Hughes's corporate interests on the Strip standing in stark contrast to the mob's waning, but still present, influence.

It was against this backdrop that the lieutenant governor embarked on his odyssey to determine Hughes's fitness. Reid's detailed notes of this journey and what he learned about Hughes have never before been revealed.

Shortly after the legislature adjourned, on June 2, 1971, Reid talked to Dr. Harold Feikes, who was largely believed to be the source of reports that Hughes was in ill health. As part of his portfolio from O'Callaghan, Reid was tasked with discovering just how sick Hughes might be, whether he was non compos mentis to control his gambling empire in Nevada, which could leave a significant portion of the Strip in limbo without clear ownership. Much has been written in other books about Feikes, a cardiovascular expert in Las Vegas, who testified about Hughes's health but was limited by doctor-patient confidentiality.

Nevada's lieutenant governor, on that day in June, coaxed the doctor to open up in great detail.

"Dr. Feikes first saw Howard Hughes in the penthouse of the Desert Inn hotel on Christmas, 1969," Reid wrote in a memo after the conversation. "At the time he saw him, Hughes weighed at or near 100 pounds. Howard Hughes' doctor that has been handling him for many years was an alcoholic and was unable to get the blood transfusions started. Feikes added that if he had continued, he would have done damage to the man's veins."

Feikes told Reid that he cared for Hughes for about three weeks and believed his emaciation was caused by "a nutritional deficiency." He was unable to do X-rays or other tests that would have confirmed his diagnosis. Feikes also told Reid that Hughes's people called him nearly a year later while he was attending a medical convention in California and he flew to Las Vegas, where he found that Hughes had pneumonia. Feikes treated him up until about three weeks before he left Las Vegas, telling Reid that Hughes "had many physical problems, including a constant sore on one of his hips caused by his latest airplane accident, which never heals, and an intermittent prolapsed bowel, which indicates minor surgery."

Feikes also confirmed to Reid that the harrowing portrait drawn of Hughes in a recent *Look* magazine article was accurate, that he had a beard and long hair. "He further stated that Hughes never wore clothes but would have a towel or sheet covering his body most of the time."

The cardiologist told Reid that he was tricked by law enforcement into signing an affidavit attesting to Hughes's bad health after he was told it was only going to be used for a search warrant. Feikes told Reid he was concerned that Hughes's "palace guard" had removed him from the outside world and "he is no longer able to demand the things he previously did."

So in his first meeting on O'Callaghan's assigned mission, Reid had heard distressing news about Hughes's health. He would later hear both confirmatory and contradictory assessments.

Just two days after his conversation with Feikes, Reid traveled to Salt Lake City to meet with Howard Eckersley, a key executive assistant to Hughes and one of the highest-ranking members of the so-called Mormon Mafia, a cadre of members of the church who were his trusted aides.

When Reid told Eckersley about the governor's desire to meet with Hughes, the aide, according to Reid's typewritten, seven-page memo of the nearly four-hour conversation, "doubted whether" such a meeting could occur. But Reid was able to glean key details about Hughes's life:

The Hughes minions, Reid learned, "work eight-hour shifts, with someone being with him constantly, even when he is asleep."

Hughes's bizarre dining habits, Eckersley told Reid, include eating "the same thing for a month or two months or three months at a time. As Eckersley said, 'it would drive you crazy.'" But Eckersley told Reid that Hughes, while "very skinny," was in good health in the Bahamas and that they had doctors flown in to see him. Eckersley also told him that unlike some pictures that had appeared, including in the same *Look* magazine piece Feikes had cited, "he does not have white hair."

When Reid pressed him about Hughes meeting with the governor, Eckersley stated "that would not solve any of the problems, as there would be those who would say, 'How do you know it is Howard Hughes and not an actor?'"

REID CONCLUDED HIS memo about the meeting thusly: "Eckersley admitted that Hughes was a very demanding, somewhat ridiculous person to work for, in that he had strange requests regarding how his bed was to be made, how his food was to be cooked and, generally speaking, all particulars about his life."

During that same time period, Reid met for two and a half hours, on June 9, 1971, with Bill Gay, another Hughes lieutenant, at his Encino, California, office. "I outlined to him the basic reasons we were concerned," Reid wrote in his memo of the meeting, "but that our prime interest was 8,000 employees and revenue for the State of Nevada."

Gay told Reid that he had lived in Las Vegas with Hughes from 1952 to 1956 and that the tycoon liked to move around, staying, without any fanfare, at the El Rancho, the Flamingo, and even a motel complex.

Reid's memo indicates that he gave Gay various alternatives, including divestiture or a conservatorship, and that Gay "appeared to be somewhat upset." Gay informed Reid of Hughes's desire to modernize the Strip resorts "so that the casino will no longer be the driving force of any of the hotels," a harbinger of what would come to pass decades later as food, retail, and entertainment became focal points. This was a fight for control of the Hughes empire, and Reid was now at the center of it.

Gay, as others had and would, told Reid that it was unlikely Hughes "would see anyone" and that state officials should be more concerned with massive losses that he claimed had amounted to as much as $22 million.

In the space of ten days, Reid had assimilated quite a bit of information about the internecine feuds within the Hughes empire and disconcerting reports about his health, all of which he appears to have relayed to O'Callaghan. What occurred next, according to a memo Reid wrote to the governor much later, was an extraordinary meeting at O'Callaghan's home with nearly all of the state's appointed gaming overseers in attendance. Governors were expected to appoint gaming regulators and then take a hands-off approach, allowing them to make their own decisions.

In the memo regarding what transpired, Reid wrote a passage that was all too revealing—and undoubtedly the reason the governor had asked for the highly unusual private meeting: "The information obtained may or may not have had some effect on the subsequent action taken by the Gaming authorities."

Shortly thereafter, on August 26, 1971, the Nevada Gaming Commission denied the applications of all of Howard Hughes's proposed corporate licensees and declared that Hughes would have to meet with the governor and one or two members of the control board or provide a letter with his confirmed fingerprints. As if he had known what the outcome would be, O'Callaghan held a news conference after the meeting and emphasized that the state had to make sure Hughes was aware of who oversaw his Nevada interests.

A direct throughline can be drawn between that series of events, catalyzed by Reid's sub-rosa investigation, and what would occur about eighteen months later: a meeting between O'Callaghan and Hughes in London early in the morning of March 19, 1973. The governor and the chairman of the Gaming Control Board, Phil Hannifin, met with Hughes and some of his lieutenants in a hotel room, with O'Callaghan emerging to tell a news conference he was satisfied the billionaire had control of his faculties and his casino holdings. Reid's serpentine travels had borne fruit.

O'Callaghan returned to the States and met with his lieutenant governor to debrief him. He told his right hand, according to what Reid recalled decades later: "Here's the deal. I'm going to tell you everything about it and how he talked but there's nothing that can be said until he dies. We stuck with that. He had long fingernails. He was not weird-looking or anything like that, very skinny, frail, quite articulate."

That was the end of Reid's central role in helping to cement Hughes's Nevada empire and to ensure the eventual transition to corporate gaming.

In late November 1973, Reid would be deposed during a lawsuit over control of the Hughes empire and the lieutenant governor would reveal just how much money the billionaire had donated to his campaign. He received four separate payments of $2,800, $5,000, $5,000, and $600 toward the end of his bid, including the latter two in November, Reid said in the deposition. All but the first donation was in cash. Reid was asked during the deposition whether the Hughes agent Tom Bell had given him $10,000 in cash in 1973, presumably for a future run for office, in the months after the London meeting. Reid confirmed he received the money but denied, when asked, that he had any business relationship with any Hughes corporations.

The campaign cash, though, would come in handy in 1974.

WHEN HE WASN'T pursuing Hughes aides and trying to set up that meeting with the reclusive tycoon for the governor, Nevada's youngest-ever lieutenant governor was acting as Mike O'Callaghan's right hand in Carson City. The relationship between O'Callaghan and Reid was so close—and their history since Basic High School so well-known—that nearly everyone knew the lieutenant governor was speaking for the governor.

Reid appeared at many events on behalf of the administration, often in Las Vegas because he and Landra had moved back there to avoid the cold of Carson City. Unless the legislature was in session, which was generally a few months every other year, Reid would be home in Las Vegas, where he could also practice law.

By the end of his first year in office, the governor praised his number two, whom he frequently called in the middle of the night, for his "support and counsel," calling him "an invaluable asset."

Reid's visibility and success in his elections caused pundits to speculate he would run against his former patron, Walter Baring, for Congress in 1972. After all, he would be at midterm and if he lost, he'd still be lieutenant governor. But Reid, who had his eye on succeeding O'Callaghan and who had just had his fourth child, Josh, quickly took that off the table. He was staying in Nevada—at least for now.

Even though he would not be on the ballot in 1972, the youthful lieutenant governor—and "youthful" became Reid's new first name in many media accounts—was acting like a party elder. At the Clark County Democratic Convention early in the year, Reid dispensed advice that would foretell his political sensibility later in his career and prescient about the electorate for years to come:

"The public will not identify with what it considers ultra-liberal politics," Reid cautioned. "If the public applies that label to us, the public will reject our party."

Despite his later protestations that he was never looking up at the next rung, Reid happily accepted invites to speak at Rotary clubs or to be a grand marshal at a parade. The *Nevada State Journal*'s Don Lynch reported Reid had "films made of himself at his work as president of the Senate. This, of course, is just basic material to have ready for any future campaign."

Reid also had arranged for his childhood friend J. J. Balk to be his eyes and ears in the legislature. He had secured Balk a job as assistant sergeant at arms in the Senate, where Reid would often preside as lieutenant governor. They would attend many capital events together, and Balk remembered that the lieutenant governor was always absorbing information:

"Every once in a while, someone would come up and try to read him the riot act," Balk recalled. "And I was always armed with a pencil and a little pad. He says—rarely did he swear—but he said, 'Write that little bastard's name down.' So he didn't forget when payback time came."

ON JUNE 22, 1971, the world stopped for Harry Reid.

The day began brightly with one of the perks of his job and one that tapped into his love of boxing. He had been invited to spend some time with the boxer Muhammad Ali, who was in Las Vegas to fight Jerry Quarry. Ali gave him an hour and a half of his time, which he remembered fondly decades later. A buoyant Reid returned to his law office and his receptionist told him his mother had telephoned. When he returned her call, she was blunt: "Your pop shot himself." Reid, ever impassive, remembered having very little reaction other than thinking, "I have to go to Searchlight."

He found his father's body laid out on the bed, the gun and the blood still there. Harry Jr. was thirty-one; Harry Sr. was fifty-eight.

Years of alcoholism and depression had taken their toll on the man who worked in dark places and often retreated to his own. "He just wanted to comfort Inez and get her into a better living situation," Landra recalled. "He also did not want to talk about it, at all."

They had a small funeral in Searchlight for Harry Sr., and Reid's friend Balk remembered it as being surreal.

"It was a scene out of a cowboy movie. The old sheriff there played the guitar. He was behind the casket in the old Searchlight community center. It was awful."

Later, Reid would talk more openly about his father's death and become engaged nationally on suicide prevention. He would succeed in getting suicide recognized as a national problem confronting policymakers.

THAT SUMMER, REID was back to getting headlines, using his familiar foil, the telephone company, working in tandem with an old friend, Jim Bilbray, now a university regent who was running for Congress against Reid's old patron Baring. They called for federal and state probes of Centel. Reid believed—and said so privately—that going after the phone company had helped elect him to the assembly and as lieutenant governor. He knew a good whipping boy and a no-lose political proposition.

By year's end, the speculation first surfaced in the media that O'Callaghan would run for the US Senate if Democrat Alan Bible retired, and that Reid would compete to succeed as governor, perhaps against Attorney General Bob List. Reid spent a lot of time in 1973 trying to get attention, sending out many press advisories—or at least many more than lieutenant governors usually issue, even identifying himself in his own release as "the youthful lieutenant governor."

On August 28, 1973, Bible made it official: the Senate seat would be open in 1974. Reid clearly believed his mentor O'Callaghan was running for Bible's seat and began to raise money for a gubernatorial campaign while O'Callaghan dithered into the new year with his own announcement. Reid opened a campaign headquarters near downtown Las Vegas, but out of deference to O'Callaghan, he did not signal what office he was seeking. But everyone knew. Or thought they knew, including Reid.

In October 1973, Reid's campaign team produced an extensive, seventeen-page "campaign outline and budget" for his incipient governor's race, an astonishing private document that is a precursor of future Reid campaigns and that, among other things, set a $120,000 budget for the primary, with the largest chunk ($30,000) for direct mail and $24,000 for television. That would be a $700,000 budget in today's dollars.

Under "image and campaign approaches," his team wrote: "It seems generally agreed that the major question mark in the Harry Reid image is his youthfulness." This was seen as a double-edged sword, but mostly an advantage for the thirty-three-year-old: "Not only is he young, he looks young, his face reflects that he is a very young man." So the suggestion was—to give him more maturity, more gravitas—to use "a drawing instead of a photograph" on billboards and signs.

ON THE "REID speaking manner," the document states: "Harry Reid is not a strong speaker. Not only is he not dynamic on the platform, but much of his material, we understand, has been dull and awkward (although thoughtful and sound), and not written in a manner that would excite an audience." And: "Reid's voice is young and youthful soft, and in fact reflects that he is a modest and nice guy. But he needs to come across as a candidate with more force and strength."

The strategy needed to be "to align himself completely with Governor O'Callaghan . . . It is a thin line. He must be close to O'Callaghan, but he also must establish that he is not a puppet. The voters won't buy a puppet—anybody's puppet."

The document also suggested Reid needed to do everything he could to avoid a primary by consolidating his political strength in the next six months. How? By courting gaming, business, and union figures; "more interest and involvement with members of the Black community"; the hermit would have to become an extrovert ("Reid should go out to lunch every day. He must be seen out publicly more."); have media folks over to his house ("Most who have met him like him, but few feel they really know him."); and on and on with recommendations to travel, go to party meetings, and harness Landra's likability.

Reid was ready to go; he was just waiting for O'Callaghan.

And waiting. And waiting. And waiting.

O'Callaghan had still not announced his intentions by the end of February 1974, just eight months before the election, and a prominent Democratic state senator, Floyd Lamb, part of a longtime Nevada ranching family, announced his candidacy for governor, assuming O'Callaghan was running for Bible's seat. So did Ralph Denton, who was prominent in Democratic politics. Publicly, Reid declared he was still waiting for the governor, saying he would give a "strong thought" to running if O'Callaghan did not seek reelection. Not irrelevant to the governor's Hamlet act was the reemergence of Paul Laxalt, the retired former Republican governor who was now a presumed candidate for the US Senate. It could not escape O'Callaghan's notice—and the media speculated as much—that a race against the charismatic Laxalt would be much more challenging than what was assumed to be a cinch gubernatorial reelection.

Finally, as the filing deadline neared, O'Callaghan announced his decision the first weekend in April, telling the Clark County Democratic Convention that he would run for reelection. He obviously tipped Reid just before his speech because at the same time in Carson City, the lieutenant governor was pivoting to the Senate race, announcing that he was filing for what promised to be a very competitive contest against former governor Laxalt.

The truth, according to both Harry and Landra Reid, was that right before his own announcement O'Callaghan had asked his protégé to run for reelection as lieutenant governor, with a promise that Reid would soon ascend because O'Callaghan would resign early for him.

Whether O'Callaghan was trying to protect Reid—"He was young, maybe he was trying to tell him to slow down a little bit," Landra thought—or whether the governor wanted his reliable sentinel to stick around, Reid clearly had grown out of the mostly ceremonial job. A race against Laxalt wasn't his first choice. Reid also wasn't the first pick of party bosses who thought former governor Grant Sawyer, who had lost his seat to Laxalt in 1966, was a stronger candidate. But now Reid felt that taking on Laxalt was his only way to move up.

Harry Reid was going to run for the US Senate. He was thirty-four years old.

CHAPTER SIX

TWO STRIKES AND YOU'RE NOT QUITE OUT

Harry Reid and Paul Laxalt could not have been more different.

Reid was seventeen years younger, not nearly as charismatic as Laxalt, and from Southern Nevada. Laxalt was not only much smoother, but he hailed from northern Nevada, the older part of the state, which held no love for the upstart Las Vegas that had grown so much larger than Reno. Despite being out of politics for four years, the former governor still had a substantial following and even in a year where the Watergate scandal promised to make it difficult for Republicans, Laxalt would be formidable. Although Reid was not the choice of party leaders, he had never lost an election and would benefit from a 139,000 to 79,000 statewide Democratic voter registration edge. Considering that Clark County now was about 56 percent of the state's nearly six hundred thousand population, and the Democrats had a sixty-thousand-voter registration edge, Reid was a solid favorite to succeed fellow Democrat Bible.

Laxalt was no stranger to competitive Senate races, having lost a heartbreaker to Howard Cannon in 1964 by eighty-four votes, two years before he won the governorship. Coaxed out of retirement by DC insiders after Bible's surprise announcement, Laxalt had been assured of support from national Republican organizations. Reid, who had proven to be an excellent fundraiser, would have the backing of organized labor in and out of state.

The youthful lieutenant governor dealt with the age issue by crafting themes designed to turn a weakness into a strength. "Send a strong, young voice to the U.S. Senate," Reid's campaign ads said. "He's younger, he's tougher, nobody owns him."

He wasted no time going after Laxalt on the central theme of his campaign: the former governor's finances.

In early April, Reid raised the issue by making his own financial disclosure and asking his opponents (Jack Doyle, an Independent American Party member, also was in the race) to do the same.

Reid's disclosure revealed substantial personal wealth amounting to $305,000—or about $1.8 million in today's dollars. He also disclosed several pieces of Las Vegas area real estate and a ranch in Lincoln County. "The public is entitled to know how a man goes into office and how he leaves," Reid told the media while boasting he had signed the Code of Campaign Practices that prohibited "scurrilous attacks." But the attacks, scurrilous and otherwise, would be plentiful in the coming months, and, ironically, an echo of the lambasting on his own finances that Reid would face later in his career.

As spring turned to summer, with a September 3 primary looming against the oil heiress and liberal darling Maya Miller, Reid received some welcome news from Washington, DC. Laxalt confirmed an account by the well-known muckraker Jack Anderson that Jimmy "the Greek" Snyder had approached Laxalt while he was governor and offered him half a million dollars for licensing an unnamed mob figure. Laxalt said he rebuffed the offer out of hand. But there was speculation that Reid's team had somehow found out about the conversation and leaked it to Anderson.

Laxalt was keeping a relatively low profile before the September primary, presumably because of the drip drip drip of Watergate revelations that culminated in President Richard Nixon's resignation on August 8. Laxalt was quietly raising money, including a luncheon with the iconic conservative and failed presidential hopeful Barry Goldwater, to fend off what he told people was Reid's attempt to say that he was "Watergated."

By the end of August, Reid had reported raising $145,000 to Laxalt's $99,000, about the same amount Maya Miller reported. But the biggest news for Reid that month was unrelated to the campaign, as his fifth and last child, Key, was born on August 19. He now had four sons and a daughter, all thirteen and under, as he traveled the state.

One week before the primary, Reid gave what would today be seen as an astonishing interview to the *Las Vegas Sun* under the headline "Abortion Controls Needed—Reid."

In the piece, Reid took issue with *Roe v. Wade*, which had been decided by the US Supreme Court the previous year, and said he supported a "right to life" constitutional amendment. Miller vehemently disagreed with Reid in the story, a move that in many a Democratic primary these days could prove fatal.

However, on Primary Day, both Reid and Laxalt won handily. Reid defeated Miller by nineteen thousand votes, with nearly 59 percent of the tally; Laxalt won by almost thirty thousand votes over two token foes, garnering 81 percent.

The general election campaign had begun, and it was expected to be close, with Reid ahead by three percentage points according to one Democratic poll. Miller initially hesitated to endorse Reid, but by the end of the month she had come around.

Only days after the primary, knowing that the capital Republican money would come in heavily for Laxalt, Reid made a handwritten list under the header "Income Projection."

The first three names were: "Glick," a reference to Allen Glick, later revealed as the front man for mob-controlled casinos, although Glick denied any involvement and was never charged; "Harrah's," which had become the first casino company listed on the stock exchange in 1973; and "Greenspun," a reference to longtime Reid supporter Hank Greenspun, the publisher of the *Las Vegas Sun*. The projections for Glick and Harrah's were $10,000 each, and $5,000 for Greenspun. Reid, according to the legal pad, expected to spend $250,000 on the campaign.

The race almost immediately turned ugly, as Reid left the Code of Fair Practices in the dust. In September, he raised questions about Laxalt's finances and implied the former governor's hands-off attitude toward Howard Hughes had resulted in a quid pro quo whereby the billionaire helped Laxalt and his brother purchase the Ormsby House hotel in Carson City. Reid was not subtle. He said he wanted to "unravel Nevada's greatest mystery: how a small-town lawyer [Laxalt] could parlay one term as governor into ownership of a $7.5 million hotel-casino."

Reid also raised another issue to put Laxalt on the defensive: why the US attorney general, John Mitchell, had asserted that Laxalt had urged him to let Hughes purchase the Dunes Hotel because it was owned by the mob—something that Laxalt denied ever saying.

This was the kind of "I'm just asking questions" technique that Reid would use to great effect later in his career, including in his most infamous accusation that Mitt Romney never paid any taxes. It was no holds barred and utterly ruthless.

Laxalt retorted that Reid had taken $13,400 in contributions from Hughes. Laxalt also argued that his approach to the tycoon had helped the state in an essential transition. But Reid would not relent, continuing to press the issue and others while believing that President Gerald Ford's September pardon of Nixon also would help his cause—"I feel like I'm running a hundred-yard dash with a hundred-pound weight on my back," Laxalt said, alluding to the pardon news out of the nation's capital.

Reid and his team believed they had gained traction with the questions about Laxalt's finances, insisting as the final month of campaigning began,

"Any man or woman who would not be completely candid about his or her finances does not deserve to be in public office." The lieutenant governor emphasized he had gone the extra mile, releasing financial information about his brothers, too—and the state Democratic chairman, Paul Lamboley, insisted, on cue, that Laxalt's brothers should do the same. Laxalt had agreed to debate the issue—and his treatment of Hughes—in late October, a masterstroke by the Reid campaign to get Laxalt in a televised confrontation about his vulnerabilities so close to the election.

Laxalt tried to change the subject, hammering away at Reid's deep support from labor and suggesting the Democrat would fulfill the national AFL-CIO's agenda of repealing right-to-work laws. That statute, passed by initiative and enacted in Nevada in the 1950s, prohibited union membership from being a condition of employment. Several efforts to repeal it by popular vote had—and would—fail.

Reid spent much of the evening of the first debate having to explain his abortion position and his criticism of Roe, as Laxalt declared his opposition to abortion but said he would not impose his views on others. The GOP contender was aided throughout by the third-party candidate Doyle, who pressed Reid on various issues.

But Laxalt was still feeling pressure on the financial questions, and days before the second scheduled debate he disclosed that banks had given him loans to build the hotel and again denied any assistance from Hughes. He also unfurled other aspects of his finances, including tax returns showing his net worth was substantially less than Reid's. His team surely hoped that would make the debate much less incendiary and potentially damaging as Election Day neared.

Having put out that fire, Laxalt was again put on the defensive in the second debate as Reid ignited another conflagration that garnered headlines. Without warning and hoping to use Watergate to full effect, Reid said that the family of Robert Mardian, the former assistant US attorney general who had been indicted for conspiring to obstruct the Watergate probe (he would later be cleared), had invested in Laxalt's Ormsby House. It was a shocking revelation that the *Las Vegas Sun*, the only newspaper in the state that had exhibited full-throated support of Reid, splashed on the front page with the headline "Laxalt Admits Mardian Ownership."

Laxalt explained that Mardian's brother's construction firm had less than a 1 percent stake in the hotel—a fact later confirmed by the Gaming Control Board chairman, Phil Hannifin. But the guilt by association tactic had done what Reid hoped—dominate the media attention in the wake of the debate and seemingly put him on the path to victory.

Reid also garnered coverage for leveling the damaging accusation that there were "possible grounds for a perjury case" against Laxalt because of his conflicting testimony over the Dunes purchase by Hughes. Laxalt constantly had to defend his relationship with Hughes from Reid's thrusts, with his only relief coming when the third-party candidate Doyle accused Reid of helping the pawnbrokers in the legislature and then being rewarded with campaign cash. Reid danced around the charge, claiming he had only received a loan, and, risibly, said he was not the prime sponsor of the bill he would brag about decades later in an interview.

Reid continued to press Laxalt on his finances despite the Republican's disclosure of his tax returns. But he was about to overplay his hand in one of the biggest mistakes in Nevada campaign history, which would be brilliantly exploited by Laxalt.

Reid insisted that the entire Laxalt family—not just his brothers—disclose their finances, without looking into who might be part of that clan, which included, it turned out, a Catholic nun. Sister Sue Laxalt, the former governor's sister, proved to be a deus ex machina in the campaign.

Reid's old friend Bryan remembered the moment, late in the campaign, when "Laxalt's people cleverly turned that issue. And they had the nun. She held a press conference and said the only thing as a member of the holy order that I committed to was chastity, poverty, and obedience."

The media piled on, turning the momentum around. The cascade of criticism continued until Election Day, as the majority of Nevada newspapers endorsed Laxalt.

The harshest condemnation appeared in the *Nevada State Journal*: "We also see disturbing signs in the campaign Reid has conducted that he does not yet possess the strength or wisdom needed for the Senate . . . It has been said many of Reid's campaign tactics have been pushed on him by campaign advisers. If this is true, he is easily influenced. If it is not, he is unwise."

And so it went in every corner of the state. Only the *Las Vegas Sun*, Reid's reliable cheerleader, came to his defense, not just arguing in an endorsement editorial that Reid would provide "bold leadership" but going so far as to say that Laxalt's actions as governor and his ties to Watergate "disqualify him for further public office." Greenspun was going all out until the end.

As opposed to Laxalt, the *Sun* said, "we have a young Mr. Clean," ironically bestowing on Reid a nickname that would echo years later on wiretaps of mob figures made by federal authorities.

It was not enough. Despite the huge Democratic registration advantage in the state and especially in populous Clark County, and a significant spending advantage—$457,000 to Laxalt's $388,000—Reid lost.

In the year of Watergate, when Democrats would do well across the country, including a net gain of three Senate seats, on November 5, 1974, Republicans Laxalt and List had eked out wins—List by 701 votes and Laxalt by 624 votes out of nearly 170,000 cast.

Reid won the heavily Democratic Clark County by fifteen thousand votes and three smaller rural counties, but he lost the twelve other so-called cow counties and Washoe County (where Reno sits), which Laxalt took by about eighty-five hundred votes. Reid had been crushed outside of Southern Nevada, and he was furious about it. "The only reason I lost was that Northern Nevada newspapers treated me unfairly," he declared two days after the election.

"It was a very dumb, stupid thing for me to say but I did it," Reid later acknowledged, but it was clear, even in 2021, that he had meant it.

The northern media did not take kindly to Reid's insinuations. The legendary Nevada journalist Warren Lerude, then the executive editor of the *Reno Evening Gazette* and *Nevada State Journal*, told United

Press International that Reid was acting Nixonian and he argued he lost "because he ran the worst Nevada political campaign anyone can recall around here."

Reid also blamed his pollster, Pat Caddell, for a survey four days before the election that showed him well ahead, causing him to withdraw from the public eye in the final week and tamp down his attacks. Reid, deeply in debt after the campaign, refused to pay bills from Caddell.

After initially balking at the idea, Reid decided that he would not accept the results and asked for a recount two weeks after the election. Legal maneuvers ensued, with Reid's lawyers demanding a hand count, claiming ballot-counting errors in Clark County. Laxalt's team insisted that it was unconstitutional. The newly reelected GOP attorney general, List, agreed with Laxalt's team in an opinion. The Nevada Supreme Court punted the decision to local officials, which caused Reid to say the matter might have to go to the US Supreme Court. But it did not, and by December 3, the recount had begun. Reid picked up a few dozen votes in sixteen counties before Washoe's count came in that weekend. Washoe, Laxalt's home base, had helped him by pushing his total higher, putting the final margin at 612 votes.

Reid considered contesting the election but conceded later that day. The damage to his reputation had been done, though, with some commentators labeling him a sore loser, an impression only reinforced when he refused to pay some of the recount costs for a time. (Carson City actually sued him over the unpaid bills.)

(In a book published years later, Laxalt suggested that if Reid had gone to Waikiki for a few weeks at the end of the campaign, he would have won. Reid sent Laxalt a note displaying his trademark wry humor after the book came out, with the benefit of time and distance, saying if he had gone to Waikiki, "think about all the fun we would have missed.")

Reid and Laxalt would, many years later, surprisingly become quite close. It would become a recurring theme for Reid to befriend his opponent after a nasty race. Some would attribute that to political expediency, but the relationship with Laxalt—and some who worked for him, including the future White House political operative Sig Rogich—clearly was genuine.

Before the end of 1974, with the race settled, Reid's friend Greenspun made one last-ditch effort to help him. In a front-page editorial, he urged O'Callaghan not to appoint Laxalt early (Bible had resigned to give his successor seniority) until financial and other questions were answered. He wanted to short-circuit Laxalt's ascension, even though the votes had been counted—and recounted. But, O'Callaghan declared, the appointment already was in the mail.

It was over. Reid had lost, without grace, and whatever political career he might have had seemed in jeopardy, if not over.

MOST POLITICIANS WHO had lost a heartbreaking race and then been labeled a sore loser would slink away into obscurity for a time, trying to avoid the spotlight and lower his or her profile. Harry Reid was not most politicians.

He had just turned thirty-five years old and was in a rush. He had never experienced a loss before—not in his high school races or his Carson City career. He was reflective in a way that was uncharacteristic of him, but he was also intent on moving forward.

First, though, came the mea culpas.

It began with a January 25, 1975, speech to the young Democrats in Washoe County, where he apologized but flashed some of his residual fury at losing to Laxalt, saying that he had considered bringing his case to the Senate because of "many voting irregularities and discrepancies around the state." Reid also told the crowd he had "to absorb a staggering financial burden," a campaign debt of $21,000.

Reid spent a significant amount of time talking about policy, saying the Ford administration had imposed tax cuts he supported to jump-start a recessionary economy. What's more, decades before he would have a chance to leave his indelible mark on two significant policy areas, he already was talking about "efforts to learn more about solar and geothermal energy sources" and "some sort of national health insurance."

Finally, at the end of his speech, Reid apologized for blaming the northern Nevada media for his loss "in the dark hours after the election," saying instead "mistakes in judgment contributed heavily to my defeat, not a vendetta by newspapers."

By March, Reid was making it clear he wanted to run for something again. He praised Laxalt, especially on immigration, declaring something that a future Harry Reid would have decried: "The fact is hundreds of Nevadans are being deprived of jobs because illegal aliens are working here."

Unsure at first what office to seek, Reid saw an opening to become mayor of Las Vegas. That election would be in the spring of the off year, 1975. It seemed an odd decision, even though the incumbent, Oran Gragson, seemed vulnerable after fending off a recall. It was hard to believe that a man who had just spent the last year talking about national domestic issues and foreign policy had found a burning desire to cut ribbons and fill potholes.

His friends thought he was making a devastating blunder. "I did everything I could to talk him out of it," his lifelong friend J. J. Balk remembered. "We didn't need another loss. And I just thought, let's let this rest for a while. And he wasn't hearing it."

Just before he died in 2021, Reid conceded the mistake. "My friends begged me not to, but my pride got in the way. I guess I was like a jilted lover. I felt I needed to rehabilitate myself . . . It was a terrible, terrible mistake."

Landra said her husband also was persuaded by his campaign consultant, Don Williams, to run for mayor so he could pay off his Senate campaign debt.

Reid's memories of the race were either a blur—or he tried to block them out. He devoted all of one paragraph to the mayoral contest in his autobiography.

The truth was that Reid looked pretty strong at the beginning of the contest. Others showed interest, including Hank Thornley, a newscaster and then city commissioner, and Ron Lurie, another city official. But when Mayor Gragson announced a few weeks before the May election that he was retiring, Reid seemed to be the odds-on favorite. Just before the filing deadline, though, Bill Briare, a former assemblyman and county commissioner who had been on the hospital board with Reid, jumped into the race. Briare, unlike Reid, was a born gladhander.

Before Gragson's announcement or Briare's entrance, Reid had been gathering support, meeting with the likes of Ben Schmoutey, the powerful leader of Culinary Local 226 who was later linked to the mob and served time for defrauding the union, and the Golden Nugget casino owner, Steve Wynn, who would later become a Las Vegas Strip visionary before being forced to abdicate amid allegations of sexual misconduct.

Reid had already sent supporters a letter in late March tipping his hand, suggesting Las Vegas was "entering a new era" and he was the man to help fight rising crime rates. He also emphasized an issue he believed had helped propel him into the legislature and the lieutenant governor job: rising utility rates.

In campaign materials, Reid touted his breadth of experience, including being O'Callaghan's number two on many issues, and he also highlighted his time as "a police officer" to establish his anti-crime bona fides—a reference to his brief stint with the Capitol Police in Washington, DC.

Reid's head start, the multiway field, and Briare's late entrance paid off in the May primary. Reid easily won with 36 percent of the vote to Briare's 22 percent, and the runoff was set. There was reason to believe, though, that Reid had reached close to his ceiling and that the 64 percent of the vote that went to other candidates would not go his way. When Gragson, a Republican, endorsed Briare, the die was cast.

One week before the election, in one of the more blistering editorials ever written about a candidate, the muckraking Las Vegas newspaper *Valley Times* endorsed Briare and castigated Reid.

The piece was relentlessly critical of Reid as a serial candidate, and it accused Reid of conflicts of interest with his law firm. The *Valley Times* also referred to "the deplorable manner in which Reid took his Senate defeat last year," understating that he "did not take it with grace and dignity."

Then the paper really lowered the boom in two startling paragraphs:

> We believe Harry Reid was once a very sincere person. But somewhere along the line in his desire for political office the real sincerity gave way to practiced sincerity—and perhaps Harry Reid himself can't tell the difference today.
>
> Somehow, to gain the money he needed to run campaign after campaign, to raise the half million dollars or more he spent last year, Reid has had to make too many compromises, has had to sell himself too many times.

A few days later, the *Las Vegas Review-Journal* did not even mention Reid in a gushing endorsement of Briare. On June 3, 1975, Reid lost by more than five percentage points.

Two losses in the space of seven months, including an embarrassing defeat for an office that was a huge step down from a US Senate contest. Many thought Election Day 1975 signaled the end of Harry Reid's political career.

CHAPTER SEVEN

A NEW JOB, A BRIBE, AND A MOB ASSOCIATE

In October 1975, Landra, her mother, and the children were involved in a devastating car accident in Las Vegas. Landra had swerved to avoid another car and the Bronco she was driving overturned, throwing her mother and fourteen-month-old Key from the car. Reid's mother-in-law died instantly, but Key and the other children miraculously survived with minor injuries. Landra was pinned in the wreckage for fifteen minutes before being rushed to Southern Nevada Memorial Hospital, the same county facility her husband used to oversee. Reid would later tell a friend that one side of Landra's face was paralyzed for three months. She, too, would recover, but the accident was traumatic for the family.

Reid retreated into his law practice, his name occasionally floated for open seats, including a state senate post. But he was focused on his job and his family, and the closest he got to politics that year was being asked by Gov. Mike O'Callaghan to try to settle a $142 million lawsuit filed by the *Sun* owner, Hank Greenspun, against Howard Hughes in a dispute over a land sale. (The case would drag on for years.)

But Reid had not completely given up on a political career. He was quietly forging relationships and mending fences, assiduously courting many of those he had alienated during the Senate and mayoral races.

In 1976, when the presidential contest reached full swing and the Democratic nominee, Jimmy Carter, was putting together state organizations, Reid took on a public role organizing fundraisers for the Georgia governor.

On June 1, shortly after one of those events, Reid wrote what could have been a pro forma letter but attached a personalized addendum to one recipient:

"I was sorry that you were unable to attend the reception in honor of Jimmy Carter with me the other evening," Reid wrote. "It was a great affair, and I am hopeful you will have a chance to meet Governor Carter at another time."

Then he added a Yoda-like PS: "Your column, I have enjoyed. Best wishes."

The warm note was to Frank Rosenthal, referring to his column in the *Las Vegas Sun*, which the *New York Times* would later label as "subliterate." By then, Rosenthal had become a notorious figure in Nevada, having been denied a gaming license by state authorities who suspected him of being, at minimum, a game fixer. Rosenthal's efforts to overturn that denial, led by his attorney Oscar Goodman, had been constantly in the media for six months. Rosenthal's Las Vegas career would later be chronicled in the Martin Scorsese film *Casino* (a character based on him was played by Robert De Niro, and Goodman played himself). Decades later, Goodman would become a popular mayor of Las Vegas.

IN EARLY 1977, Governor O'Callaghan called his protégé. The governor said he wanted Reid to chair the part-time gaming commission, the five-member board that oversees regulation of the state's most prominent industry. In Nevada's two-tiered system, the full-time Gaming Control Board investigates and makes recommendations; the part-time gaming commission reviews the control board's findings and decides whether to accept or reject them. The statutes were written so that a unanimous commission vote is required to veto the control board. The commission truly is the final word, barring any court intervention.

Pete Echeverria, the flamboyant chair, was retiring and O'Callaghan said privately that he wanted someone tough at a time when the federal government was still sniffing for mob influence in casinos. He knew that if the state didn't keep its house in order, the feds would step in—as then attorney general Bobby Kennedy had once threatened former governor Grant Sawyer. Instead of elevating a current member to helm the critical commission, O'Callaghan bypassed the incumbents and asked Reid to chair the panel.

Reid would say later that the governor came to him for two reasons. "Number one, he wanted to do something for me," Reid said. "Number two, he needed somebody to be at that gaming commission that he could trust implicitly."

The governor rescued Reid from political oblivion, giving him arguably the most high-profile state appointive post but one that didn't necessarily guarantee a return to elective life. Reid knew something of the industry by virtue of his legislative experience and certainly his months spent chasing down the Hughes coterie. But even he would later say—and others would agree—that he was naive about the job and the dangerous forces arrayed against him.

This was a time in which the mob had installed associates in casinos in lower-profile positions—entertainment director or food and beverage boss—to conceal its involvement. The gaming authorities were determined to ferret out these Mafia plants and expel them from the industry by calling them forward for licensing and exposing who they really were.

Before he began his new role, Reid went to Reno to meet with Echeverria. The outgoing chairman pointed outside to a car with men in it. "He told me, 'Those are spies. They are there to do what they can to make me look bad,'" Reid recalled. "I thought he was full of BS, but he wasn't. He was telling the truth."

So when Reid took the reins of the state's gaming regulatory apparatus on April 27, 1977, he knew this was not the same as being on the hospital board, or in the legislature, or lieutenant governor. He spent weeks reading old meeting transcripts and case files to get ready. "I don't intend to be tough," he told the *Las Vegas Sun*. "I want to be fair, but if I have to be tough, I will be."

He would have to be. And more than once.

Reid's appointment was welcomed by the media. He secured a rare positive mention from the *Las Vegas Review-Journal* editorial board, and Rosenthal, in his *Sun* column, lashed out at Echeverria, who had blocked his gaming license, and welcomed "a new era with Harry Reid."

Not everyone, though, was immediately persuaded that Reid would hold the line. Jeff Silver, a respected member of the control board at the time who went on to a successful legal career, said there was skepticism about O'Callaghan appointing a former politician to such a sensitive post.

Almost immediately, Silver thought his fears were validated in one of Reid's first meetings when the commission considered the control board's rejection of Paul Lowden. A former musician and bandleader, Lowden had put together a complex set of financial maneuvers to purchase the Hacienda Hotel on the Strip.

Silver was adamant that Lowden had not been forthcoming and had participated in "sham transactions." He raised the possibility that Lowden had hidden investors. Some of those dealings had to do with Allen Glick and the Argent Corporation, which had wanted Rosenthal in charge of the Stardust before his licensing was rejected in 1976 and he had to take lower-profile jobs that did not require the state's imprimatur.

Reid, though, was having none of it. In a lengthy statement at the meeting, he eviscerated the control board's investigation, said it relied too much on a convicted felon, and concluded, "The evidence that we are asked to hold him over on wouldn't hold water in anything, in an eighth-grade government class, in my opinion."

Reid's screed swayed his colleagues and Lowden received the unanimous vote he needed to overrule the control board.

"That was one of the few times that I could recall that the board was turned away," Silver recalled. "In fact, the only times that I can recall that the board was ever rejected [during his tenure] in its recommendation were items that were engineered by Harry Reid."

However, Silver said that since Reid had come from nothing, he might have sympathized with Lowden, "a person who had worked in Nevada as a musician and [Reid] kind of saw him as a little guy trying to make a score in his life by buying this property. And he was able to cobble together financing that might have been a little questionable, but [Reid] wasn't going to turn him down."

The reaction was positive. "Reid came on strong, put his chin on the line somewhat, but we liked what we saw in Harry Reid last week," the *Review-Journal* wrote. "In only his second month on the job, Reid made it clear that he will not accept any nonsense from his gaming staff or the applicants."

In at least one sense, Reid was proven right. Lowden went on to even greater success in the industry, eventually purchasing the Sahara Hotel. Reid believed—and others, including Silver, agreed—that without Reid's intervention, Lowden's career in gaming would have been over. He saved him.

"Then the bastard turned on me," Reid would say later, a reference to how Lowden's future wife, Sue, would challenge him for the US Senate in 2010. "What a terrible lack of loyalty and appreciation they had."

IF REID WENT out of his way to help Lowden, that was nothing compared to what he would do less than two months later. He flouted the attorney general's advice to help a client and close friend of a former law partner and sowed the seeds for an FBI probe of him. Reid essentially changed the rules to push through the approval of the California oilman Jack Urich, who wanted to invest in the Tropicana Hotel. The Tropicana had gone from being the "Tiffany of the Strip" to hard times and needed a multimillion-dollar investment from the chemical heiress Mitzi Stauffer Briggs to save the place. But even that did not seem to be enough, and the argument was that Urich's money would help rescue the Tropicana. His multimillion-dollar investment had to be cleared by gaming authorities.

Urich was represented by Jay Brown, a close Reid friend from the Jemison law firm. Brown would become as tight with Reid as anyone outside his family, helping him raise money and utilizing his friendship with Reid to good measure. Brown also would become one of the most powerful and successful local government lobbyists in Nevada history, harnessing his cultivated relationships with key public officials to help his clients.

The day before the September 15 meeting, the Gaming Control Board rejected Urich's attempt to invest in the Tropicana. Urich had not appeared before the board and the Tropicana failed to persuade the members that an emergency existed. On the day of the commission meeting, Gaming Control Board member Silver flew up to Carson City and none other than Harry Reid sat next to him on the plane.

"I said, 'Well, is there anything that you think you want to discuss with me with respect to your agenda and the actions that we've taken,'" Silver recalled. "And he said, 'Well, tell me about this Tropicana thing.' And so I went through the thought processes of the board, and the report. And I really said to him, 'You know, this guy is a bad actor.' And I was concerned about it."

When the meeting began, Silver said, "It's like nothing I ever said registered." Indeed, Brown immediately asked for a private session to discuss proprietary information about the Tropicana's finances, which Reid granted. When the chairman emerged from that closed session, he said he was convinced a state of emergency existed and that Urich's money was needed.

"The fact is the Tropicana Hotel has been limping along for a long while, and it appears to me that the limping is about to be cured, and I don't think that the commission should cut them off at this time," Reid declared at the meeting. Fellow commission member George Swarts, a respected CPA, vehemently disagreed with Reid's characterization of what they had learned in the closed meeting and suggested it was outrageous that no financial statements were provided to back up the assertions. But Brown had done his job and all he needed was for Reid, who also served as chief parliamentarian, to rule that only a majority vote was required in this case to overrule the board. That is exactly what happened, over the objections of the attorney general's office, and Urich's stake in the hotel was approved.

Reid defended his decision in the media as necessary to save the hotel and scoffed at suggestions he had a conflict because of Brown. He also wrote a letter to Attorney General Bob List defending his ruling on the majority vote, insisting the move was legal in cases involving emergencies. List, responding to a control board request, produced an opinion by year's end that declared Reid's ruling had been in error, that the legislative intent was clear that a unanimous vote was required. But the ruling was not retroactive and was too late to stop Urich's emergency investment, which already had been made.

Six months later, Urich was gone. He had been rejected by the control board again, and this time Reid could not save him.

REID'S FIRST NINE months on the commission had brought him into the public eye again, and he was being mentioned as a potential candidate for governor in 1978 to succeed O'Callaghan. He denied any interest. In private correspondence, he told people he wasn't making any political plans. Indeed, the new year would bring an entirely new set of challenges for the chairman that would give him very little chance to think about his political future. It also commenced with sad news as Reid's mother, Inez, died at the age of sixty-nine in January 1978. Now thirty-eight, Reid had lost both of his parents.

A few months later, a controversy occurred that would become the stuff of Nevada lore. On July 20, 1978, the commission voted four to one to override a denial by the control board of a new slot machine. The machines, the control board believed, were more like arcade games and more appropriate for carnivals than a casino floor. Reid voted with the majority, but Commissioner George Swarts's no vote, thwarting unanimity, doomed the proposal.

Six days later, Reid received a phone call from Joe Daly, a publicist active in Democratic politics. Daly said he represented one of the slot machine principals, Jack Gordon, a former wedding chapel owner at Circus Circus casino, and urgently needed to meet with the chair. Reid, who said he smelled a rat when Daly contacted him, immediately called former control board member Silver, who he knew had contacts with the FBI. "He said, 'Jeff, you got to help me with this because this guy is trying to bribe me,'" Silver said. He advised Reid to put off Daly until the next day, which he did, in time for the FBI to wiretap his phone.

Over the next five days, under the monitoring of the FBI, Reid took phone calls about the prospective bribe and set up a payoff meeting. After an initial offer of $3,000, the FBI advised Reid to tell the principals that was too paltry a sum for him to risk his career and to ask for four times that amount. Gordon and another associate, Sol Sayegh, a carpet salesman, readily agreed. They planned to go to Reid's law office late on the afternoon of July 31 to consummate the deal. By then, the FBI had his office wired for sound and video to present compelling evidence at a trial.

"Well, I guess we're all set to go," Reid said to Gordon and Sayegh as the FBI watched and listened. "As I understand it, there are two things that are important. One is to get back on the agenda. And the second is to try and pick up another vote. Fair enough?"

When there was some hesitation about the logistics of getting the item back on the commission agenda, Reid, who would later be described as appearing nervous on the videotape, seemed to lose his patience. "I'm not gonna screw around anymore," he told the men. "Either we go ahead . . . I'm just not gonna horse around with it. I thought we had a deal tonight."

Unbeknownst to Reid, the men had locked his office door behind them. So after he accepted the payoff, the FBI agents could not get in.

His law partner, Bruce Alverson, was in his nearby office watching on monitors the FBI had set up, along with the agents. "All I could hear was some rattling of the doorknob," Alverson recalled. Alverson had a key so he walked over and opened the door. "These three [FBI] guys grabbed Gordon and threw him up against the wall."

Reid leapt out of his chair and put his arms around Gordon, choking him. "You tried to bribe me, you son of a bitch," he yelled, uncharacteristically and histrionically. The agents had to pull him off Gordon, who along with Sayegh was arrested. Later, Daly was taken into custody in California.

"We're All Proud of Harry Reid" was the headline the next day in the *Las Vegas Review-Journal*'s editorial praising the chairman for his actions.

Even though the federal government would obtain convictions the following year—the case against Sayegh was dismissed in a bizarre twist after his son was kidnapped and the government argued he had suffered enough—Daly and Gordon alleged in court that they were trying to prove Reid was corrupt and then turn over the evidence to Oscar Goodman, the well-known criminal defense attorney. Assistant US Attorney Larry Leavitt scoffed at such an argument in which defense attorneys compared Reid to the snake in the Garden of Eden tempting their clients.

Former commissioner Silver, who had concerns about Reid's susceptibility to be influenced by his friends in gaming matters, nevertheless came to believe that he was fundamentally honest. "The fact of the matter is that he never would take any kind of bribe," Silver said.

The bribery brouhaha was not even the most memorable incident from Reid's second year on the commission. Reid did not realize that as he and O'Callaghan were railing about the federal government regulating Nevada enterprises, the FBI was already hard at work investigating the casinos. They were closing in on Argent Corporation, which controlled several Las Vegas casinos, and by midyear, the FBI was alleging that the company was a puppet of the mobster Anthony Spilotro and other underworld figures. (Spilotro was also fictionalized in *Casino*, as a character played by Joe Pesci.)

Rosenthal's association with Spilotro was part of the reason that he had been denied a license by gaming authorities and why he had shifted to food and beverage director at the Stardust. But Nevada's regulators were not relenting and were about to call him forward for licensing again, suggesting he was no mere food and beverage director.

The commission had plenty of evidence that Glick, the head of Argent, which owned the Stardust, was a front for the mob, and the feds were investigating this, too. During a lengthy proceeding in which Goodman, Rosenthal's attorney, made multiple threats to go to court, the commission voted unanimously to move forward with a licensing hearing. Reid said he believed Goodman should have been able to present more evidence, but still voted for the motion. After Reid adjourned the meeting, a furious Rosenthal approached the dais and confronted Reid, who he said had come to the Stardust, promised him a "fair hearing," and was a "hypocrite" presiding over a "kangaroo court."

The video of the confrontation, later dramatized in *Casino* and which appeared decades later in the Las Vegas CBS affiliate's special *Mob on the Run*, shows a calm Reid being confronted by a fuming Rosenthal.

"Mr. Rosenthal is being very typical to this point: he's lying," Reid said into the TV cameras and microphones assembled before him. "The only time I have ever been to the Stardust was with Brian Greenspun [the eldest son of the *Las Vegas Sun* owner], long prior to me getting on this commission."

Rosenthal immediately walked up to Reid and declared that the two had had "lunch with me. Is that a lie, too?"

"You were wandering around," Reid acknowledged as Rosenthal lit up a cigarette.

Rosenthal then told the media to ask Reid about contacting Jay Brown "to seek my influence" to kill a damaging story about the Stardust Hotel and Casino giving freebies to incipient governor Bob List before the election. Reid, who did not break monotone while Rosenthal became angrier and angrier, acknowledged he did approach Brown to contact Rosenthal to use his influence because "I thought it would be terrible for the state of Nevada for a story like that to break."

After Reid's confirmation, Rosenthal sneered, "Thank you very much for not calling me a liar. More bullshit. You and the O'Callaghan gang."

He then walked out of the room.

On December 19, the control board and commission declined to license Rosenthal. Reid delivered a lengthy speech in which he acknowledged that some had called him too soft and that he was seen as "voting for people that maybe didn't deserve my vote, but I voted for them and I'm not going to change that procedure when there's some reason given to me to do so." But he added that Rosenthal and Goodman had not given him reason to overrule the control board.

The vote was unanimous. Reid and gaming regulators had essentially kicked Frank "Lefty" Rosenthal out of the gaming industry, his past and future legal protestations notwithstanding. The significance—the watershed moment—should not be underestimated. Rosenthal, tied to the mob yet embraced by some of polite Vegas society, had tried to mask his stewardship of the casino, hiding in plain sight.

"Rosenthal was the perfect test case for gaming laws around the world, and especially in Nevada, because he was such a bad plaintiff," Silver said. "He tested every single imaginable law and was rebuffed every time he went to court . . . And, you know, if you just looked at the reference letters that Frank Rosenthal submitted in connection with his original licensing application, it read like the who's who in Las Vegas, respectable people."

The same people, some of whom later were found to be disreputable, whom Reid the candidate raised money from, whose judgment Reid would have trusted. But, Silver believed, even if Reid had been influenced by community luminaries and his friends, he had his eyes wide open now.

"[Rosenthal] was the only man I was afraid of," Reid said. "I wasn't afraid of him personally. I was afraid of what he would do, have done to me."

Reid, a movie buff, claimed he never saw *Casino*.

"I read the reviews on it, and they said the movie made Rosenthal look good." (It did not.)

By this time, List had become governor, and there were questions about whether the Republican would replace Reid on the commission. List said he never considered booting the Democrat as the state's top gaming regulator because he was on a four-year term appointment and because he trusted him.

The pair had worked together on the Rosenthal case because List was the attorney general at the time. List argued the case in the Nevada Supreme Court that upheld Reid and the commission's decision to deny Rosenthal a license. A bond was forming that would become very important.

CHAPTER EIGHT

CLEANFACE, MR. LAS VEGAS, AND OL' BLUE EYES

On April 17, 1979, a few months after the Rosenthal hearing, the FBI began investigating Harry Reid.

According to a redacted FBI file that Reid apparently requested and put in his archive at the university in Reno, it was related to a case called "STRAWMAN-TROPICANA" and it involved "hidden LCN [La Cosa Nostra] of the Tropicana Hotel in Las Vegas . . . During extensive Elsur [electronic surveillance] activities in Las Vegas and Kansas City, numerous references to a 'Mr. Clean' and 'Clean-Face' were intercepted. These nicknames obviously referred to a high state gaming official who would allegedly do the bidding of the LCN in gaming matters. A careful analysis of the context in which these references were made during the telephone conversations revealed that they could only relate to subject Reid."

The chairman of the Nevada Gaming Commission had come under the FBI's scrutiny because of his actions in the Tropicana cases and his close relationship to Jay Brown, who had acted as both the resort's lawyer and that of Joe Agosto, the controversial producer of the Folies Bergere show at the hotel.

"The conversations referred to Reid receiving money from the Tropicana disguised as legal fees to [the name is redacted, but it had to be Brown] as well as to Reid 'fixing' certain decisions relative to the Tropicana . . . Investigation to date has revealed that Reid has in fact made several controversial decisions on the Tropicana, including attempting to overrule a vote of the Commission prohibiting Los Angeles [redacted, but it had to be Jack Urich] from investing in the Tropicana."

Reid's actions, including his insistence that the commission could overrule the control board in the Urich case, where Brown also was the lead lawyer, and where Attorney General Bob List eventually opined the chairman was wrong, had caused the FBI to open a file on him.

The probe into Reid would eventually become broader and deeper and last much longer than has been previously disclosed, for five years and into his Capitol Hill tenure. Wiretaps would become public about a month after the investigation became public and catalyze a pivotal point in Reid's life, threatening to end his career and destroy any confidence in the state's casino regulatory process. It's no exaggeration to say that if events had gone just a little differently, Reid would never have held elective office again.

Shortly before the wiretap transcripts became public, and in what can only be seen as a breach of judicial ethics, Reid received a phone call from an old friend, Harry Claiborne, who had become a federal judge. Claiborne didn't want to talk about details on the phone and told Reid he wanted to meet in person.

"He came to see me and said, 'The word going around is the mob is calling you 'Mr. Cleanface.' And there are wiretaps in that regard," Reid recalled the judge telling him. Reid assumed the US Attorney's Office had tipped Claiborne, who would soon demand that the wiretap affidavits be unsealed.

"Can you imagine, a federal judge told me that?" Reid said in a moment of unbridled candor decades later. (Claiborne was later impeached and removed from office on tax evasion charges.)

"And I was so, so out of my mind. But I hadn't done anything wrong, so why did I care if there were wiretaps?"

He would soon care very much.

In late May, Ned Day, a reporter for the *Valley Times*, broke the news that would eventually rock the state and change Reid's life: the wiretaps revealed that despite the state's best efforts, the Kansas City mob still had pervasive influence in the casino industry in at least four hotels, including through the Folies Bergere majordomo, Agosto, at the Tropicana. But there was more: Agosto was caught on the tapes boasting of having a relationship with "Cleanface" and "Mr. Clean," the direct implication that it was through Brown.

Agosto initially denied he was talking about Reid, but it was evident to everyone, including Reid, that he was. The name was an echo of what Hank Greenspun had bestowed on him in a complimentary way years earlier, and that was Reid's reputation. As affidavits were released, all doubt was erased.

Reid denied any wrongdoing, saying Agosto was just "one hoodlum boasting to another hoodlum," and the chairman even threatened to sue the mob associate for slander. (He never did.) In one affidavit, from a wiretap of a September 19, 1978, conversation between Agosto and the Kansas City organized crime lieutenant Carl DeLuna, Agosto said Frank Rosenthal was "really abusing . . . Cleanface."

Reid also was persuaded by the repeated references to his longtime friend and law firm colleague Brown as the "Cleanface" connection that he was the person being talked about. In one instance, Agosto said that Reid had agreed to not yank licenses at the Stardust and Fremont casinos and impose a $100,000 fine instead, which Reid vehemently denied, saying, as he did at the hearing, that there was not enough evidence to pull the licenses.

Reid's commission colleagues defended him, insisting he did not sway their votes on the matter. But in doing so, Clair Haycock, a friend of Reid for two decades, was not exactly helpful.

"I'm sure they were talking about Harry Reid," Haycock said. "Jay Brown was continually saying he controls Harry Reid . . . But it's nonsense. I don't believe Harry Reid can be corrupted." He would call Brown "an influence peddler" to another outlet and added he "wouldn't be surprised if he told friends like Agosto he controlled Harry."

(Brown denied he ever boasted about any influence with Reid to clients.)

As the media frenzy ensued, Reid prepared a statement to read at the next commission hearing: "We as gaming regulators . . . cannot stop those that peddle influence and boast and lie to others about this influence except to state that we are not impressed . . . Gaming authorities will not be intimidated or influenced by the criminal elements or those evil ones in our society . . . Gaming officials of the state of Nevada are not for sale."

Governor List immediately came to Reid's defense, or at least said he deserved the benefit of the doubt because he believed Agosto had "very little credibility." But because of the potential taint on the industry, he also vowed that there would be a thorough investigation.

The immense pressure prompted Reid to go see his mentor and tell him he was resigning. O'Callaghan talked him out of it, and List rejected his half-hearted and pro forma attempt to depart.

Reid and Landra were worried about his and the family's safety. But he decided to stay.

Reid knew he would have to ride out the bad publicity and the looming state investigation, and he realized the probe would be broad and deep into his life, his finances, his connections. But before it all began, he received one phone call, amid some public pleas in the media for him to resign, that had a profound effect. It came from his onetime rival Sen. Paul Laxalt, according to Brown.

"He said, 'Harry, if you did something wrong, you resign,'" Laxalt told Reid. "'If you didn't do anything wrong, and knowing you, I can't imagine you did, don't you dare resign.'"

He was going to tough it out.

LAW ENFORCEMENT AGENTS surely read an investigative series by the *Reno Evening Gazette* in August with great interest. As part of a seven-part series on gaming control, the paper published a story headlined: "Gaming Chief Reid: Is He Tough Enough?"

Based on interviews with current and past gaming officials, the piece painted Reid as too soft, too kind, too weak, too political for the job. Former Gaming Control Board chairman Phil Hannifin was critical of Reid and Brown, who, he reiterated, frequently bragged about Reid's "juice" with the commission. But, the story said, "Over the weeks, those interviewed often ended critical discussions of Reid with: 'But Harry Reid is honest. He's not a crook.'"

Reid began meeting with federal strike force attorneys almost as soon as the wiretaps were discovered, and by October, the probe had become public because of affidavits filed to try to get Brown and Goodman to disclose financial information. Reid told the media that he, too, had turned over documents, and said he welcomed the probe because it would exonerate him.

By the end of the year, according to an FBI file, the bureau had "uncovered" other allegations against Reid:

During his 1970 run for governor he was given a $25,000 contribution (from whom is redacted but is believed to be Agosto). The FBI document said the contribution "was allegedly not reported by Reid." There was no reporting requirement until 1975.

"When Reid ran for the Nevada State Senate prior to being elected Lieutenant Governor, he was alleged to have received five separate checks from Argent Corporation." After a small redaction, the document again says Reid did not report the money. Also, he never ran for the state senate; this surely meant the assembly.

"When Reid ran for the U.S. Senate [against Laxalt], a party was thrown for him in which numerous 'backroom' cash contributions were personally made to him which were not reported."

"Reid was allegedly given a $25,000 cash payoff in 1974." The details are redacted.

The FBI's suspicions clearly intensified when it discovered that Reid had done legal work for Growth Industries, the parent company of Royal Reservations, a show ticket sales firm affiliated with Argent, which owned the Stardust and Fremont Hotels. Reid would later disclose that he had been paid $250,000 by Growth Industries, which translates into seven figures today. He abstained on gaming commission matters involving Royal Reservations as soon as he was appointed to the commission, records show.

A raw FBI file is just that—a series of allegations. The bureau, though, was far from done with Reid, and the investigation continued into the 1980s.

Reid never gave an inch as both the federal and state investigations continued. The Gaming Control Board, led by Richard Bunker, an inside political player close to List who would later become the lead lobbyist for the casino industry, appointed two retired Texas Rangers to probe Reid's finances. A national accounting firm also was retained.

The probe was very intrusive as Reid was forced to provide invoices for clients as well as home purchases. He would later say that "no one has ever been investigated as much as I was."

"For everything I bought, a couch, a TV set, whatever it was I had to prove how I paid for it. Anything over $200 I had to prove how I paid for it . . . That was really very difficult for me."

Finally, on February 26, 1980, five months after the state investigation had begun, Reid was greeted by the headline he wanted, needed: "Mr. Clean Clean as a Whistle—Top Gamer Reid Totally Cleared," the *Las Vegas Sun* said.

"There were no improprieties on the part of Mr. Reid," Bunker said. "The investigation we put Mr. Reid through was certainly more inclusive than that given any applicant for the [control] board."

What is perhaps most remarkable about all of this, at least in political terms, is that "Cleanface" was never used by opponents in any of Reid's subsequent campaigns for office—at least never beyond whisper campaigns. No ads were aired, no mail pieces sent, no press conferences called. The vindication by state and eventually federal authorities would turn a potentially fatal political issue into a nonexistent one.

For Reid, the Bunker press conference meant the ordeal was over. But he still had a job to do, at least for another year until his term expired. He was about to play a major role in the casino careers of arguably the two most famous entertainers ever to play Vegas—Wayne Newton and Frank Sinatra—and once again, allegations of mob influence would play a role.

IN 1980, WAYNE Newton made a bid to buy the troubled Aladdin Hotel, which had been shut down and then reopened. Newton's bid came to the fore after the talk show host Johnny Carson failed in his quest to buy the property.

By midyear, Newton had made his interest known and had to come before regulators. He was represented by a Reno lawyer named Frank Fahrenkopf, who would later become the general chairman of the Republican National Committee and the head of the American Gaming Association. The commission gave Newton a deadline to consummate what would have been a $100 million purchase. But Newton could not finalize the deal, and by mid-July, the resort was shuttered.

Finally, in September, with Reid leading the charge for Newton, he was approved to own the Aladdin after recruiting a former Riviera Hotel general manager, Ed Torres, to run the place. Reid brushed aside criticisms of both men's alleged ties to organized crime figures—Torres to the infamous Meyer Lansky and Newton to a man named Guido Penosi, who was affiliated with the Gambino and Lucchese crime families.

"I personally commend Wayne Newton for hanging in there after the place was closed," Reid said at the meeting. He later said that he didn't believe that Newton's relationship with Penosi was a big deal. He pushed it through because "I felt that he had been coming to Las Vegas, ever since he was a boy, and his standing in Las Vegas was really good. I thought that had he been denied a license, it would be detrimental to the gaming industry generally."

Reid was "almost bubbly" in his praise, as the *Reno Evening Gazette* would later describe the chairman's demeanor. But ten days after Reid led the commission to approve Newton, NBC News broadcast a segment called "Wayne Newton and the Law." The segment raised questions about Newton's ties to Penosi, implied he had been less than candid with the commission, and even went so far as to intimate Penosi might have a financial interest in the Aladdin.

In what would become one of the most celebrated libel cases in American history, Newton sued and was eventually granted a $19.2 million award, which was later reduced to $5.2 million before the verdict was overturned by the Ninth Circuit Court of Appeals. (The US Supreme Court eventually declined to hear Newton's appeal.)

Reid would be deposed in the case and asked why he had dismissed concerns about the singer's relationship with Penosi. In fact, when he was questioned about Newton's call to Penosi when his only child was threatened with violence—and he did not explain why he thought Penosi could have helped—Reid said bluntly, "He called Penosi. And from that point forward, he had no more threats regarding the safety of his only child."

Newton was forever grateful for Reid's role in getting the Aladdin purchase approved, even though Torres would eventually buy him out in 1982.

The two remained good friends until the senator's death in 2021. Reid helped Newton, who spoke fondly of Reid after he died, get a USO lounge at the Las Vegas airport. Despite being a big Republican donor, Newton attended DC fundraisers for Reid. "Life has no blessing like a prudent friend (Euripides)," Reid wrote in a handwritten note to Newton in 2002. "You are, for me, giving up some of your valuable time to come to D.C. for me. I hope in some way, some day, I can repay your act of generosity."

North Dakota's Byron Dorgan, Reid's longtime friend and colleague in the Senate, knew of the friendship. So when he was running for reelection and Newton was helping fund a Republican effort to defeat him, Dorgan gave Reid a simple message at an event: "Tell Wayne Newton to go fuck himself." Reid said he relayed the message, and the two friends shared a laugh.

SHORTLY THEREAFTER, REID presided over a hearing on an even bigger celebrity. Frank Sinatra had given up his Nevada gaming license almost two decades earlier after the Mafia boss Sam Giancana had been seen at the crooner's Cal-Nevada resort near Lake Tahoe. When questioned about it by then control board chairman Ed Olsen, Sinatra had launched an abusive, profanity-laced tirade. He was done with casinos, he said, and was going to focus on singing and acting.

But in 1980, Ol' Blue Eyes was back seeking another license. Sinatra was not seeking to buy a casino—at least not yet—but he needed the license to become a consultant to Caesars Palace. In early February, the control board had granted Sinatra a limited six-month license after more than a year of investigating him and his potentially unsavory associations with the likes of the mobsters Giancana, Lucky Luciano, and Jimmy Fratianno.

Reid's speech at a September hearing was nothing if not memorable.

"I went into these hearings some 13 months ago . . . with the preconceived notion, I hate to admit that, that's a fact, the preconceived notion that you're the type of a person that shouldn't receive a gaming license," Reid told Sinatra. "And I still had feelings in that regard eight days ago."

That was when he read the voluminous testimony and investigation by the control board and realized, "I have to be very candid and honest in saying that I was totally wrong."

The self-flagellating chairman then felt it necessary to read an entire poem a woman had submitted in support of Sinatra and recounted Sinatra's awards and charitable endeavors. He concluded his fawning tribute by declaring, "I started out [by saying] that I was a Willie Nelson fan, not a Frank Sinatra fan. And even though you both perform at Caesars Palace, I have to honestly say that after having learned about you as a person, I'm now a Frank Sinatra fan."

Sinatra received his license to be a consultant and the ability to earn a reported $20,000 a week from Caesars Palace.

Some gaming executives and former regulators worried about the precedent the Reid-led commission had set, overturning previous assumptions that associations mattered. But Reid had no regrets.

When he was asked whether the character testimonials from fellow actors and entertainers, and one from President Ronald Reagan, had swayed him, Reid deadpanned: "I was more impressed with Gregory Peck's recommendation."

Reid said he never met Sinatra before or after that meeting but that the singer once sent him a campaign contribution for one of his Senate races. "I still have a check that he gave me," Reid said. "I never cashed the $1,000 check."

For Reid, that seemed to be the exclamation point on his gaming regulatory career. A couple of weeks later, he announced that List had offered him a reappointment but that he turned him down. Reid also declared he would not take any gaming clients for a year, a cooling-off period that others had not taken.

His departure was greeted with almost unanimously positive editorials. "Reid Leaves Gaming Post with Respect, Integrity" was the headline in the *Valley Times*, writing that he served with "dignity, good grace, integrity and common sense. He was gutsy when the need arose; but for the most part he was even-handed and reasonable."

Even the *Nevada State Journal*, which ran the headline "Mixed Performance" and lambasted Reid for embarrassing Nevada when he "read a silly poem" at Sinatra's hearing, credited him for not taking gaming clients and said he was "leaving in high style."

By mid-July, Reid was telling the media he was considering a run for governor in 1982 against List, the man who had supported him during his darkest hours. He suggested that the only person he would not run against was his father figure, O'Callaghan, now executive editor of the *Las Vegas Sun*, a position Reid had negotiated for him with the publisher, Hank Greenspun. Reid announced that he wasn't sure whether he wanted to run for governor or for a new congressional seat in Southern Nevada created by the legislature a few months earlier.

It was clear that after six years away from an electoral run, at the age of forty-one, Harry Reid was ready to get back into the fray.

CHAPTER NINE

MR. REID GOES TO WASHINGTON

Three months after Harry Reid left the gaming commission, on the evening of July 29, 1981, Landra Reid had to take one of their sons, Leif, to a scouting event at a local chapel. The family car, an Oldsmobile, had been acting up, but the Reids' only daughter and oldest child, Lana, had not had time to take it to the dealership.

On the way home, the car seemed as if it was about to break down, Landra said. "The car was just missing, just shaking and doing all this stuff. And I was almost to the house."

That's when she recalled what George Swarts, the former gaming commissioner, had told the Reids a few weeks earlier over dinner. Swarts said his car had been behaving strangely and when he looked under the hood, he found a makeshift explosive device, wires running from the sparkplugs to the gas tank.

Landra was worried: "So I pulled into our driveway and opened the hood of the car, and I could see some cords and I could see the cords going into the gas tank. And so I ran in the house and called him [Reid] because he was still at the office. And I said, 'Don't start your car!'"

Reid hung up the phone and called the authorities. Police and firemen descended on the Reid house on Lacy Lane in a tony part of Las Vegas. The police would later say they were not sure whether it was an assassination attempt or just a scare tactic because the device was so crude and unreliable. They offered rewards, but the police never found out who had planted the device. Reid always assumed it was Jack Gordon, who had tried to bribe him. That was probably not a bad guess because Swarts, whose car had been rigged identically in May, had cast the lone vote against Gordon when he was on the gaming commission.

Reid and his wife had the same searing memory of that evening, the police cars and fire trucks with their flashing lights and five-year-old Key staring out their picture window at the scene. "The next thing that we did was cover up those bare windows," Landra recalled. And from that day on, until they left Las Vegas, the Reids used remote devices to start their cars.

That was certainly not the way Harry Reid wanted to get his name back in the news after he left the commission. He had decided about this time to run for the newly created southern congressional district. Nevada had been growing in population—it was now more than eight hundred thousand, enough to sustain a second congressional seat. The new district was also drawn to be heavily Democratic, so the opportunity was ripe for Reid.

This was not a simple decision, though, because Reid was part of a phalanx of lawyers who had sued the MGM Grand on behalf of plaintiffs after a devastating and fatal fire in 1981. Neil Galatz, a prominent lawyer at the time, told Reid he was foolish to run for office. Decades later, Reid remembered the conversation verbatim, he said.

"I think you're making a big mistake running for Congress," Galatz told him. "You're going to get a million bucks out of the MGM fire case. Why don't you just not run for anything? Do it another time."

Reid responded: "You know, Neil, there may not be another time. That's the way it is in life. You take your shots when you can. If I had waited around, I may never have gone to Congress."

Galatz was not exaggerating. Four years later, MGM settled the case for

$76 million. Lawyers for the plaintiffs received a sizable share of that sum, including Reid's ex-partner, Bruce Alverson.

Reid was right, too. If he had listened to Galatz, he may not have been able to get to Capitol Hill for quite some time, if ever. It was a new, open seat, a rare opportunity. A Democrat almost surely would have won, and Reid would have been blocked.

By October, Reid had filed federal documents so he could start raising money, and he announced his candidacy. He asserted he was a moderate, although he refused to cite any issue positions, and he insisted the Cleanface episode had only burnished his image. He also hired Sig Rogich, a Republican who had been with Paul Laxalt and would soon become part of President Reagan's "Tuesday Team."

But Reid was not just relying on the best local talent for this race. He also hired Chris Brown, a Santa Fe, New Mexico, consultant who had worked in the Jimmy Carter campaign with Rey Martinez, Reid's childhood friend who was also involved. Brown would be the first of many highly skilled data analysts Reid would hire over the years, trusting the conclusions of his own experts over polling, which he distrusted since the survey before Election Day in 1974 showed that he had the Senate race locked up.

By November, Brown had already prepared a detailed strategy memo for the campaign. Given Reid's high name recognition and background, and the lack of any high-profile opponents expressing interest in the race, Brown saw Reid as the "clear front-runner and favorite" in the primary. He also believed the district was a Republican target and that Reid would face a serious general election foe. He outlined Reid's advantages, including his reputation for having "honesty and energy," and even came up with a slogan: "Nevada know-how."

The registration figures seemed to heavily favor Reid in Clark County—all but a sliver of the county that housed Las Vegas was encased in the new district. Reid had defeated Laxalt by fifteen thousand votes in Clark in 1974, the last time he was on a statewide ballot, and the Democrats now had 58 percent and the Republicans only 35 percent of registered voters.

Polling conducted in August by Fairbank, Canapary, and Maullin, a respected California firm, showed Reid had emerged from his gaming commission tenure with high marks. He had a 47 percent positive rating in Clark and only 16 percent negative, and when asked about his performance as a regulator, the numbers were similar: 53–26.

Brown, though, thought this was all misleading. In a later memo, titled "Profile of a marginal district," Brown pointed to Reagan's two-to-one victory over Jimmy Carter in Clark in 1980 and an "incredible 14.4 percent cut off the Democratic registration edge in just four years."

This was no slam dunk.

Brown also argued in the initial thirty-three-page memo that Reid should maintain his stance on issues such as abortion and gun control, even if it would hurt him with some portions of the district's electorate. The danger of his appearing to flip-flop, or worse yet appearing "mealy-mouthed," was much more likely to damage his candidacy because of his image for rectitude.

Reid already had begun doing what he did better than almost anyone at the time—and this would be a feature of nearly all his campaigns—and that was to raise money. By the end of 1981, Reid had already raised $104,000 for a campaign Brown thought would cost $500,000. Much of the money came from companies and individuals he had just recently regulated, including past and present Tropicana executives. (He had also accepted thousands of dollars from Stardust executives, and even after the FBI alleged skimming at that casino in January, Reid said he would keep the money or the men would appear guilty. This was not a standard he would adhere to in later campaigns.)

As the year turned, Reid had a sizable financial foundation, no major foe in either the September primary or the general election, and despite Brown's cautionary words, he seemed to be a heavy favorite as he planned a formal May announcement. Then, in March, he picked up the morning newspaper and read a career-threatening story: among a list of 183 names intercepted by FBI wiretaps in conversations with the alleged mobster Tony Spilotro was the former chairman of the Nevada Gaming Commission.

ON FRIDAY, MARCH 5, 1982, the federal strike force prosecutor Stan Hunterton had an unannounced visitor in his Las Vegas office. Reid insisted that he had never talked to Spilotro, that the newspaper story was wrong.

"I didn't even know what he was talking about," Hunterton recalled. It was, the former prosecutor said, "one of those rare mornings when I hadn't read the newspaper. Otherwise, I would have put two and two together."

When he looked, Hunterton saw why Reid was so upset. The story in the *Review-Journal* said Spilotro was caught on the federal wiretap at his known hangout, the Gold Rush, talking to Reid. Hunterton realized this was an explosive and very damaging revelation, a potential career-ending story for the incipient congressional candidate Reid. Hunterton told Reid he would look into it.

What he discovered was exculpatory. Neil Beller, an attorney in the law firm representing Spilotro, had been at the Gold Rush and called Reid into his office about a bankruptcy case. It was a mistake, and Hunterton made sure he knew right away. A follow-up story pointing out the error ran the next day. Campaign disaster averted.

By the time he officially entered the race on May 4, Reid had a quarter million dollars and two potential foes: the head of the Clark County school board, James Lyman, and a former assemblywoman named Peggy Cavnar, whose husband, Sam, had already embarked on a longshot bid for the US Senate.

In announcing his candidacy at the Henderson Convention Center, introduced by the man who defeated him the last time he was on a ballot, Las Vegas Mayor Bill Briare, Reid sounded at times almost like a moderate Republican and nothing like the partisan attack dog he would eventually become. He fretted about the economy and the deficit, suggested most of the Reagan tax cuts should stay in place, and declared: "This is not the time to attack the other side for its failings."

His final plank was to rail against violent crime, saying he had seen "both sides of this issue—as a prosecutor, as a defense attorney, and as a policeman." No one pointed out that Reid's putative law enforcement experience was as a Capitol policeman and Henderson city attorney. He eschewed any labels in the campaign, assuring the public there was no "liberal or conservative answer to all the issues."

By the time he arrived at the state Democratic convention later that year, though, Reid was, albeit playing to that audience, giving a twist on the Gordon Gekko greed speech: "Government is good. Government is necessary."

It was the kind of speech that Bishop Marlan Walker said showed Reid's true ideology, and Reid went on to talk about being "a Democrat by choice" because he believed in working people and helping the poor and caring about equality and justice. He would conclude by invoking his mother's embroidered wall plaque from his Searchlight hovel with FDR's call to action: "We can. We will. We must."

He was asked about the Equal Rights Amendment, which he said he supported until a Nevada referendum failed, so he no longer did as a potential representative of the people. He was asked about gun control, which the man who once proposed a waiting period as a state lawmaker said he was generally against and pointed to New York, which had such laws and high crime rates. He was asked about abortion, and Reid said he supported returning control to the states; he also said it should be illegal after six weeks in Nevada, that a wife would need the husband's consent, and minors would need parental consent. (In one newspaper list of issue differences during the general election, Reid's stance on abortion was distilled thusly: "Opposes abortion because he says it has 'gotten out of hand' and should not be used as a contraceptive measure.")

By September, just before the primary, his media consultant, Rogich, began airing TV bio ads that upgraded Reid to "former lawman" who would "get tough on criminals." In a radio ad, Reid declared, "As a former prosecutor and policeman . . . we can't keep letting criminals loose."

Each ad ended with the kicker "That's Nevada know-how." Similar themes appeared with the bold-faced slogan in print ads as Primary Day approached; newspaper ads were much more important in the pre-digital days.

Reid, facing only token opposition, easily won his primary on September 14, and Cavnar, despite spending almost nothing, crushed Lyman to become the GOP nominee. Reid was considered a prohibitive favorite to win the contest, and even Laxalt said publicly that it would be an upset if Cavnar won. Both Las Vegas newspapers endorsed Reid.

On November 2, 1982, Reid won with just under 60 percent of the vote. He boasted on Election Night that he had "never said a bad word about the president. I don't believe in that." Not yet, at least.

After the election, Reid insisted he would be able to work with the Republicans in the four-person Nevada delegation—he was the only Democrat amid Laxalt, former Laxalt aide Rep. Barbara Vucanovich, and new senator Chic Hecht. Reid had carefully cultivated Laxalt's supporters and aides since 1974, and a couple of them besides Rogich were involved in his campaign.

Even though it was a natural race to speculate about, Reid took running for the Senate off the table, saying, "You can quote me as saying, 'Harry Reid will never run against Paul Laxalt.' I have no illusions, inspiration or whatever you might call it to become a member of the Senate."

WHEN REID ARRIVED in Washington, DC, in 1983, he was still under investigation by the FBI. With the first federal probe moribund, the FBI had opened a new file on Reid after he was elected to Congress, looking into allegations of "bribery" and "conflict of interest," according to a June 7, 1983, memo. The allegations in the document were whether Reid was guilty of "furnishing false information on his annual disclosure statement." The information was shared with DOJ attorney Steven Shaw, who "opined that an investigation be implemented to determine if Reid may have violated Securities Exchange Commission law violations."

This document shows that it was expanded to include "mail fraud regarding possible ownership of stock by Harry Reid."

In 1981, Reid pal Jay Brown had been charged by the SEC with securities fraud because, it alleged, he had helped mislead board members in an attempt to merge the Tropicana with a Minnesota company. After Brown's law firm, which included Oscar Goodman and others, agreed to implement practices designed to prevent any violations, the complaint against Brown was dismissed in February 1982.

But the FBI was still sniffing around Reid, and on April 6, 1983, the sitting congressman was interviewed by the Kansas City division of the FBI. None of this was reported in the media, but Reid was asked about the supposed $25,000 payment from show producer Joe Agosto. "During this interview, Congressman Reid stated he never received $25,000 in cash or check from [name redacted] for Agosto and if [name redacted] did receive money from Agosto, then "'he must have kept it because I never got it.'" (The redacted name is almost certainly Brown's.)

More than two months later, Shaw, now the head of the DOJ's Public Integrity section, criminal division, "opined that an investigation be implemented to determine if Congressman Reid may have violated Securities and Exchange Commission and Election law violations, and/or furnished false information on his Annual Disclosure Statement." They were still looking into that $250,000 payment to Growth Industries that Reid had listed on his 1982 disclosure to determine its provenance and whether Reid had lied about it on the form.

The FBI documents indicate that the Las Vegas, Kansas City, and Washington, DC, offices of the FBI were involved in the investigation. In August, an agent traveled to Minnesota to check out the company, El Dorado, that Brown had been working to merge with the Tropicana. The bureau was expending significant resources, with a congressman in its sights.

But after the FBI advised the SEC of the allegations that Reid had somehow obtained an illegal commission (the $250,000 from Growth Industries) and perhaps stock, the SEC informed the bureau that "after checking public source documents . . . [they] could find nothing other than purely technical violations of an illegal manner." The Las Vegas FBI office also pored over the documents and concluded: "Nowhere in that information, which was comprised of 10K and 10Q reports, was Harry Reid's name mentioned."

For all intents and purposes, the FBI investigation was done. Shaw found he did not have enough evidence to go to a federal grand jury. But it would be more than half a year later, on May 1, 1984, well into Reid's first term and not far from his reelection date, that Shaw decided he "was declining prosecution in this matter inasmuch as it appeared no federal statutes were violated."

It was finally over, five years after the Kansas City tapes had surfaced; both the state and the FBI had found that Harry Reid was . . . clean.

How much of this affected Reid during his first term in Congress is unclear. But what is clear is that Reid became a crusader against the FBI's behavior in Nevada, railing against the special agent in charge, Joe Yablonsky. Yablonsky had been accused of using his position to try to help his friend, Democratic US Attorney Mahlon Brown, in his race for attorney general against Republican Brian McKay. (McKay won.) Reid decried that but also lambasted the FBI for its investigation of his friend, US District Court judge Harry Claiborne, and "Operation Yobo," which ensnared a slew of local officials in a sting.

From his Capitol Hill perch, and beginning in March 1983, Reid began criticizing Yablonsky and the FBI as well as questioning how a new FBI hotline for citizens to give the bureau corruption tips might work. By October 1983, Reid had recruited fellow Nevada representative Barbara Vucanovich, a Republican, to the cause as they both publicly called for investigations into the investigators.

Reid did all of this, we now know, while *he* was being investigated by the FBI. In none of the letters that he wrote or cowrote about his concerns over investigations in Nevada did Reid mention that he, too, was being probed.

It's possible he was unaware of the depth of the FBI's interest in him, even after submitting to that spring interview. But in hindsight, his public attacks against the FBI in Nevada cast a different light.

REID'S FIRST YEAR in Congress was eventful. After declaring himself a pragmatist the day he was sworn in, Reid became a regional whip, a job that involved gathering votes from colleagues on the leader's behalf, which he claimed was a key role for a small state. It may not have been, but it was an early glimpse of his upward mobility, always reaching for the next rung.

Reid also secured a spot on the Foreign Affairs Committee, which he explained was important for Nevada, especially because of the impact of tourism across the southern border. He also landed on the Science and Technology Committee—he mentioned turning Las Vegas into Silicon Valley—and eventually the Select Committee on Aging.

Laxalt graciously included Reid in all delegation meetings, and Reid would never forget how well his former foe treated him. But he was still a Democratic island in those gatherings.

Reid found a safer haven when he was asked by California Democrats to caucus with them. Reid realized that with California's forty-five members, he could develop important and lasting relationships that could pay off later. He helped the California members, too, whether it was flying back from Nevada to be there for Rep. Howard Berman during a leadership fight or urging the casinos, through their DC lobbyist Jim Ritchie, to help defray the legal fees of the ongoing reapportionment battle being fought by California Democrats. Reid was listed on the California delegation's letterhead and eventually was even elected secretary-treasurer of the California Democratic Party delegation in the House.

Reid also was named to the important steering committee of the Travel and Tourism Caucus, which would be a critical perch for the gaming industry. It was the beginning of a long career protecting the casinos, one that he would always justify because they are Nevada's number one employer.

The freshman congressman also soon learned of the lure of Las Vegas for members, and he secured a July visit from House Majority Leader Jim Wright, ostensibly to talk about flood assistance but also to attend a fundraiser in the Texan's honor. In a letter to his friend Jay Brown, Reid invited him to the dinner, saying he was "one of only six people chosen and accepted to be a member of the Speaker's Club." The parade of congressmen and senators to the Strip would continue unabated for decades—helping both Reid and his gaming patrons.

Reid retained his moderate label through his first year, even though he and Vucanovich would often cancel out each other's votes, including on a nuclear freeze resolution he supported. But on the most high-profile, Nevada-centric vote of his first year, Reid, after expressing skepticism about President Reagan's plan to site MX missiles in Nevada and other Western states, voted with the White House. Reid had changed his mind after he and another two dozen holdouts were invited to have dinner with the Great Communicator.

In a note to the president after the dinner, Reid asserted he was leaning toward voting for the MX. "Your presentation at the dinner convinced me that the nation would be well served by Congress approving funding for the MX," he wrote in a typewritten missive to the president on May 24, 1983. "In short, my vote was made resolute."

Reid would later receive a personal thank-you from Reagan for his support. But he would break with the president shortly thereafter by voting to cut off support for the rebels in Nicaragua.

Reid would continue to confound the label makers late in the year when he was one of only thirty-eight Democrats to help kill the Equal Rights Amendment, which fell six votes short of House ratification. Reid also was a reliable pro-life vote in his first year, repeatedly voting against using federal health plans to pay for abortions and for an amendment that would have defined the word "person" to include unborn children from the moment of conception.

Nevertheless, Reid was not exactly a rogue Democratic vote despite some high-profile defections. *Congressional Quarterly* found he voted with the Democratic leadership on 85 percent of 206 votes examined, placing him seven points above the House average, and he supported the president only 26 percent of the time.

Reid received almost uniformly favorable media coverage in 1983, too. He met in the House dining room with Don Reynolds and Fred Smith, the top two executives at the *Las Vegas Review-Journal*, and wrote Smith a thank-you note saying he looked forward to working with them, adding, "If I can ever be of any help to you, your family or any of your friends, please feel free to contact me at your convenience."

Going into his second year in Congress, Reid was wondering, as he said to one reporter, why he was even getting paid to be doing what he enjoyed so much. (He didn't need the money, actually, as his first congressional disclosure revealed he was one of the House's twenty millionaires, with assets of about $1.1 million, or about $3 million today. Most of it was in land holdings in Searchlight, Henderson, Las Vegas, and Bullhead City, Arizona.)

ON JANUARY 17, 1984, the American Institute of Mining, Metallurgical, and Petroleum Engineers, Southern Nevada section, passed a resolution in support of storing high-level nuclear waste at the Nevada Test Site, where nuclear bombs had been detonated for many years about ninety miles from Las Vegas. The resolution argued that the test site had "suitable geological subterrain for nuclear waste storage in the Yucca Mountain area. Present technology allows for a safe, geologic containment . . . The residents of Clark County are accustomed to nuclear activities at the Nevada Test Site."

The resolution was signed by the University of Nevada, Las Vegas (UNLV) professor Robert Summers, the chairman of the group. Less than a month later, on February 19, Reid forwarded the resolution to President Reagan, saying it was "self-explanatory. If you or any of your staff have further questions, Professor Summers will make himself available."

The message of the note seemed unmistakable: this is my view, too, Mr. President. This is a startling revelation about a man who would eventually become known for strangling the project. But this was early, Yucca Mountain had barely been mentioned in the media as an important issue, and Congress had just passed the Nuclear Waste Policy Act, which ultimately would single out Nevada.

By the end of the year, with Nevada targeted as a priority site for study, Gov. Richard Bryan remained unalterably opposed. Reid sounded a slightly different note, saying that while he opposed Nevada as the site, "we better start thinking about" the reality that it could be located at Yucca Mountain.

IT WAS ABOUT this time that Reid received the call that no politician wanted to get, that Mike Wallace of *60 Minutes* wanted to interview him. The program had been working on an investigative piece about Laxalt and his supposed organized crime–linked campaign contributors—some of the same people who had donated to Reid. The segment, which was slated to be included in the season premiere in September, also focused on the controversial FBI chief, Yablonsky, and his role in indicting Judge Claiborne, a close friend of Reid and Hank Greenspun's. Greenspun, not coincidentally, had been crusading in his newspaper against Yablonsky and defending Claiborne.

Against this backdrop, Reid did one of the last things he wanted to do during a campaign for reelection and sat down with Wallace in the congressman's Las Vegas office in the summer of 1984, with the prospect that the segment would air a few weeks before the election.

Wallace wasted no time coming after Reid, asking him whether there was still organized crime in Las Vegas and whether it controlled the gaming industry, according to a never-before-reported transcript of the interview that was taped by his staff. The segment would never air after ABC interviewed Yablonsky, and Laxalt demanded a live interview and threatened to sue CBS. But Reid didn't know that as he answered the barrage of Wallace questions.

Reid conceded that he would have said no when he first joined the commission, and acknowledged some people approved for licensing "we learn[ed] later did have some problems."

"Nevada, Las Vegas is not clean," Wallace declared in his famous confrontational style.

Reid countered that a cash business is going to have some malefactors involved, which played into Wallace's hands as he asked about political contributions: "From what known mobsters or people close to mobsters or good friends of mobsters or people who are a front for mobsters, have you, through your campaign, taken cash?"

This moment crystallized the reality of Las Vegas during this time, the reality that the remnants of the Mafia were still around and that people with questionable backgrounds were often the city's leading lights and major campaign contributors.

Reid didn't answer the question directly, and what he said was not true: "Mike, I have never taken any money from anybody who has been convicted of a crime." This, of course, was easily disproven by the cash he had taken from Benny Binion, patriarch of the Horseshoe Casino downtown, who had been convicted of murder in Texas before he arrived in Nevada. Wallace knew this and would later in the interview press Reid on this fact, to which the congressman replied that he had no idea when the conviction occurred and that he had "the highest regard for the Binion family."

Wallace also pressed him on Moe Dalitz, whom Reid described as a great community benefactor, but who had long been tied to organized crime figures including Meyer Lansky; Herb Tobman, who had just had his licenses suspended; and Ed Torres, Wayne Newton's partner at the Aladdin whom Reid had helped investigate as chairman and who had been charged with an illegal wiretap in the 1950s. Reid defended all of them as reputable citizens, closing out the discussion of Torres in Reid-like fashion: "By the way, his daughter just won a gold medal at the Olympics."

Undaunted and in his performative style, Wallace said, "The question that one asks is why is it that Nevada political figures have to depend heavily on men whose ties to organized crime are so ripe in this thing?"

Reid pointed out that of the $500,000 he raised for his race in 1982, a very small percentage came from the men Wallace mentioned, to which the *60 Minutes* star replied, "Good, then my apologies."

Wallace pressed on, though, asking Reid about Yablonsky's public assertion that he and Laxalt and *Las Vegas Sun* publisher Hank Greenspun were part of the "old boy network here."

Reid told Wallace that he had a problem with Yablonsky calling news conferences and trying cases in the media, which led Wallace to ask him about Claiborne. Reid pointed out that the judge was convicted on tax issues, not on bribery charges involving the brothel owner Joe Conforte.

Wallace asked Reid again about Yablonsky and whether he knew whether Laxalt tried to have him ousted in 1981; Reid said he had no knowledge of that. Then Wallace asked why he went to the FBI director, William Webster, and told him to get Yablonsky out of Nevada. "No, of course I did not, Mike," Reid replied, elaborating and perhaps sanitizing that he went to see Webster to make him aware of information about the Las Vegas FBI chief, and that it was "up to him after the reviews to make the appropriate decision." Reid also acknowledged that he had raised the issue of Claiborne and that Webster told him "that is out of our hands now."

At the end, Wallace brought the interview back to Laxalt and his associations, to which Reid retorted: "Paul Laxalt isn't tied to organized crime. That's foolish."

Even though Reid had made no startling admissions during the interview, he and his team surely sighed with relief when the segment did not air as planned after the primary. When Laxalt sued the *Sacramento Bee* over similar allegations that he had allowed skimming at his Ormsby Hotel because of ties to organized crime, the speculation began that the senator would not run for reelection in 1986.

Shortly after the Wallace interview, Reid reported his latest campaign funds, which included the second donation from . . . Moe Dalitz.

THE GENERAL ELECTION campaign was relatively uneventful. By October, the Reid team believed he was a heavy favorite, and their only worry was that Reagan again was likely to easily win Nevada. Reid, fortuitously perhaps, engaged in a public feud with the Democratic nominee, Walter Mondale, over the terms of a nuclear freeze, which probably helped his "independent like Nevada" campaign, a new slogan from Chris Brown in a likely Reagan landslide year. His opponent was once again Peggy Cavnar, who had a hard time distinguishing herself from the incumbent on many issues. He also neutralized her on abortion with this position outlined in a *Review-Journal* comparison chart: "Supports constitutional amendment banning abortion as an affirmation of life."

On another social issue, Reid returned a check from the Human Rights Campaign shortly before the election, later saying he was opposed to federal legislation protecting homosexuals from discrimination. (This was many years before Reid would be honored by HRC and deliver the keynote address before the group in 2010.)

A UNLV poll in early October showed Reid was ahead 54–34 over Cavnar. It seemed only an act of God could cost Reid the race—and one almost occurred in late October when a suicidal man jumped from atop a hotel and crashed through the roof of the Holiday Inn Center Strip right above a doorway where Reid had been greeting guests. Reid had been a mere six feet away but was uninjured.

It wasn't until five days before the election that Cavnar received a letter from President Reagan endorsing her candidacy—it did not mention Reid. Laxalt also did not criticize the incumbent and told the media that his friend in the White House would not be visiting because Nevada was in the bag for the Democrats.

All of Reid's media alliances also came to the fore toward the end. The *Sun*, as expected, endorsed him; the *Review-Journal*, for the second straight cycle, endorsed Reid, calling him the "clear choice." And his friend Jim Rogers, who owned the NBC affiliate, starred in an on-air editorial that was eviscerating and . . . sexist: "As charming and attractive as Peggy Cavnar is . . . we simply cannot see that Peggy has the background to serve as our congresswoman."

When Election Day came, Reid won by an almost identical margin as 1982, garnering 56 percent of the vote. Reagan easily won reliably red Nevada again and crushed Mondale in heavily Democratic Clark County with 63 percent. Southern Nevada voters were indeed independent.

Shortly after the election, when asked about the Senate race in 1986, Reid insisted Laxalt would run again because of pressure from Reagan and national Republicans not to risk the seat. “I wouldn’t run against Laxalt,” Reid said. “He’s going to run.”

CHAPTER TEN

A SECOND CHANCE

On August 19, 1985, Harry Reid, more than halfway into the first year of his second House term, was overseas when the call that would change his career trajectory came from his press secretary, Valerie Wiener.

"Congressman, Paul Laxalt has just announced he's not running for reelection," she recalls telling him. "I could tell he turned away from the phone, and he shared it with the other congressional members who were with him. And I could hear them say, 'Congratulations, Senator Reid.'"

When he returned to Las Vegas around Labor Day, Reid knew he would run for Senate, so he summoned his senior staff to a meeting and told them to keep his decision confidential for now.

One thing to learn was who Reid's opponent would be. The most obvious choice was Republican representative Barbara Vucanovich, Laxalt's protégée, who clearly was interested. She represented Reno and rural Nevada in a very safe seat. News had leaked before the 1984 election that she had commissioned a survey from the Houston pollster Lance Tarrance to gauge her statewide drawing power.

The memo from Tarrance suggested Vucanovich already had made up her mind, advising her on "how to behave politically for an orderly transfer from the U.S. House of Representatives to the U.S. Senate." Tarrance suggested that Vucanovich had decent statewide name identification (60 percent), but he also emphasized how important an endorsement from her mentor, Laxalt, would be. Little did she know then that not only would Laxalt not give her his imprimatur, but he would deliver a similar message to her that he would deliver in February 1986 to the Philippines strongman Ferdinand Marcos on Reagan's behalf: cut and cut cleanly.

Laxalt and others close to him did not believe Vucanovich could defeat Reid, the poll notwithstanding. She was not a dynamic campaigner, they thought, and had no Southern Nevada presence, which was where the votes and campaign money were.

But if not she, who?

Quietly, Laxalt had been coaxing a former Democratic congressman, Jim Santini, to switch parties and take on Reid. Santini had become persona non grata among Democrats after running in a 1982 primary against Sen. Howard Cannon. He fell short but he was widely blamed for Cannon's eventual loss to the unknown haberdasher Chic Hecht in 1982.

Santini hesitated at first, but when it was clear Vucanovich was out, he agreed.

The Republicans were feeling good about their choice. Santini was known as a dynamic candidate, facile on the stump and with statewide name identification because his congressional seat had encompassed all of Nevada before the state was awarded a second seat in 1981. Reid was seen, as one Republican put it, as a "milquetoast" contender. The state had been turning more Republican—LBJ had been the last Democratic presidential nominee to win the state, in 1964—except for Bill Clinton who was twice in the 1990s aided by Ross Perot's third-party candidacy—and the magnetism of Laxalt coupled with Reagan's popularity was a substantial plus for Santini.

But before he could even focus on the race, Reid was about to learn—again—that the Faulknerism about the past never being dead was certainly true for him as the specter of Cleanface returned.

"**REID MAY HAVE** intervened for mob figures."

Such was the headline on an Associated Press story on November 12, 1985, less than a year before the US Senate race would be decided. The ghosts of the past had returned.

In the eighth week of a trial of organized crime figures in Kansas City, focused on hidden interests skimming at Argent casinos in Las Vegas, the jury listened to a tape of now deceased mob associate Joe Agosto talking about a meeting he had with Reid along with the then commission chairman's good friend Jay Brown. Prodded by Allen Glick, the mob frontman at the head of Argent, Agosto and Brown had been assigned to see whether they could get the commission to fine the company and not revoke its license. Agosto claimed they met with Reid, and the chairman promised to round up the votes to block revocation, and instead, the company would pay the $100,000 fine Agosto and Brown had suggested.

Agosto: "I talked to my friend, put in a good word."
Kansas City underboss Carl DeLuna: "Clean?"
Agosto: "Yeah."

The congressman issued a statement about what he called the long-ago and debunked allegations and how thoroughly he had been investigated. This was all too familiar for Reid, but he and his team knew the potential damage to his incipient Senate campaign, so they sprung into action. Larry Werner, a star reporter for the *Review-Journal* who had just gone to work for Reid as his press secretary, wrote a memo to the congressman on November 14 on how to address the issue.

"I would suggest for Round 2 of the Mr. Clean battle we take the stance of a party aggrieved, that is, HMR, a man of integrity, has been dragged into a Kansas City courtroom without the privilege of fairness of the thugs who are spouting falsehoods," Werner wrote. "I also think we should add an element of righteous indignation to our stance."

The urgent tone of Werner's memo underscored the potential impact on Reid's nascent campaign.

"Specter of 'Mr. Cleanface' Still Haunts Harry Reid" was the headline at the top of Ned Day's well-read and influential column in the *Las Vegas Review-Journal* four days later. Day acknowledged the history, that Reid had been cleared by state and federal probes, but then he lowered the boom: "But the question of whether or not he took payoffs is not the only question germane to a candidate for U.S. Senate," Day wrote. "What about his judgment?"

Day wondered whether Reid had been thoughtful in his decisions on key cases involving the mob-infiltrated casinos: "Did he measure up to the test when confronted with difficult choices?"

The column was stinging and potentially lasting. The response came swiftly. George Swarts, a Republican stalwart and Reid's commission colleague who strongly disagreed in 1978 with the Reid-led decision to go easy on the Tropicana, wrote a column in the *Review-Journal* defending the former chairman. Swarts pointed out that the commission aggressively pursued Rosenthal, Spilotro, and others but also had to take into account the jobs at each of the casinos. "Harry Reid and I had many differences of opinion and engaged in public debate, but at no time did I question his integrity," wrote Swarts.

Even as the media storm swirled in November, Reid held his first major fundraiser, hosted by none other than Paul Lowden, whose career the congressman had saved when he chaired the gaming commission, and his wife, Sue, a popular news anchor at the CBS affiliate.

THIS CAMPAIGN WAS going to be different.

Reid had the scars of 1974. He knew that the state and the country had swung Republican—other Democratic elected officials had switched parties right before Santini had. He knew the power of the Reagan-Laxalt tandem in Nevada. The state was still Democratic in registration (by six percentage points and twenty-six thousand voters), and Clark County, where he had run so strongly in every race, was still a Democratic bastion (by twenty percentage points and thirty-seven thousand voters) and had more than half of the state's electorate. But he was not going to leave anything to chance, leave any stone unturned. Indeed, this campaign would sow the seeds for much of what was to come in the three ensuing decades.

He hired elite national talent. He greenlighted the precursor to the voter registration/turnout apparatus that would become the Reid Machine. He employed data-driven models that would reveal just how divided Nevada was becoming and how the margin for error was not large. He would use his personal touch, in letters and notes to the powerful and the unknown, and his attention to the smallest detail of the campaign, seen in short missives to his campaign aides. He would begin harnessing the techniques of newspaper letter-writers to burnish his chances and calls to radio shows to bolster his case, his friends and aides masquerading as average citizens. In this race, the first signs of Reid the environmentalist emerged as he pushed a wilderness bill and faced a siege from mining advocates, even as he quietly helped the industry. All of his long-cultivated media relationships would matter, too, with the Greenspuns and O'Callaghan (he essentially was part of the campaign, present for Reid's announcement and for a tour of the rural counties where his surrogate son needed help) at the *Sun*, Jim Rogers at the NBC affiliate, and Don Digilio, the former editor and then columnist at the *Review-Journal*. The question was whether the 1974 hangover in northern Nevada with the news media would haunt him.

Even with the glimmers of a modern campaign, Harry Reid would still be Harry Reid, prizing loyalty to friends and family above all else. It was during this same period that he pushed (unsuccessfully) for a pardon of his longtime contributor Benny Binion, whom Mike Wallace had asked him about and who had become a community luminary after being convicted of murder and, later, tax charges. Reid also was temperate in his remarks about his old friend Harry Claiborne, who was convicted and impeached, and served time. (Despite their close friendship, to preserve his electoral viability, Reid would vote to impeach the man who tipped him off to the

Cleanface wiretaps after he initially said he was "pulling for" his longtime pal when the charges were first brought.)

Nineteen eighty-six also was the first high-profile campaign in which "Reidisms" surfaced, the unfortunate utterances that would make staffers cringe and consult their damage control handbooks. He called the Contras in Nicaragua whom Reagan wanted to aid "Nazis." He referred to a state GOP chairwoman cashiered by her own party as the best one the Republicans in Nevada had ever had, partly because she was "pretty and rich."

Santini, of course, had all the resources Laxalt could get him, including Sig Rogich (a Reid friend, now turned enemy) and his company, R&R Advertising, and the president's pollster. This was going to be the biggest and most important Senate race in Nevada history, perhaps deciding control of the US Senate, then in Republican hands, 53–47.

The groundwork for Reid's campaign had been laid in 1985, even before he announced his candidacy. Chris Brown, the data guru who had sounded the alarm about Nevada's decreasing Democratic voter registration, prepared a plan to change that trend. He pointed out that Republican registration in the urban areas was "at an all-time high as a percent of total registration," which threatened all major Democratic candidates. He also noted that Nevada had a high percentage of unregistered voting-age residents. Adding voters was essential, he argued, but tracking them and getting them out to vote in November 1986 was critical—the model that would make the Reid-era Democratic Party so formidable. It was also dependent on another factor—Reid raising money for the cause. The memo went on to say that Reagan's popularity and the relative unpopularity of the national Democratic Party had caused the GOP surge and made the plan even more urgent. Brown presented a blizzard of figures and analysis and suggested that adding ten thousand new Democratic voters in Clark County to the eighty-eight thousand already registered could make a decisive difference. A few months later, Brown had a plan for Washoe County, home to Reno, where Republicans had always run well. Reid, surely with Brown's data in mind, had argued in his annual speech to state lawmakers for a motor-voter bill, one that would allow voter registration at the Department of Motor Vehicles when people renewed their licenses, an idea that would fail for decades in Nevada before its enactment.

This was the beginning of Reid's impact on the state's voter trends that would last for nearly four decades—and perhaps beyond.

THERE ARE THOSE who believe that the 1986 US Senate race ended the day Jim Santini formally announced his candidacy on March 24. Most announcement news conferences are banal affairs. The candidate reads a prepared speech; reporters toss softballs. But not this one.

The Reid campaign, using spokesman Werner's connections to his old employer, had prepared a former *Review-Journal* colleague now working for the local ABC affiliate with an old Federal Election Commission inquiry from Santini's 1982 campaign. There were questions about what he had done with money earmarked for the general election—Santini had lost in the primary—and whether donors had ever received or cashed the refunds. The reporter kept peppering Santini with questions about the FEC probe to the point that the former congressman jokingly asked whether he was working for the Reid campaign. What happened next became a defining moment for the campaign.

"We learned early on that Santini was a sweater," Reid recalled. "He would just sweat all the time."

Sure enough, Santini began to perspire, at one point wiping the sweat off his brow. A Reid campaign film crew was there to capture the moment, and from there, Michael Kaye, who had worked for Disney, created a brilliant set of devastating ads. The spots juxtaposed something Santini had said as a Democrat—with a picture of him as a congressman—with something he had said as a new Republican, along with that shot of Santini wiping his sweat away as the narrator intoned: "Which Jim Santini do you believe?"

Reid could not stop smiling as he recalled it years later. "Every time we would have a debate or town hall together, we would make sure that we turned the heat up as much as we could," Reid said. Indeed, Werner furtively adjusted the thermostat at a debate to make it hotter for Santini.

The ads resonated because they had the ring of truth. Santini did not ever seem quite comfortable in his GOP garb—and many of his friends, including Reid's former Gold Dust Twin Richard Bryan, who was now governor and unsuccessfully tried to talk him out of switching parties, noticed this, too. He was not the same Jim Santini who had been a congressman for four terms.

Even if the Reid campaign thought they had scored a blow, they did not believe it was a knockout punch, especially with what they knew was the Reagan-Laxalt onslaught to come. But they had plenty of opposition research to work with, from newly minted Republican Santini saying as a congressman that Jimmy Carter "has the potential of being the most cohesive and impressive president of the 20th century" to a column in which he declared, "I am a Democrat and I always will be."

Meanwhile, the Reid campaign was humming along. He had recruited major casino industry figures to his finance committee, and when Reid first scribbled names for his money team on his yellow pad, what once took a few lines now gobbled up three and a half pages.

At a strategy meeting in February, the Reid team discussed its first poll, which showed him with a 36–31 lead statewide, but with a third of voters undecided. Reid was easily winning Clark County, his home base, 47–21, but was losing the rest of the state.

A few months later, Chris Brown produced what he called the "Victory Vote Model," which "called for Reid to garner 62 percent of the vote in Clark County, 44 percent in the Carson City/Washoe County region, and 33 percent in the remaining Rural Counties." In that remarkably prescient model, Reid would receive 51.5 percent of the statewide vote.

"OBVIOUSLY, A STRONG VICTORY IN CLARK COUNTY IS THE SINE QUA NON OF OUR ENTIRE STRATEGY," Brown wrote.

Fall below 60 percent and jeopardy accrues. This is, ironically, part of why Laxalt and Co. chose Santini: Reid would almost surely have crushed Vucanovich in Clark, but Santini, a former Democratic statewide congressman who lived there, might be able to compete—or at least hold down the margin.

Brown understood, as he wrote that there was "NO MARGIN FOR ERROR" in any of Nevada's three regions, but he knew, like a political Willie Sutton, to go where the votes were. So Reid would campaign in Clark and a bit in Washoe; Landra and Rory would be sent as surrogates to Reno and the rural areas.

Reid also was intent on protecting his right flank, especially on a couple of hot-button issues. In a Western state such as Nevada, the National Rifle Association was very popular, and Reid's attempt in the state legislature to impose a waiting period was a distant memory. In April, he voted against extending the ban on the interstate sale of handguns, saying gun control had failed in most states. "I'm generally opposed to the regulation of guns," Reid told the *Review-Journal*.

This paid off. Two weeks before the election, Michigan representative John Dingell, an influential Democratic House member, wrote a note to Reid telling him he had spoken to the NRA chief, Wayne LaPierre, "on your behalf. Wayne informed me that the NRA is staying out of your race and is not backing Jim Santini. They will be giving both of you an A rating."

With the NRA's resources, this was no small thing. Such was the beginning of what would become a decades-long cozying up to the NRA by Reid until it fell apart in 2010.

ONE ISSUE WHERE Reid's right flank was exposed was abortion, despite his 100 percent pro-life voting record as a congressman. The Santini race would highlight the separation of church and ideology that would cause a schism in the LDS community, where many Mormons opposed Reid for what some perceived as his encroaching liberalism, even as a member in good standing. (Santini was Catholic, although his wife, Ann, was Mormon.)

On April 24, the First Presidency of the church in Salt Lake City issued a statement of political neutrality: "In this election year we emphasize anew the long-standing policy of the Church of strict political neutrality, and of not endorsing political candidates or parties in elections, and of not using Church facilities for political purposes."

This edict would be violated in spirit or actuality in Nevada campaigns for years, and the message from Salt Lake was simply a fig leaf for the many LDS activists involved in politics. A split among Mormons, who played an outsized role in Nevada politics in the 1980s because of their high registration and turnout numbers, would soon become evident.

In the June edition of the Pro-Family Coalition newsletter, *The Circle*, President Carol Carlson, whose husband was a Mormon bishop, sent out an "Alert on Crucial U.S. Senate Race."

Carlson wrote that in the group's interview with Reid, he said that he would generally vote to confirm Supreme Court justices even if they differed from his positions on various issues because of a president's prerogative to nominate. She said the group "had determined that Congressman Reid would never under any circumstances oppose the appointment of any justice, even to the Supreme Court, though the appointee stood against everything we believe in."

Carlson then revealed that after being confronted about the interview, Reid "immediately called me for another appointment and the following morning very angrily read a letter dated June 1, his new 'official position' on abortion and the appointment of Federal judges. In 48 hours, he had completely reversed his position on this critical issue."

Reid had indeed penned a June 1 letter to Carlson in which he reiterated his commitment to separation of powers, but added "that I would have to in good conscience be consistent with my record on abortion, which is quite clear." Saying he had run out of time during the interview, Reid added his flip-flop: "I wish to inform you, as a matter of record, that I could not, in good conscience, confirm a judicial candidate who is a proponent of abortion."

But it was too late. Carlson wrote that the board voted unanimously that evening to endorse Santini, with some members crying because of their affection for Reid. "He has given us cause to question his integrity," she concluded. "He has lost our trust."

Reid mobilized his Mormon friends, some of whom wrote a letter to Citizens for Responsible Government, another Mormon-dominated group that went against him. Other supporters, including Sandra Jolley, a Reid supporter and key activist in the LDS community, met and decided to try to counter the move toward Santini with hundreds of people signing on to a "We believe in Harry because . . ." campaign.

"Make sure we use a variety of people from all over the valley," a memo of the meeting said. "Not just the LDS. Have a black person represented."

The attacks on Reid's integrity created fissures that never healed. Reid was able to hold on to friends such as Jolley, who always believed in Reid and helped him organize in the Mormon community. But Jolley said people became hopelessly entrenched against him and she lost friends over her support of Reid. "Its legacy spread a negative contagion among Mormons who knew little to nothing of Harry Reid the man," she said.

REID ALSO REALIZED how popular Reagan was in Nevada—the president had won easily both times and had even produced landslides in Clark County, which was a possible warning sign. He was careful not to attack the president, continually reminding people that he was running against Santini. Privately, he wanted people to know he supported Reagan at times.

In one of his many "if there is anything I can do for you please don't hesitate to call" notes to powerful Nevadans, Reid wrote to the state's most prominent casino mogul, Steve Wynn, suggesting he would be a budget hawk in the Senate. "In short, I think I would do a better job than most of the people in his own party in supporting the president . . . I support him almost 50 percent of the time," he scrawled on a handwritten addendum to a typewritten missive to Wynn about a *Washington Post* story.

Reid was expert at managing his major gaming donors in Las Vegas—he had most of them on his team, even those who leaned Republican, such as the Palace Station president, Frank Fertitta. When Fertitta wrote to Reid soliciting an ad in a brochure to be presented at a St. Jude's Ranch for Children fundraiser, Reid reacted transactionally in a memo to campaign aide Rey Martinez: "I okay the $125 ad. Have to do it because Fertita [*sic*] had donated huge amounts of money to my campaign."

From the Strip to downtown, Reid was a gaming industry darling and would be for as long as he was in office. Reagan made his first visit of the campaign in June, raising what would later be an estimated $700,000 for Santini's campaign. By now, though, Reid and his campaign had made such a big deal out of the possible nuclear waste dump site in Nevada that Reagan had to address the issue at length, insisting it would not be a political decision. After suggesting to Reagan a few years earlier that he was not opposed to the dump, Reid had seen the political light and had become an evangelist against the project.

Reid and other Democrats, including Bryan, would often use incendiary rhetoric in talking about the repository. On the day of Reagan's visit, Reid compared it to Chernobyl, the site of the Russian nuclear reactor meltdown that had occurred that April. Reid would continue to use the dump as an issue for the rest of the campaign, implying, over Santini's protests, that the ex-congressman was not as strong as he was and that Laxalt, Hecht, and Vucanovich had not been forceful enough. For many years, one of the parlor discussions among Nevada pols would be the failure of Laxalt, if he even tried, to persuade Reagan to short-circuit the nuclear waste repository from coming to Nevada, leaving it as a hammer for Reid and Democrats for many cycles to come.

Reid's team believed that Reagan's support of Santini would drive up turnout in the so-called cow counties, perhaps skewing the statewide vote toward the Republicans and mucking with Chris Brown's victory vote projections. So Reid sent his eldest son, Rory, on a summertime reconnaissance mission through rural Nevada in the then law student's Cutlass Supreme. The younger Reid picked up on a trend that would become only more problematic for Reid in future races. Nevada was becoming more and more divided, and Reid's margin for error was dwindling even back then.

In a "Rural Nevada Report" memo he penned when he returned, Rory Reid said he had interviewed fifty of his father's supporters and discovered:

> "HMR is perceived as a Las Vegas politician who has done little or nothing for rural Nevada."

> "Without doubt, HMR's biggest liability in the rural counties is WILDERNESS. The people of rural Nevada do not understand wilderness legislation and they do not want to make the effort to understand it."

The senator called his son almost every night for updates. "It was hard because they hated him," Rory Reid said, mostly because of his attempts to set aside land for wilderness, earning him the moniker "Sierra Harry." "They were nice people, until they found out who I was."

The congressman was worried about his son's safety because of the virulence of the animosity, and he eventually sent Mike O'Callaghan Jr., his mentor's son, as a bodyguard to travel with Rory.

Nevertheless, the younger Reid suggested in the memo that his father make a visit to rural Nevada to mitigate the damage, perhaps with Mike O'Callaghan Sr., "a legend in rural Nevada."

Reid would follow his son's advice, and with O'Callaghan, the former governor turned newspaper executive, introducing him and trying to soften the blow in several rural counties, the congressman would spend a week or so in places where he was disliked.

In reaction to coverage of Rory Reid's rural tour, Santini criticized the candidate himself for not being there, which resulted in a Reid retort about his opponent criticizing his family. This sparked a rare occurrence during any campaign, a personal note from one candidate to another: "Goodness, lighten up," Santini wrote to Reid. "My feeling about family members campaigning for their favorite candidates is, God bless them. In no way would I make your family an 'issue' in the campaign. The issue is your wilderness bill, and I still think it's 'unfair of Harry' to send your family around Nevada to answer questions you should be answering. That's all."

Reid would not spend much time in rural Nevada in future campaigns, even as he continued to work behind the scenes to bring federal largesse back to the smaller counties just as he did for the larger ones. In July 1986, for example, he was trying to persuade the House Ways and Means chairman, Dan Rostenkowski, to not let a tax bill damage his and Governor Bryan's attempts to erect a power project in tiny White Pine County. However, those efforts would go unrewarded at the ballot box. White Pine would vote against him by about 60 percent to 40 percent in November, emblematic of how rural voters treated their pork benefactor. Years later, Reid would marvel at how much time Bryan, when he was a senator, would spend in rural Nevada campaigning compared to him, only to earn a minuscule percentage more of the vote.

Similarly, despite the mining association's attempt to raise money to scuttle his wilderness proposal, Reid also was quietly assisting the industry. In that same tax reform legislation, Reid helped insert a provision to protect the Kennecott Bingham Copper Mine Modernization Project, which resulted in a thank-you letter from the company.

Reid the legislator was still distinct from Reid the candidate, but for how much longer if his good deeds would be relentlessly punished at the ballot box?

BY SEPTEMBER, REID appeared to have the race pretty well in hand. He had built up a large lead, especially in Clark County, to hold off whatever Reagan and Laxalt were primed to do to juice GOP turnout at the end. On September 12, a UNLV poll showed he had a 56 percent to 24 percent lead in Clark County, not far from Brown's target. In a private note to fellow Democratic representative Gary Hart ten days later, Reid confided: "The race goes well. Pollster Peter Hart now has me up to ten points—my biggest lead yet."

The Republican panic had reached the corridors of the nation's capital, and by mid-October, Laxalt returned to Nevada to essentially take over the campaign in the final three weeks to try to keep his promise to his friend in the White House to save the senator's seat. Laxalt immediately acknowledged that Santini was behind by six percentage points in polls he trusted, but he hoped two Reagan visits in the final days could help erase that margin.

Laxalt's handiwork was evident when the *Review-Journal* endorsed Santini a few days later, well in advance of the election. The paper's editorial page editor, Rafael Tammariello, confided that a call had come to the newspaper's higher-ups—presumably pressured by Laxalt—to get an early endorsement, and he had been instructed to get it done quickly so the campaign could use it. The lacerating editorial was everything Santini could have hoped for, portraying Reid as weak on national defense, in the pocket of Big Labor, and a tax-and-spend liberal. It was reproduced and passed out the same day at Santini events.

Reid had cultivated the paper's owner, Don Reynolds, and exchanged notes earlier in the year with him about a flattering profile in *Forbes*. Reid had even accepted an invitation to Reynolds's birthday party in September and provided a fawning letter as part of a packet of remembrances to be given to the newspaper mogul. How disappointing the cut that came a month later must have been.

Reid, of course, landed a strong endorsement from his friends at the *Las Vegas Sun* as the Greenspuns and O'Callaghan tried to counter the *Review-Journal* and its much bigger circulation. Despite worries at the beginning of his campaign from Reid's team that the northern Nevada media would remember his petulant attacks on them from 1974, the *Reno Gazette-Journal* wholeheartedly endorsed Reid two Sundays before the election and excoriated Santini as a hypocritical opportunist.

Two October debates were essentially nonevents, with Reid exceeding expectations.

One notable moment from that first debate was Reid's answer when asked about an immigration control bill before Congress that would eventually be signed by Reagan. "It's a bad, bad piece of legislation," Reid answered in a way that might seem shocking today to his Democratic base. "It grants amnesty to millions and millions of people who came here illegally. That's wrong. How can we as a country justify an illegal act and reward them with the greatest thing we can reward anyone with and that is citizenship in this country?"

There were no major gaffes in either debate, nothing for Santini to use to devastating effect in the final stretch. A few days before the election, Reagan signed a bill, ironically, that would be remembered as one of Reid's lasting triumphs, the creation of a national park in northern Nevada at Wheeler Peak. Laxalt and Hecht had insisted the size of the Great Basin National Park be slashed by two-thirds to 44,000 acres, and Reid eventually negotiated down from his original 129,000 acres to 76,000. But this was the state's first national park and a victory for environmentalists and the only Democrat in the delegation.

Reagan made good on his promise to visit twice in the final weekend—once to Las Vegas and once to Reno—but the die was cast, as it perhaps had been for the entire campaign. On November 4, Reid won by fourteen thousand votes, or 50 percent to 44 percent, including by thirty-two thousand votes in Clark County. Reid would lose every other county, except tiny Mineral. Brown's projections had been remarkably close, with Reid garnering 63 percent in Clark, 46 percent in Washoe, and 37 percent in rural Nevada. The machine had worked.

It also turned out that Laxalt's seat was not that critical. The Democrats netted eight seats in the midterm, capturing the Senate majority by a substantial margin (55–45). It was the first time the Democrats had control in five years. In one of several races where a freshman elected in the 1980 Republican landslide was defeated, a Democratic congressman named Tom Daschle defeated Republican James Abdnor in South Dakota. The significance of that outcome would later become evident and have an important effect on the new Nevada senator's career.

After the election, Reid received a handwritten note from an old friend congratulating him: "As the old Indian saying goes, 'May your moccasins make many happy tracks in the snow.'"

The return address was "Federal Prison Camp" in Alabama. It was from Harry Claiborne.

CHAPTER ELEVEN

A BYRD IN THE HAND

Before he was sworn in as a US senator, Harry Reid knew what he wanted most—a seat on the Appropriations Committee.

Reid was savvy enough to realize how powerful such a perch would be for him as well as for such a small state that otherwise would have had, essentially, zero clout. It was a long shot, though, with only two seats available and Reid ranking near the bottom in seniority. His ultimately successful attempt to win the seat would reveal all the abilities that facilitated his path to power—harnessing whatever allies he could find, using his personal connections, and playing both sides, if need be.

During the campaign, Reid had played footsie with J. Bennett Johnston of Louisiana, an expert appropriator and influential senator who was planning to challenge the legendary Robert Byrd of West Virginia for majority leader. Johnston was accumulating votes from those who believed the party needed someone younger and more dynamic to take on the telegenic actor turned president.

After a fundraiser Johnston hosted for the Nevada congressman in Washington, DC, in July, he wrote a warm letter to candidate Reid, saying, "By all indications your campaign has the organization and the momentum necessary for a victory this fall." It did not matter to Reid at that time that Johnston was the ranking member of the Senate Energy Committee, which was pushing forward with a plan to dispose of the nation's high-level nuclear waste quite possibly in Nevada. He wanted to be on his good side should he become leader.

When Byrd called to get Reid's commitment to support him as majority leader, the congressman refused to give it. Reid saw that Johnston might have the upper hand and knew enough to keep his options open. It was clear from one of their conversations that Byrd was not happy, but shortly after the election, Byrd promised his colleagues he would give up the post he had held since 1977 in two years. He would eventually trade it for the chairmanship of the Appropriations Committee—causing Johnston to lose support. One week after Reid was elected, Johnston dropped out of the race.

Reid pivoted quickly. On the same day the media reported Johnston had dropped out and Byrd's reelection as leader was assured, Reid penned a letter to the West Virginian. Reid began his November 12 missive to Byrd with a hard sell by informing the leader that he needed a committee, "a prominent, major committee on the level of [Laxalt] who held a spot on the Appropriations Committee," Reid wrote. "An assignment of this kind would not only greatly help me in my attempt to unify the state, but it would have positive repercussions for Nevada Democrats in the next Senate race in two years."

There it was, the classic Reid salesmanship: help me, help my state, and help the party. He then asked Byrd for Appropriations, with Finance and Commerce as his backups. Reid added a handwritten note to the typewritten letter, congratulating Byrd, who was on Appropriations, too, on becoming leader.

Reid wasn't done lobbying for the slot. He also recruited former Nevada senator Alan Bible to make his case to the Appropriations chairman, John Stennis of Mississippi. Bible and Stennis had served together for two decades.

Reid also wrote to other Democratic senators to help with his request, including the incoming Judiciary chairman, Joe Biden, who wrote back telling Reid he would do "all I can."

By the end of November, Reid's maneuvering had paid off. Byrd informed him he would get the coveted Appropriations seat, a decision that was the first step in Reid's eventual ascension. He would soon show Stennis his work ethic and strategic mind and display what would become a signature feature of Reid's tenure, his ability to funnel money and jobs to his usually ignored state. By mid-1987, Reid erased a House provision to limit the size of nuclear explosions at the Nevada Test Site, a provision designed to close it down; saved $100,000 for the Stillwater National Wildlife Refuge, preserving an Indian site; and restored funding for an environmental research center at UNLV that would later be named in his honor because of his efforts.

Within six months, Reid would become a respected inside player, and he would use the panel as a place to funnel what would eventually become hundreds of millions of dollars of projects to Nevada, and no one else in state history even came close.

For now, Reid was learning the process and developing relationships. One of those was with another freshman Democrat who had snared a seat on the powerful committee, Maryland's Barbara Mikulski. This would become a lifelong friendship, a symbiosis in the Senate that would help advance both of their lots. Mikulski remembers seeing the hints of Reid's talents and his eagerness to learn in those early days.

"He watched the masters," Mikulski recalled. "He watched Bob Byrd. He watched Bennett Johnston. He watched them, the way they maneuvered and got the job done . . . And he learned all of that with how you move the agenda. That's what he became one of the experts at, and he also learned a lot about the people."

Byrd was the most important relationship Reid developed in those early days despite their tiff during the campaign, one that was long forgotten after they got to know each other. It was father-son (Byrd was sixty-nine, Reid was forty-seven), teacher-pupil (Reid would later address him as "friend and mentor" in handwritten notes), and it became much more. Byrd had secured Reid's loyalty by the Appropriations appointment, but for the rookie it was a chance to learn at the feet of a seasoned senator. Byrd didn't just show Reid the ropes; he taught him which strings to pull.

"He really liked me," Reid recalled. "I became kind of his pet." From her vantage point, Mikulski saw one other aspect of the cohesion between them: their similar beginnings.

"I think he bonded with Bob Byrd so early on [because] these were two men who had known not only poverty, but desperate poverty," she said. "And Harry was, along with Bob Byrd . . . they really liked the night school crowd over the prep school crowd."

Reid said Byrd appreciated his determination and work ethic, including during that first year when he filibustered nuclear waste for about eleven hours.

"I took the floor as a brand-new senator, and I was told it was the longest filibuster for a freshman senator," Reid said. "I talked about Searchlight, about anything that came to my mind." In fact, Reid said, when the majority leader realized Reid was determined to go past midnight, he recessed the Senate for the day.

Byrd also protected his mentee, such as when he simply forgot to put an appropriation for water research in a bill. "I told him what my problem was and how embarrassing it would be for me not to get that," Reid remembered. "He saw and took care of it."

Beyond their love for Senate rules and legislative legerdemain, and their impoverished backgrounds, they shared a love of history. They would often exchange books and send each other notes about them. Reid thought he was "quirky" and "eccentric," but those words could be used to describe him, too.

From Byrd, Reid also learned the large power of small favors to colleagues, a Byrd trademark. Like Byrd, he would never be a powerful TV presence, but he knew how to get things done by courting colleagues. As much as Reid always thanked Byrd for his mentorship, he also tried to emulate the ruthless, calculating, and transactional Johnston, the man who would become most responsible for singling out Nevada as a nuclear waste dump. In a way, Reid would have appreciated how Johnston got that done.

But Reid truly loved Byrd and told friends as much. There is a throughline from that first letter that Reid wrote to Byrd in November 1986, before Reid took the oath, to almost exactly eighteen years later when the protégé would be nominated by the master to take the majority leader position he once held.

"My role model is Sen. Byrd," Reid wrote to him on one of his note cards on November 16, 2004. "What an honor to be nominated by the 'Babe Ruth' of the Senate."

REID'S FIRST YEAR in the Senate culminated with a devastating legislative loss as Johnston pushed through a bill singling out Nevada for the nation's high-level nuclear repository. Reid protested publicly at hearings about Johnston's attempts to stack the deck, including a move to pay off any state that would take the dump with $100 million a year. Reid would receive credit for nicknaming Johnston's bill to narrow the site selection process from three to one—which he and others presumed was Yucca Mountain—as the "Screw Nevada Bill." This crass but effective moniker would echo through the coming decades, its provenance coming from the man who used a "David vs. Goliath" theme in his Senate campaign and now was finding another iteration because Nevada was the "little kid on the block." This underdog dynamic, this Nevada versus the world, would animate much of what Reid, the David from nowheresville, would do in his career. Reid, who claimed in a 1988 interview that he didn't think the dump could be stopped, knew in this seminal defeat that there was only one way to entomb the dump and that was to somehow amplify the state's power, which could only be done from a leadership post. Reid never acknowledged this was the moment he decided to climb the Senate's rungs of power, but it had to have been on his mind, no matter what his long-term plans and ambition had been before December 21, 1987. In a memorable postscript to the ignominious defeat, the *Review-Journal*'s newest columnist mocked Reid's lack of effectiveness, saying he and Congressman Jim Bilbray were "ambushed" in the conference committee, and he praised the perpetually ineffectual GOP senator Chic

Hecht for his legislative efforts. That rookie columnist's name was Jim Santini, Reid's 1986 foe.

The year may have ended on a bitter note for the freshman senator, but Reid had begun to build and bolster relationships at home that would serve him—and others—for many years. Reid could be even more indispensable to the gaming and mining industries in the Senate than he had been in the House.

The casino industry was going through a metamorphosis, too, with the last remnants of the mob giving way to corporations, and skilled operatives who understood campaign finance replacing more thuggish types who handed out cash.

The issues for the casinos, by the time Reid ascended to the Senate, were not about squashing Henderson dog tracks but heading off federal intervention in their business, something then gaming commission chair Reid had frequently warned about. Now he was in a position to do something about it.

Reid began to use his budding relationships, including with Senate Finance Committee Chair Lloyd Bentsen of Texas, to scuttle a plan to tax the winnings of foreign nationals, some of whom were known as "whales" (big money gamblers) in the casino business. Reid also was able to slow down plans to expand gambling on Indian reservations, which the Nevada-based casinos then saw as an existential threat but, just as they would do with New Jersey, which had legalized casinos in 1977, would later see as an opportunity to make money. Reid would be as flexible as they were.

But for now, with Congress forced to act by a 1987 Supreme Court decision that allowed Indian casinos, Reid, as he would later say, "did everything I could to stand in the way of Indian gaming" to protect Nevada's semi-monopoly.

Reid played a major role in crafting the 1988 Indian Gaming Regulatory Act, which set up a strict oversight framework, ostensibly to keep organized crime from corrupting the tribal casinos, but which also forced them to negotiate with the states and form compacts before they were allowed to operate. For a man who later evolved into a fierce advocate for tribes, his loyalty at this point was obviously to the Las Vegas Strip.

That was not all Reid would do for gaming in his first term. In 1988, for example, Reid called for a Senate investigation into the IRS, alleging the agency violated its own rules when seeking information from Caesars Palace about dealer tips. When David Souter was nominated to the Supreme Court in 1991, Reid was a lone voice raising concerns that he had bragged about stopping New Hampshire from having casinos. (Reid spoke to Souter and eventually supported him, and the two actually became friendly. When Reid took up the cause of judicial compensation twelve years later, Souter wrote him a long, handwritten thank-you note.) Later, when President Bill Clinton tried to put a 4 percent tax on casinos to help finance his welfare reform plan, Reid, along with the rest of the delegation and Gov. Bob Miller, stood up for the industry. The idea died.

ALTHOUGH REID WAS paying attention to parochial issues during his first year, the one that would suck the air out of the Senate chamber was the nomination by President Reagan on July 1 of Robert Bork to the US Supreme Court. This would be Reid's first experience with a controversial nominee, and the freshman would find it more than a bit challenging as he strove to be independent like Nevada. The nomination would eventually be considered a watershed moment in Supreme Court history as special interest groups mobilized to block Bork's nomination because they believed he would roll back civil and abortion rights, among other criticisms.

This was a difficult political predicament for the freshman, who had told the Pro-Family Coalition that he would respect presidential prerogative and not oppose any high court nominee unless the person was corrupt. As the weeks went on, and the Democratic leaders indicated they were going to try to defeat Bork, Reid dithered in announcing his stance.

As the number of undecided senators dwindled, Reid tried to explain that he didn't fully appreciate the Senate's role in confirming nominees when he made those statements during the campaign. "I viewed the role of a senator as much narrower than it is," he said. "This has been a real educational process."

Reid knew that politically, he was at risk in Nevada. He was also jeopardized with national special interests and the Democratic leaders he was trying to cultivate if he voted for Bork. By October, 85 percent of senators had declared their intentions and only two Democrats had said they would vote for Bork. Reid all but acknowledged that he was hoping Bork would withdraw to save him the trouble, claiming to a reporter that he "lost interest" in deciding because he thought the issue would be off the table. He urged the White House to send another nominee to the Hill, but Bork vowed to fight on, forcing Reid's hand.

On October 13, when he finally announced he would oppose Bork on the Senate floor, Reid's speech was a serpentine marvel. He began by saying that he wanted to confirm Bork, that he originally believed a senator's role was quite limited, and that he entered the process with what he called a bias: "I wanted a conservative justice to fill that vacant seat. It has long been my belief that the Court has gone much too far in its judicial activism, and I hoped to see a restraining brake applied."

These were remarkable words for a Democratic senator to assert. But Reid then pivoted and said he opposed Bork because of his "lack of consistency" and a confirmation conversion that contradicted his earlier writings on civil rights, one man one vote, and a host of other issues. On Bork and abortion, Reid restated his own pro-life credentials and said he was not sure of Bork's: "I have a 100 percent pro-life voting record . . . There simply is no logical basis for predicting his decisions in this vital area."

As Reid reached his peroration, he was his blunt, unedited self: "Judge Bork says his views have changed. I do not believe him."

On October 23, 1987, Bork was rejected by a vote of 58–42. The presiding officer in the Senate who announced the result: Harry Reid.

OUTSIDE OF HIS legislative role, during his first two years in the Senate, Reid had two goals: rebuild the Nevada Democratic Party into a fine-tuned machine and ensure his friend Gov. Richard Bryan replaced Republican Chic Hecht in the Senate.

Reid's attempt to secure control of the party was hampered by his early advocacy for the presidential campaign of Tennessee senator Al Gore, which caused a rift with many of the activists who backed Massachusetts governor Michael Dukakis. Gore and Reid had become allies and the families had become connected when Tipper Gore, who had written a guidebook for political wives, helped Landra during the 1986 campaign. Reid was so all-in for Gore that he publicly predicted in March 1988 that Gore would defeat George Herbert Walker Bush forty-nine states to one. That display of oracular boldness came a day after Gore edged Dukakis and Jesse Jackson to win the Nevada caucus. Gore was out of the race a month later.

As the Nevada Democratic Party roiled, though, Reid was quietly putting into action a plan that the consultant Chris Brown had started in 1985 to change the dynamic of a red state. By July, the voter registration efforts were paying off and the Democrats had boosted their margin in Clark County significantly. This was the beginning of the firewall to protect statewide Democrats from losses outside of Southern Nevada, which would help nearly every statewide Democrat, including Bryan in 1988 and, not coincidentally, Reid in coming campaigns.

That same month, Joe Trippi, a veteran of Democratic presidential campaigns, created a "Nevada Plan" that pointed out how well Democrats had done in legislative races compared to their abject failure at the presidential level. Trippi also noted that it was harder to organize Hispanic voters because, unlike the African American community, they were not confined to one geographic area in Las Vegas, and especially because fewer than half of the eighty thousand voting-age Latinos were registered. This is one of the first documented instances, and adjacent to but not directly tied to Reid, of the recognition of the nascent power of the Hispanic vote in Nevada that would be essential in future campaigns for the senator and all statewide and federal candidates.

The nineteen-page memo contained detailed proposals for voter registration along the lines of what Reid's data man, Brown, had recommended. Trippi was way too optimistic about the chances for Nevada to be in the

Democratic presidential column in 1988, but the document nevertheless was a blueprint that built on Brown's modeling for the future.

Bush won Nevada in a Reagan-like landslide (59–38) even as Bryan defeated Hecht by four percentage points. Nevada was still a deeply red state, and an early iteration of the Reid-led Democratic Party was not quite what it would become. But by virtue of Bryan's victory, Reid was now the state's senior senator, after only two years in office.

In his inaugural entry as a senator in the *Almanac of American Politics* in 1987, Reid was described as a "quiet, almost mousy man, a religious Mormon and straight arrow, but he also has a quiet sense of humor and a considerable ambition."

CHAPTER TWELVE

FRIEND OF ENVIRONMENTALISTS AND MINERS

When it came to legislating, Reid was patient. The senator used to tell his staff that if a bill or an amendment failed, they should not despair, he would get it . . . next time. Reid's chess playing had no timer; he just remained confident he would always have the last move, whenever it came, the checkmate.

He would show that he knew how to make friends *and* make friends out of enemies, how he would use the power of personal connections, through doing what no one else would do to help colleagues (including during a scandal), or by essentially legally extorting a private company (in this case, a telephone monopoly to change its board). On all of this, he was happy to be the tortoise, hiding in his shell for the most part, and slowly but surely getting the job done.

There would be enduring political ramifications of these actions, especially on his ever-diminishing appeal in rural Nevada, from whence his next opponent would spring. Even as he was assiduously standing up for mining, the most important industry in the cow counties, against continuous, attempted federal incursions, his growing environmental bona fides, mostly because of his wilderness bill and a massive water settlement, infuriated small-county residents who increasingly saw him as the city slicker taking their public lands with no understanding of their way of life. Indeed, Reid had not given up on establishing a wilderness area in Nevada, a measure that had been stymied by the Republicans in the delegation since he first introduced it as a House member. With Republican Chic Hecht gone and fellow Democrat Bryan in his place, Reid saw an opportunity to go beyond what he had initially requested and finally get a bill passed. With Bryan and Bilbray on board, he introduced a 733,400-acre wilderness bill that would set aside thirteen different pockets of land; Vucanovich's bill was about one-sixth that size. This was still a tiny fraction—less than a tenth of a percent—of the public lands in Nevada that would be protected in their pristine state, off-limits for mining claims and other commercial ventures. With Democrats in control of both houses of Congress, Reid predicted it would sail through the Senate and the House.

He was wrong.

A new fly in the ointment was Wyoming Republican Malcolm Wallop, who held up the measure because, he said, the Fallon Naval Air Station in rural Nevada was concerned about training flights being blocked. Reid thought it was a pretense, perhaps even a stalking horse for a former navy admiral, James Watkins, who was now the head of the Department of Energy and was furious with Nevada for blocking the nuclear waste dump. Whether Reid was posturing or his conspiracy theory was correct—Wallop never brought up the dump in negotiations—the Bush administration got involved in the person of Defense Secretary Dick Cheney. A compromise was reached, and Reid wrote a note to Cheney thanking him "for your time and efforts . . . it all worked out well . . . You are doing a good job for our country."

But it wasn't quite soup yet. The measure remained on hold when Minority Leader Bob Dole delayed passage until Bryan agreed to release his hold on Department of Energy nominees because of the nuclear waste dump push. Bryan agreed to relent so Reid's pet bill could move forward.

After Reid agreed to a provision allowing the navy minimal access to the wilderness areas—he insisted it was a nonevent, while some environmental groups claimed it was devastating—the bill sailed out of the Senate on a voice vote. But Vucanovich would not go quietly, calling for public hearings in the affected areas, which Reid knew would cause an uproar. By July, even the *Review-Journal* was on board and lambasting Vucanovich for her stalling tactics. If ever proof were needed that this was an urban-rural issue and not a partisan wedge, the *Review-Journal*'s support provided it. Reid blasted Vucanovich, with his usual gift for hyperbole: "It's the most heard bill in the entire history of the state of Nevada going back to the Civil War."

Vucanovich had no leverage to stop the bill from passing the House just before Congress adjourned for the year, by a vote of 323–75. On that day, Reid wrote a handwritten note to Wallop.

"You are a tough adversary!" Reid wrote, noting the House passage. "This ended 5½ years of frustration. You are to be commended for your deep concern about the military preparedness of our country."

But there was still one more hurdle—President Bush's signature—and Vucanovich insisted she would press her case with the Republican president. That's when Reid made his last move.

Sig Rogich, who was then an adviser to Bush in the White House, remembers getting the call from his old friend asking for help after he had compromised with Wallop. Rogich approached Bush's chief of staff, John Sununu. "'We're not signing that,'" Rogich said Sununu told him. "Barbara Vucanovich does not want us to sign that bill." Sununu told Rogich he would have to go to the president and make his pitch if he believed in it that strongly.

"So I went to the Oval Office," Rogich recalled. The meeting featured Sununu, Vucanovich, and others. "So they all made their pitch," Rogich said. "And the president said, 'Sigly wins this one.' And I remember Barbara Vucanovich was looking at me like she wanted to kill me."

Reid, though, was grateful to Rogich, who was his friend before he ran

Santini's campaign against him and now was his friend again. No permanent friends, no permanent enemies in Reid's quest for results, even if it took five years. Rogich was on a list on one of Reid's yellow legal pads for thank-you notes to send after the president signed the measure on December 5, 1989.

A day later, Reid sat and wrote several of those handwritten missives, including one to Bush: "Last night you signed S. 974, the Nevada Wilderness bill. This legislation will be remembered, most favorably, long after we are gone. It will leave a legacy of the beauty of nature. As a Democrat, I have been criticized for being too complimentary of you. They won't be able to quote me now! Thank you for what you did for America and the state of Nevada."

Bush was under other pressures, too, and had some desire to be seen as an environmentalist on a bill that, if vetoed, would probably have been overridden in both houses. But Reid had pushed past all the setbacks since he was first elected to Congress and knew what a seminal moment this was. He had created a national park, preserving hundreds of thousands of acres.

It was just the beginning. By the time he was done, millions of acres would be set aside, including two national monuments. Reid beamed with pride every time he talked about his accomplishments in this area.

He knew the political cost, too. In 2008, for instance, Esmeralda and Mineral County commissions voted against a lands bill that the elected officials knew would help the counties but were afraid to upset constituents. (In a memo on the subject, Reid scrawled, ". . . so be it. They can continue to live in poverty.")

Despite the tens of millions of dollars Reid would eventually earmark for the rural areas, though, many of which boosted the local economies, the so-called cow counties were unforgiving. That made his margin for error in a competitive race that much smaller—he needed to win by a large enough margin in populous and Democrat-heavy Clark County to offset losses elsewhere.

———

IF PASSING A wilderness bill after so many tries was no mean feat, what Reid was able to do on the perennially thorny issue of water rights in northern Nevada made that look like child's play. The issue was hopelessly complex: how to allocate the waters of the Truckee River, which runs through northern Nevada and California, among a panoply of interested and often competing parties, from a power utility to an Indian tribe to municipal water authorities, and to ensure the survival of Pyramid Lake, located about forty miles northwest of Reno. The various disputes, which went back a century, had been the subject of dozens of lawsuits, some that reached the US Supreme Court. Endangered trout species were also involved, which made it even more complicated.

Reid was an environmentalist, perhaps, but when he got to the Senate, he had little interest in the northern water issue, especially after a deal Paul Laxalt had negotiated failed to make it through Congress.

Marcus Faust, the capital lawyer/lobbyist who would eventually become a close friend and ally, was lobbying on the issue for Sierra Pacific Power, the northern Nevada electric utility, when Reid was elected. Most of those involved thought it was over after Laxalt failed, but Faust went to see Reid anyhow.

"I went in and sat down with him and kind of walked through it," Faust recalled. "And he said to me, 'Why would I want to pick this up when Paul Laxalt, the most influential senator Nevada's ever had, couldn't get it done?' And my answer was: 'Because when you get it done, it will become a part of the Harry Reid legacy.' He said: 'Let's do it.'"

The rookie senator was about to learn what sometime Nevadan Mark Twain meant about whiskey being for drinking and water for fighting. Reid began a new chapter in the settlement attempts, bringing in all of the disparate players and his legislative director, Wayne Mehl, who would attend countless meetings.

Reid was relentless and steadfast, and his strategic mind was deployed at various key junctures. Faust said it was "the mastery of his legislative skills. He knew how to cut the deal. He knew instinctively what the other side needed to get to get to a yes [vote] and he would work those deals out."

Sue Oldham, a Reno attorney who was involved in the negotiations, later recalled: "Reid essentially told the parties to stay in a room until meaningful agreements were reached," a process she said took some three days. "He said basically 'don't come out until you have some way of approaching and getting to settlement.'"

Decades later, Reid could still recite details of the negotiations and the political consequences for himself. He believed that Laxalt and others had given short shrift to the tribes, and he took their side in many of the disputes with farmers. Part of it stemmed from his imperative to divert water to ensure the future of Pyramid Lake and an enduring water supply for the tribes.

"The farmers just hated me," Reid said. "They hung me in effigy. They were our biggest enemies, because number one, they didn't like Indians. Number two, they didn't want any of the environmental staff to check their water."

Reid also was proud of being able to reroute water to marshes to help migrating birds and preserve the ecology of the region. But, as he put it, "It came at a price. All that was good for the environment wasn't good for me with farmers."

By August 1989, Reid thought he had enough agreement to introduce a bill in the Senate that would give something to all of the parties in Nevada and California—establishing a drought reserve for the cities, preserving the lake, and forcing officials to provide a plan to protect the fish, provide money for the wetlands, and settle outstanding water claims against the state and the federal government.

"Harry Reid's water bill is a massive achievement, one of the few truly monumental pieces of Nevada legislation in many years," the *Reno Gazette-Journal* gushed in a long editorial on November 21, 1990, after the bill passed. The newspaper credited Reid with overcoming "insurmountable odds" to reach "an accomplishment that remains amazing to this day." And then the kicker: "Future generations will look upon this as one of the truly amazing accomplishments of any public official in Nevada history."

Just as Faust had foretold.

It was not over yet—lawsuits and implementation issues would delay a formal signing ceremony by all the parties for almost two decades, and all the lawsuits would not be resolved until 2015. Reid's nonpareil staff, including state director Mary Connelly, kept their eyes on the ball all those intervening years after the original bill passed to ensure it came to fruition.

Mehl, who died in 2011, considered the compact one of his proudest accomplishments. So did Reid, who said in 2015, "There is nothing I have done for the state of Nevada that is as important as this."

EVEN AS HE was beginning to pour the legislative concrete for the foundation of his environmental legacy, Reid also was standing up for the industry that had fought him on it: mining. This would be a hallmark of his career, his ability to be both a darling of environmental groups and the mining industry's foremost defender. It was a trick few could have pulled off.

When T. Boone Pickens, the Texas hostile takeover king, showed an interest in Newmont Mining, North America's largest gold producer, with deep Nevada holdings, Reid was the strongest among the state's elected officials in fretting about corporate raiding. When Congress showed an interest, especially because of Newmont's South African part-ownership, Reid tried to affect the tender offer through legislation, which drew Pickens's ire. His bid for Newmont eventually reached $6.3 billion, but the company eventually was able to fight him off.

When Pickens later supported clean energy, Reid and he became allies.

Protecting Newmont from Pickens was small potatoes compared to what began in Reid's first term and would continue until his retirement, and that was fighting off efforts to reform a mining law that was almost a century and a quarter old. The Mining Law of 1872, written after the gold rush, gave broad authority to private companies on public lands, extracting no royalties and providing no environmental protections. For decades, environmentalists had agitated for it to be reformed, and the mining companies lobbied against major changes. They could not have found a more hard rock champion than the son of a miner from Searchlight. "No one in the country—no one—did as much for mining as I did," Reid would later boast.

There are few who would disagree, from the environmental lobby he consistently frustrated to the companies he protected to the man he consistently and improbably defeated in floor fights, Democrat Dale Bumpers of Arkansas.

Bumpers believed the law was an archaic giveaway to the mining industry, and he introduced many bills to reform the anachronism, starting in Reid's first term. He was a formidable opponent for the freshman senator. Bumpers was known for his oratorical skills, often mentioned as a presidential contender, and he took to the floor to give stem-winders about the unfairness of the 1872 law. But Reid defeated him every time, not by being Cicero but by counting votes.

Reid worked the floor, even persuaded Democrat Kent Conrad of North Dakota to change his vote. He then stood up and averred that mining was the "soul" of Nevada's economy. When the tally came, Bumpers's bill died by a 50–48 count. Bumpers would then approach Reid and call him a "son of a bitch," Reid recalled. This would become a familiar pattern, and the votes were almost always very close.

"Senator Bumpers just kept coming forward with his floor amendments once a year, and Bumpers would give these incredibly eloquent speeches," recalled Michael Brown, a longtime executive with Barrick Gold who became part of Reid's inner circle. "And then he would stand at his desk at the back of the chamber during the vote count, but Reid was down in the well, buttonholing his colleagues and putting the votes together."

Reid took some of what Bumpers said during the many floor debates personally. Reid often said Bumpers was an easterner who did not understand the Western way of life, but one time, recalled longtime Reid aide Jimmy Ryan, Reid thought he had gone too far.

"He said, 'People need to understand my father was a hard rock miner. And if we're sitting here in a historic building in the Capitol and the Senate chamber, if somebody told my dad that there was gold underneath the floor, he'd start digging.'"

The primal, personal nature of the argument, and Reid's rare loss of composure on the floor—or anywhere—surprised those in the chamber. He was truly passionate about the issue, and he would not let Bumpers win. Later, when Reid became leader, and mining reform bills passed the House a number of times, they were dead on arrival in the Senate.

IF THE FIRST-TERM senator was willing to take on unpopular legislative causes such as killing measures the environmental lobby desired, he also was showing a knack for taking on tasks no one else wanted and for sticking his nose where others would not dare. On the former, Reid took on the role of being Alan Cranston's emissary when the California Democrat became embroiled in the so-called Keating Five scandal; on the latter, Reid decided to continue his decades-old war with the Las Vegas phone utility, Centel, by telling the company who it should have on its board.

Reid had known Cranston since before that unusual arrangement whereby he became part of the California Democratic congressional delegation when he was the sole Democrat in the Nevada caucus. Cranston had even helped funnel $80,000 into Nevada to help with voter registration during Reid's first race for the Senate. (Reid, ironically, would later say of Cranston that "all he cared about was raising money for his campaigns.")

That money, though, was later found to be part of a PAC that Charles Keating contributed to, and Keating's name became radioactive in late 1989 when his company, Lincoln Savings, collapsed as part of a widening industry scandal. Five senators—Cranston, John McCain and Dennis DeConcini of Arizona, John Glenn of Ohio, and Don Riegle of Michigan—were accused of using their positions to influence regulators to go soft on Keating's company. The Senate Ethics Committee launched an investigation in November 1989 that would last almost two years.

That's where Reid, who had taken $4,000 from Keating that he later returned, came in. He helped behind the scenes, especially because four of the five were Democrats. He remembered Glenn being brought to tears in a Democratic caucus meeting because of his besmirched reputation.

So Reid agreed to be a go-between among the senators, especially Cranston, with the ethics panel. In one letter to the tribunal he wrote on October 24, 1990, and marked "personal and confidential," Reid invoked his trial lawyer experience and said he hoped "that each of the five senators would have the right of confrontation and be able to cross examine witnesses." Reid also listed other procedures, common in trials, that should be afforded the senators, including witness lists and depositions, before they went before the panel. "I know that you will do your utmost to be fair and impartial, but I thought the above suggestions may be of help to you and the committee staff and counsel," Reid concluded.

Reid did more than just write to the panel. He called Alan Dershowitz, at that time a premier defense attorney, to help in the case. "I called him cold and he agreed and he was terrific," Reid remembered. None of the Keating Five was ever prosecuted. The ethics panel found four of the senators had acted improperly or showed poor judgment, and issued a reprimand for Cranston rather than a full Senate censure, partly because he was ill with cancer and had announced he would not run again. Nevertheless, this was seen as a victory for his lawyer, Dershowitz, and his go-between, Reid.

The Nevada senator's role came to light during the hearings, and the Republicans, who did not have a seemingly viable candidate against him, seized on the news to lambaste Reid and say he should be investigated by the full Senate. That went nowhere, but Reid had burnished his credentials as an inside player acceptable to both parties, willing to undertake an unseemly task. The ethics panel came under withering criticism for what were seen as a series of wrist slaps, but the *Las Vegas Sun* publisher, Brian Greenspun (Hank Greenspun had passed away in 1989), reliably came to Reid's defense, saying he was a dealmaker helping "the sick and aging Cranston."

REID WAS SLIGHTLY less subtle in another contemporaneous power play in which he was able to renew his long-running—and, not coincidentally, politically advantageous—feud with the phone utility. He had attacked Centel in his legislative and lieutenant governor campaigns—and they had responded in kind—and now he saw another opening. This time he was in an even more powerful position, and it would not be the only time he tried to intimidate a private entity to submit to his will on behalf, he would say, of the interests of Nevadans.

In mid-1989, Reid discovered that the utility had no Nevadans on the board of directors, so he had his staff write a letter to the CEO, John Frazee, and persuaded Bryan and Bilbray to sign on.

"A significant amount of your revenues are generated in Nevada and frankly, we feel it is an embarrassment and slight to the state of Nevada that you do not have a Nevadan on the board," the letter said. "It would be appreciated if you would give us your reasons for there not being a Nevadan on the Centel Corporation Board of Directors."

The letter was conveniently leaked to Reid's old friend at the *Review-Journal*, Don Digilio, who wrote a favorable column (he had moved to the *Sun*) that ended, "Give 'em hell, Harry."

Frazee declined to write back, instead passing on the letter to Robert Huntley, the head of the board's nominating committee, who responded a few weeks later saying geography was one of many factors considered, but "except for competence and integrity, no single criterion is controlling."

Four days later, Reid responded—there were no cosignatories this time—and he pulled no punches.

"Your letter of June 12 is an insult to the people of Nevada. You should have answered the question of why there is not a single Nevadan on the Centel Board of Directors. You did not. The people of Nevada deserve better than a letter from an out-of-state law firm that says little, offers nothing and sidesteps an issue of great public importance."

Reid, so mild-mannered in public, was just getting started.

"Your company has taken millions of dollars out of Nevada . . . Without going into more detail, it seems like your out-of-state company still does not consider Nevada as anything more than a place to make money. Shame on you. You know better . . . and the people of Nevada deserve better."

It took a while, but the strikingly different tone of Reid's solo letter clearly had an impact. On January 10, 1991, Bill Creech, a retired air force general living in Nevada, was appointed to Centel's board.

Six days later, Reid wrote to Centel's president, James Kropid, expressing his appreciation for the Nevadan's appointment "with all best wishes."

CHAPTER THIRTEEN

DOUBTING THOMAS

Reid really wanted to elevate Clarence Thomas to the US Supreme Court. Soon after President Bush nominated Thomas, who would be the second Black justice ever to sit on the high court, in July 1991, Reid said he would vote to confirm him. The Democrats were in control of the Senate, 57–43, and Richard Bryan also committed to back Thomas.

But in early October, after the law professor Anita Hill shocked the country with her assertions that Thomas had harassed her, Reid said publicly he would reconsider given the troubling nature of the allegations. He and Bryan both supported delaying the vote to consider Hill's testimony. Reid said the Senate would be "grossly insensitive to women" if it did not consider the charges, a telling statement from someone who had worked hard to appeal to female voters as a pro-life candidate by holding hearings on domestic violence and women's health. (Reid would work throughout his career to offset the political damage to him with Democratic women on abortion by advocating for other women's issues such as domestic violence.)

On the day of the vote, October 15, 1991, Reid and Bryan were declared undecided by their offices, accompanied by front-page headlines. But that day, at 8:08 a.m. Las Vegas time, Reid's speechwriter and close aide, Evan

Wallach, faxed to his personal number in McLean, Virginia, a speech the senator could give that day to confirm Thomas.

"Judge Thomas is on trial before us for honor, for life, for his very soul," the speech said. "Equally unfortunately, we do not know, I believe we can never know, what happened between these two people ten years ago."

The speech then went on to say that "ten years is a long time," suggesting memories can fade, a clear implication that perhaps Hill did not recall the events correctly. It quickly pivoted to Reid's support of sexual harassment laws and his "hope, most fervently, that out of these hearings will at least come increased sensitivity to the problem of sexual harassment in the workplace."

The speech continued that the statute of limitations on the federal sexual harassment law had passed and then quoted Thomas Paine: "Suspicion is the companion of mean souls and the bane of all good society."

Then the decision: "What I have seen in these last few terrible days has not given me sufficient evidence to change my mind [to support Thomas] . . . I announced that I would vote to confirm someone whom I believed was a good man. I still believe that, but now I would add that I believe that this man whose mettle has been tempered by the flames of Hell will profit by that terrible journey . . . I believe this good man has been given the opportunity to become a great man. Not a great Black man, not a great representative of his people upon the Supreme Court, but a kind and compassionate person who tempers justice with mercy and who matches scholarship with wisdom, a person who exemplifies the best qualities of that race to which we all belong as brothers and sisters, the human race."

Reid would never deliver that speech.

A few hours later, he voted against Thomas, who was confirmed 52–48. Reid told reporters that he had called his wife shortly before the vote, and she asked him whether he was at peace with himself and he told her no. He hung up but called her back one more time forty-five minutes before the vote and said he was going to vote against Thomas.

"He agonized about Clarence Thomas a little bit because he didn't listen to all the hearings, he didn't have time to listen to all the hearings," she said. "I watched everything."

What did she tell him?

"I told him I believed her, I didn't believe him," she said bluntly.

Reid insisted publicly that "every political bone in my body said I should vote for Clarence Thomas . . . But in the end, I couldn't vote for him. My conscience wouldn't allow it."

Those words were a stark departure from the speech Wallach had sent him that morning, and the politics were far from as simple as Reid made them sound. Even then, there was speculation in Democratic circles that Reid was terrified of a pro-choice candidate surfacing against him and the possibility that Thomas might vote to toss out *Roe v. Wade*. It had appeared as if only an obscure rural rancher named Demar Dahl would challenge Reid in 1992, but why give anyone, including the abortion rights darling and moderate Republican lieutenant governor Sue Wagner, any reason to reconsider?

Reid and Bryan also made their decisions after it was well-known on Capitol Hill that Thomas had the necessary votes, context that would not be lost to the mists of history. Reid's relationship with this "good man" would become nastier over the years. In 2004, he would call Thomas "an embarrassment to the court," something no other sitting senator would have the gumption to say, and in 2018, after the court decided a controversial contraception case, Reid decried the actions of "five white men," earning him scorn in right-wing circles for the flub.

For now, though, he had come within a hair's breadth of voting for Thomas and lauding him to the world before deciding his conscience—or the politics or his wife—would not bear it.

DAHL NEVER HAD a chance in the 1992 election, but Reid made it interesting by taking the race for granted, including a primary challenge from a badly disfigured millionaire businessman with an eye patch named Charles

Woods. Woods took nearly 40 percent in the primary, a possible canary in the coal mine that Reid was weaker than he thought with the base. (Reid, who privately called Woods "Scarface," also defeated an only-in-Nevada candidate named God Almighty.) Even Dahl's poll that he released after winning his primary showed him eighteen points behind. The national Republicans put their best face on it, but they knew this was not their year to unseat Reid. Not even God Almighty could defeat Reid, as the joke went.

Reid had plenty of national support, too, not just from Big Labor but from the teachers union. One revealing aspect was that, according to his answers on a National Education Association questionnaire, Reid stuck to his guns. Literally. The only two questions where he checked that he disagreed with NEA's position was on guns ("NEA supports safe and weapon-free school environments and supports federal legislation to limit access to cheap, readily available handguns and semiautomatic assault weapons, and a waiting period and background check prior to the purchase of handguns") and abortion ("NEA supports reproductive rights without governmental intervention").

The results on November 3 were not surprising:

Reid won by eleven percentage points, or 51 percent to 40 percent, and nearly fifty-four thousand votes.

ONE BENEFIT CONFERRED on Reid from becoming the senior senator with Chic Hecht's loss in 1988 was that once a Democratic president was elected, he would have immense power to recommend nominees from judgeships and other federal posts. Over time, Reid would select dozens of people who would eventually be nominated and confirmed, one of his proudest accomplishments. He would always strive for diversity—or, as some of his critics would say, identity politics. Reid recalled the catalyst. He was at the federal courthouse for a ceremony shortly after his reelection, and he looked around on the dais. "There's all these judges, all white men," Reid said. "I said to myself, 'Maybe someday I can change that.'"

Once he had a chance, that's exactly what he did. His most controversial recommendation was Johnnie Rawlinson in 1997. "I wanted to get a Black woman," Reid recalled. "So I found a woman who was working in child support [in the Clark County district attorney's office], which is about as low a rung as you could get. And I named her the first [Nevada] federal judge who was a Black woman. I took so much heat for that."

Reid's gamble paid off, though: Rawlinson became a well-respected judge and eventually ascended to the Ninth Circuit Court of Appeals. Many years later, he would reveal another factor in his choice: "Here's the one thing she had going for her. She was from North Carolina, where my son-in-law is from. They knew each other."

Later, he would choose a Hispanic woman, Gloria Navarro, and then, "I wanted an Asian. I got Miranda Du, who was born in Vietnam."

He knew what a powerful—and lasting tool—he had been given, one he could even use to his electoral benefit. Reid would later choose as a federal judge Brian Sandoval, an up-and-coming star in Republican politics and a Hispanic former legislator and attorney general who also had once held a job Reid had, chairman of the Nevada Gaming Commission. "He did a good job," Reid said. "He was a good judge. But I did that, of course, to make sure he wouldn't be running against me. No need to play around. That's the way it was."

Remake the court, sideline an opponent, and change the course of Nevada history.

REID ALSO WOULD show in the first two years of his second term that he was not afraid to take on a Democratic president, criticizing Clinton for trying to increase mining and grazing fees to help fund his fiscal 1994 budget, and gaming taxes to pay for welfare reform. Reid helped scuttle both proposals.

When the *Almanac of American Politics* was released in August 1993, the word "mousy" was gone, replaced by a description of Reid as "mild-mannered but proven that he can be tough." And the following year, in the popular "Walter Scott's Personality Parade" feature in the *Washington Post*, the author answered a question about who in the Senate was in Harry Truman's "class as far as integrity and guts are concerned." Scott answered that he talked to Washington veterans, and they could only name six. Reid was one of them.

With his emerging national reputation, Reid also began to feel more comfortable at home after his reelection. He began flexing his muscles in local elections, telling candidates whether or not they should run. When a promising young assemblyman named Matthew Callister wanted to run for attorney general, Reid sent the message that it was a bad idea because of a legislative pension vote scandal. Callister did not run. He often anointed candidates for statewide and county offices, too, including making some poor choices along the way as the party's kingmaker or meddler-in-chief. He infuriated some Democrats when he persuaded a far-right conservative state senator, Bob Ryan, to switch parties and run against a county commissioner, Don Schlesinger, he did not like. Ryan got crushed.

This was the beginning of a pattern that would be repeated scores of times in the next two decades as prospective candidates would seek to be vetted by Reid, who could not help but meddle in down-ballot races.

As with Ryan, his choices did not always work out. He succeeded in obtaining a speaking slot at the 2000 Democratic National Convention for Clark County Commissioner Dario Herrera. But Herrera's career later would implode with ethics questions and eventually a federal corruption conviction in a sordid case that sent him to prison in 2007. Reid also hyped a former aide, Ruben Kihuen, who served in the legislature before winning a congressional seat in 2016. But his career quickly disintegrated amid sexual misconduct allegations, and he was forced to retire after only one term.

Years later, Reid was defensive about his protégés, whom he had picked more for their ethnicity than anything else, insisting it did not reflect on his judge of character. Reid said Herrera was a UNLV quarterback, "had a great pedigree but he had a zipper problem and he couldn't handle that." Reid said Kihuen was "a totally different deal. He was not a lecherous man . . . he patted some lady on the leg while they were sitting at a table . . . That was the beginning of the Me Too movement and men couldn't treat women the way they used to . . . Ruben just got caught in that trap and he did not react to it well at all." (Despite Reid's characterization of what occurred, multiple women had come forward to accuse Kihuen of misconduct.) Reid was so enamored of Kihuen that he had put him in another congressional race four years earlier against Dina Titus, who outraised Kihuen and forced him to withdraw, causing the senator and his staff to scramble to find Kihuen a job. "Senator Reid wants to find a paid appointment or employment opportunity for Ruben Kihuen. Needs to happen somewhat quickly. Can you start looking to see if there are paid appointment or administration opportunities?" an internal staff email read a few days after Kihuen dropped out. He was eventually hired by the Community College of Southern Nevada in a sinecure.

TWO ELECTIONS IN late 1994 changed the trajectory of Reid's political life, even though his name was not on the ballot.

The first occurred on November 8 when his close friend, Congressman Jim Bilbray, who had held the senator's congressional seat for four terms, lost in a sensational upset to Republican John Ensign. Bilbray was not just a pal dating to their days as Capitol policemen together; he was a backstop for Reid—Bilbray ensured that Reid never had to worry about a Republican challenge from the First Congressional District.

Reid had futilely tried to save his friend when a bill the congressman had proposed to expand the Red Rock Conservation Area was caught up in controversy because it would have made millions for Bilbray's closest adviser.

As the news broke of the land deal, Reid did something few others would have done: he called Bilbray's opponent. In a typewritten memo on September 30 signed "HMR," Reid said he had spoken with Ensign four days earlier and "he indicated he had no problem with the Red Rock expansion going forward," so long as any negotiations were made public and Clark County had to approve any exchanges.

With that quickly handled and memorialized, the next day Reid met in his Las Vegas office with executives of Del Webb to try to calm the waters—and protect Bilbray. The company believed that Bilbray was a handmaiden of Summa, the latest iteration of Howard Hughes's original company that owned prodigious tracts of land in Southern Nevada and was frustrating Webb's attempts to expand.

The Del Webb executive Phil Dion began, in what a memo by Reid staffer Hugh Ferree described as "an adversarial tone," fulminating about how "we've been screwed by Bilbray" and that unless Reid can specifically come up with a solution, "this meeting is worthless."

Dion went on to say "the real estate community has known for a year about [the exchange being sought by Bilbray's consultant Don Williams, who also had worked for Reid]." Del Webb's Don Moon chimed in, according to Ferree's memo: "Bilbray knew (with emphasis) about this too before (with emphasis) the bill proposal."

During the meeting, Reid tried to mollify Dion, saying how much he "admired his tenacity" and expressing a "general dislike of Summa," according to the memo. Dion was not to be deterred, threatening more public disclosures and lawsuits if Reid did not amend the bill to allow Webb to get more land. When Reid asked toward the end of the hour-long meeting to lay off his friend, Dion promised not to "go after Bilbray" if Reid could get the bill amended.

A week later, the expansion bill passed, with Del Webb given preference in land swaps. Reid had worked meticulously to get holds removed from the bill. The measure had passed, Bilbray was crowing, and Reid had done all he could behind the scenes to protect his flank. It was not enough.

Bilbray lost in one of the biggest upsets in state annals during the year of the Newt Gingrich Revolution by 1,400 votes out of 150,000 cast. Ensign, young (thirty-six) and dynamic, was an immediate threat to Reid in his next election in 1998.

The other election that would have a dramatic impact on Reid's future took place a few weeks later on December 2 in Washington. If it had gone the other way—and it almost did by the slimmest of margins—Reid's course would almost certainly not have been what it became.

The balloting was for a new Democratic leader, and the contest had begun in March when Maine's George Mitchell announced his retirement. Reid's name was floated as a possible successor, and he did nothing to discourage the speculation, surely realizing it gave him more leverage. One staffer said that Reid actually encouraged South Dakota's Tom Daschle to run shortly after Mitchell retired, and he was never serious about seeking the position himself, simply thinking a few moves ahead. By April, Reid announced he would not seek the post and would endorse Daschle.

Daschle and Reid had been in the House together since 1982 and had formed a real bond. The day that Reid endorsed Daschle in April, he received a handwritten note from his friend: "I want to reiterate my gratitude for what you did this morning. I don't think it could have come off any better. You are a great friend. This could be a difficult race—but I am feeling better and better."

When the vote finally came after the election, only two contenders remained: Daschle and Connecticut senator Chris Dodd. When the votes were counted, Daschle had won . . . by one vote, 24–23. Daschle immediately appointed Reid to the chairmanship of the Democratic Policy Committee, which Daschle had held and was a clear rung up the leadership ladder—even though Reid had previously questioned its importance when Bryan landed on it. (Daschle technically was the cochair with Reid, but this was the Nevadan's baby now.) A few days after the vote, Dodd penned a handwritten note to Reid:

"Just a note to tell you, my friend, I understand your vote for Tom last week," Dodd wrote. "Harry, we've been friends too long to let this difference linger."

They would remain good friends until Reid's death, occasionally talking on the phone and reminiscing. After Ted Kennedy's death in 2009, Dodd and Reid ventured together one early morning to the Massachusetts senator's grave. "Harry said, 'Do you mind if I say a prayer?' And I said, no, if you don't mind if I give Teddy a drink." He poured a little vodka on Kennedy's grave.

Both men would remember the moment for a lifetime.

HARRY REID WAS always looking ahead. He wanted to sideline Ensign before he could run against him in 1998, but by midsummer of 1996, the only Democrat who had taken the bait was a state senator named Bob Coffin, whose last name seemed an unfortunate harbinger of his electoral chances.

How far was Reid willing to go to derail Ensign? The Republican congressman had been working with Democratic senator Bryan on a lands bill that would have freed up Bureau of Land Management parcels and infused millions into local coffers. This was revolutionary legislation that was right in Reid's environmental wheelhouse. It was included in an omnibus bill and seemed likely to pass. Even Reid had signed on as a cosponsor.

But then it mysteriously died, depriving Ensign (and Bryan, too!) of a huge legislative victory just over a month before the election. Reid had put a hold on the language, saying he didn't want any of the money used to buy habitats for the endangered desert tortoise in Utah. He would later say he did not have the power to stop the bill, and besides, he was a cosponsor.

But a letter dated September 26, 1996, from Frank Murkowski, the chairman of the Senate Energy Committee, to House Resources Chairman Don Young, said the Nevada lands bill would not be included in the final package "due to opposition from Nevada's senior senator."

When the measure finally passed a few years later, Reid would happily take credit for it. And his maneuver did little good: Ensign won, and he was coming for Reid, and they both knew it.

IN HIS SECOND term, Reid was cementing his standing as a Senate institutionalist like his mentor, Robert Byrd. When some of his colleagues, including Bryan, wanted to change the threshold of votes needed to break a filibuster from sixty to fifty-one, Reid spoke up. "The filibuster is all we've got to defend our rights," he said at the time. "The founding fathers knew what the tyranny of large states could do to small states like Nevada."

His position on the filibuster would evolve over time.

Reid also would take full advantage of his cochairmanship of the Democratic Policy Committee to provide weekly briefings for senators and a yearly issues conference. Reid was building goodwill for his next step up the leadership ladder.

It came sooner than he might have imagined when Democratic whip Wendell Ford announced in early March 1997 that he would not run again. That meant the number two spot in the Democratic caucus was about to come open, and Reid wasted no time. Reid's alacrity and aggressiveness in pursuing the whip's job so long before it would become open is evident in thank-you letters to those who had committed to him, all handwritten, that he was sending only a few days after Ford announced his retirement. He didn't care that some suggested it was unseemly to campaign for the job so soon; Reid wanted the number two slot, and he knew how to press his colleagues' buttons, sometimes in an obviously obsequious manner. He called Maryland's Barbara Mikulski "the best orator we have in the Senate," he told Delaware's Joe Biden he had been "my role model," and he praised Bob Kerry for "your service to our country in the military."

It didn't hurt, of course, to have these notes as memorialization of commitments.

REID ALSO WAS busy in the mid-1990s standing up for the state's two preeminent industries, which brought him into conflict with a high-profile Clinton administration official.

Bruce Babbitt, who would serve as Clinton's Interior secretary for the president's entire tenure, was, in many ways, a man after Harry Reid's environmental heart. They both wanted to protect and preserve public lands, and Babbitt came to Nevada a few times when Reid had an announcement to make on that front. But when it came to protecting and preserving Nevada's two key industries, the two were at loggerheads.

Babbitt wanted his department to be the final arbiter of compacts between the Indians and states that Reid had written into the Indian Gaming Regulatory Act of 1988. "Substantive changes to IGRA should not be made by unelected bureaucrats at the Department of the Interior," Reid fumed.

The two crossed swords even more over mining, with Babbitt on the reform side and Reid on the status quo side. In May 1995, Reid went public with his concerns in an interview with *Mining World* magazine: "I think Bruce Babbitt has not done as good a job as he's capable of doing. He's made some tremendous mistakes. He focused on mining and grazing in a critical fashion. I don't think he served the president well."

The blunt, brutal assessment provoked an immediate phone call from Babbitt, who was obviously not pleased and probably fretted about his standing with Clinton. After hanging up, Reid scrawled one of his handwritten missives to the cabinet secretary.

"What is in the article is what I have told you personally," Reid wrote to Babbitt. "I think you have been to [*sic*] strident on the mining issue." And a classic Reid addendum:

"If you still have hurt feelings, remember I am your best friend you have in the Senate."

Reid would also approach Babbitt on behalf of mining companies with Nevada interests. In 1995, he wrote to Babbitt about a delayed patent application in Washington state for Battle Mountain Gold Company, which also had holdings in northern Nevada. "The delay is troubling, and I would appreciate your ideas about why it has occurred," Reid wrote, adding that the company had received varying explanations from the Bureau of Land Management on why it had been on hold for two years. (It's unclear what, if anything, occurred after Reid wrote the letter.)

Babbitt was not the only prominent capital official who became Reid's target during this period. In mid-1996, Reid began what would become a nearly decade-long war against Federal Reserve Chairman Alan Greenspan by declaring he would vote against a third four-year term because Greenspan kept a "slush fund"—i.e., $3.7 billion set aside to cover potential losses. (The Fed had not suffered a loss in seventy-nine years.) With Daniel Patrick Moynihan of New York calling Greenspan a "national treasure" and Connecticut's Chris Dodd saying it would be a "tragic mistake" not to confirm him, Reid was among only seven senators to vote no.

Reid voted against a fourth Greenspan term in 2000 and then five years later, in a broadside that shook DC and snared a spot in the legendary *New York Times* columnist William Safire's political dictionary, Reid called Greenspan "one of the biggest political hacks we have here in Washington."

Daschle, by then out of office, emailed Reid. "Your comments about Greenspan were the talk of the luncheon I attended today. Everybody, including me, loved them! Nice job."

BY EARLY 1997, Team Reid was preparing for a race against Ensign the following year, and almost everything he did would be refracted through that prism. He had a million dollars in the bank, almost ten times what Ensign had.

About this same time, Reid, who had hired Paul Maslin as his pollster, commissioned a survey to gauge where he was in relation to Ensign—and, just in case, northern representative Jim Gibbons. The results were encouraging: Reid led Ensign, 50–33, and Gibbons, 50–34. Reid's approval numbers also were robust: Only 17 percent of respondents had an unfavorable view of the senator, and 69 percent approved of his job performance. Ensign was still not known by more than a third of the electorate. These were the numbers of an incumbent in excellent shape.

This was also going to be the first cycle that Reid would begin to recognize, if not harness, the potential of the Hispanic vote in Nevada, although it would be some time before the cohort would prove critical. Reid had been a hard-liner on immigration, while the Hispanic population in Nevada was relatively unimportant. In 1993, he had given a speech that could have been given by Ted Cruz or perhaps even Donald Trump today. Reid introduced what he called the Immigration Stabilization Act to outlaw so-called birthright citizenship—that is, a child born in the United States to undocumented parents is considered a legal citizen of this country, according to the US Constitution.

"Paring immigration to more manageable levels would necessitate some long-overdue changes in the way immigrants are selected," Reid said on the floor. "The ever-growing pressure to expand immigration levels is a byproduct of a system that grants immigration preferences to extended family members."

Reid was not prepared for the reception he received at home that evening as Landra laced into him for the bill, reminding him that her father had come to America, probably illegally, from Russia to escape anti-Semitism. She also reminded him that his grandmother had come to America under the cover of darkness from Eastern Europe. Reid would shift gears on the issue, but it would not be until 2006, when Hispanics had become a powerful force in Nevada politics, that he would repudiate his previous efforts in a Senate floor speech. He said, in part:

> A group of people came and talked to us and convinced us that the thing to do would be to close the borders between Mexico and the United States; in effect, stop people from coming across our borders to the United States. This period of time for which I am so apologetic—to my family, mostly—lasted about a week or two. I introduced legislation. My little wife is 5 feet tall. We have been together for soon to be 50 years. As I said here on the floor a few days ago, her father was born in Russia. He was run out of Russia. His name was Goldfarb, his family. They were Jewish. My wife heard that I had done this. She does not interfere with my legislation. Only when I ask her does she get involved in what I am doing. I didn't ask her about this. She, in effect, said: I can't believe that you have done it. But I had done it.

Four years later, Reid had begun to mend fences and develop relationships in the Hispanic community, including a friendship with Eddie Escobedo, the publisher of *El Mundo*, Las Vegas's main Hispanic newspaper, and Fernando Romero, who ran a popular Hispanic political group.

His staff advised him that there was no utility in courting Hispanics because the community was not that large, many were not registered to vote, and they did not all live in one section of Southern Nevada, as the Black community did in a concentrated area called the Westside of Las Vegas.

By 1997, on the cusp of his bid for a third term, Reid held a Hispanic Leadership Summit. The language in the brochure he handed out was hardly subtle.

"As the largest and fastest growing minority in Nevada, Hispanics are expanding their presence throughout the State," Reid wrote in the introduction to "Hispanic Americans in the Silver State."

Hispanics made up 12.5 percent of Nevada's population; by 2025, the brochure projected, Nevada would have the fifth-largest population of Latinos in the country. The piece featured graphs showing the Hispanic growth in various areas in Nevada and contained a picture of Reid with former Housing and Urban Development secretary Henry Cisneros. The brochure also pointed out that only 15 percent of the state's Hispanic population voted, but the remarkable growth could make them "a deciding factor in local, State and national elections."

Reid presciently saw how decisive the Latino vote could be—for him and for other statewide contenders, including presidential nominees.

By November, Ensign had finally announced he would take on Reid, citing as his key reasons the senator's votes for a 1993 tax increase that passed by one vote and against a Balanced Budget Amendment that failed by one. The most expensive and what would prove to be one of the closest Senate races in Nevada history had begun.

CHAPTER FOURTEEN

A NEAR-DEATH EXPERIENCE

The race that almost changed everything, and then *did* change everything, was one that almost ended Harry Reid's career and then laid the groundwork for so much of what was to come.

The 1998 Senate race highlighted Reid's disdain for campaigning, showed how a newspaper that had doubled as the senator's press organ desperately tried to secure a win for him at the end with an astonishing breach of journalistic ethics, and would also end in a recount that became a model for others, with its focus on public relations to amplify as well as blunt legal actions.

All of this came against the backdrop of a parallel, albeit sub rosa, campaign that Reid, now fifty-eight, was running to assure himself of becoming the assistant Democratic leader, a contest that would be moot if he didn't defeat Ensign.

It's almost impossible to overstate what a seminal year 1998 was in Reid's political life.

Who was Harry Reid in 1998? With two Senate races behind him and a substantial record of votes after a decade and a half on Capitol Hill, his team decided to prepare a private, detailed compilation of his record and vulnerabilities. In the series of documents, a rare glimpse behind the scenes emerges of strategy and preemptive damage control, including quotes and citations from stories and columns since 1982, as well as summations from the staffers assigned to each section. They knew Reid's record better than he did, and they were unsparing.

For example:

- *Gaming:* "We have been nothing but a friend to the gaming community. The trouble, of course, arises from the fact that Ensign (the son of a casino owner) has his own personal ties to the gamers."

  The document listed Reid's efforts to fight federal taxation of gaming, his efforts to neuter a federal gaming commission, his opposition to Indian gaming expansion, and his blocking IRS proposals to tax casinos and their workers on tips.

- *Environment:* "Environmentalists should be our biggest supporters. They don't call him Sierra Harry for nothing."

  The list of Reid's environmental accomplishments to brandish was long, including the national park, the wilderness bill, and Red Rock National Conservation Area. The document also pointed out he received "a lot of positive press" for his Lake Tahoe summit.

  Reid's efforts that might have upset environmentalists also were included. There was a section titled "Reid's Anti-Environment Side," which included his activism for the billboard industry that won him plaudits from the *Las Vegas Review-Journal*, whose parent company owned billboards, too.

  On helicopters flying over the Grand Canyon, which many environmentalists hated, Reid shucked what the document called his "Mr. Environment" mantle to fight for the tour companies, many of which were based in Las Vegas. That section ended with this parenthetical: ("Check to see if the Scenic Tour industry has given us any money").

- *Defense/Foreign Policy:* The document begins with criticism Reid received for opposing land withdrawals for the military in rural Nevada, which had added to animus there that first sprung from his wilderness legislation. It then pivots to his foreign policy stances, including initially opposing troops in Bosnia in the early 1990s before acceding to President Clinton's wish for an extension. The document also brags about Reid being the first Democrat to support George H. W. Bush's invasion of Iraq and indicates he would back military intervention in Iraq again if the Pentagon determined it were necessary.

- *Crime:* "Reid is tough on crime. This is one of those where we shed the typical democrat image and align ourselves very closely with conservatives." The document points out Reid supported the controversial 1994 crime bill, including the assault weapons ban, "and we can expect criticism of this vote along with his Brady Bill vote from the NV Gun Nuts."

  Under "gun control," the document says Reid was endorsed by the NRA in 1992 but his flip on the Brady Bill is "cause for concern." (Reid justified his switch by citing escalating crime rates and his belief it would not hurt "honest gun owners.")

- *Trade:* "Our opposition to NAFTA and GATT resonates well with labor, but not as well with the business community. Something to downplay as we court this constituency." His team hoped to use his partnership with the conservative Republican Don Nickles of Oklahoma on business regulations as inoculation.

- *Abortion:* There may be no clearer description of how Reid navigated these stormy political waters than in the document prepared by his team.

  "Senator Reid has been consistent in his pro-life stance over the years, never wavering from his bottom-line statement that he fundamentally believes abortion is wrong . . . He has taken various stances over the years, for example his vocal support of family planning and his outrage over abortion clinic violence, which paint him, in the eyes of some, as undedicated to the cause of stopping abortion."

The rest of the document details Reid's various votes, including for the partial-birth abortion ban, for freedom of access to clinics (he spoke out against bombings on the floor), for overturning the gag rule, against federally funded abortions (he supported the Hyde Amendment), for parental notification, for a measure with the Republican Olympia Snowe to make prescription contraceptives more available, and for (in 1974) a constitutional amendment prohibiting abortion (that he subsequently backed off from).

The document concluded: "The only possible problems lie in his abortion stance weakening our position with a couple of base support groups: pro-choice women who are likely to accept his pro-life stance and not hold it against him since he is good on so many other women's issues and Mormons who think he's too soft on the issue."

- ***Immigration:*** Reid was an immigration hawk in the 1990s, introducing bills to slow legal and illegal immigration. In 1993, Reid had lamented in that infamous floor speech, "The United States admits a population roughly equivalent to the population of my home state of Nevada every year and will continue to do so every year for the foreseeable future without any clear idea of what it is we hope to achieve." He went on to say, "Nobody has consulted with them [the American people] about whether they want to see the social and cultural makeup of their nation radically altered."

  The document brags about how Reid is "consistently tough on illegal immigrants" but warns how his positions could cause him problems with the minority community. "While this is one of those issues that makes our man look good with the conservatives, our friends in the minority community are not too thrilled with his tough stances," the document stated.

  This is who Harry Reid was as his reelection year began, with polls showing him well ahead of Ensign but his team acutely aware of his vulnerabilities.

"I THOUGHT HE was such a nothing," Reid would say decades later of Ensign. "But I was wrong about that one."

Ensign's team, assembled at the end of 1997, knew how Team Reid felt about the young congressman challenging the senator who was already on a leadership track. "At the time, you could feel it," said Mike Slanker, a key consultant on Ensign's campaign who would later become a staple in major GOP campaigns in Nevada. "He was annoyed by us. It was very dismissive."

The early fundraising numbers favored Reid—he had $1.7 million on hand at the end of 1997 compared to Ensign's $900,000. An internal survey for Reid's campaign at the end of the year conducted by a national pollster showed him well ahead, 51 percent to 34 percent. But there were signs early in 1998 that Reid's campaign would leave nothing to chance, including a story about how his aides—and his mentor and *Las Vegas Sun* executive Mike O'Callaghan—had hectored right-wing radio for commentaries excoriating Reid, trying to mute or even squelch them.

Ensign's campaign knew the two-term congressman had an uphill climb, but they believed their candidate was a perfect foil for Reid. "Our feeling was that there had been very few candidates like John Ensign: good-looking, articulate when he put his mind to it, passionate, a breath of fresh air in the political scene, and an exciting, young guy," said campaign spokesman Jack Finn, who had left a television job to helm the campaign's communications strategy. "And we thought that made a nice contrast to Harry Reid, who we were committed to depicting as out of touch, entrenched in DC, addled with Potomac fever, living in the Ritz-Carlton [Reid had moved into a condo there], old, out of step, and liked our chances, image-wise, and message-wise."

The first public poll of the campaign was released February 26 by the *Review-Journal* and still showed Reid with a robust advantage, 45–36. His campaign also pushed out a story, with the data compiled by his relentless press secretary, Jenny Backus, that he had brought home $800 million in projects (Reid always hated the common political term "pork," which he saw as pejorative)—about seven times what Ensign could claim.

Reid had built a formidable fundraising machine, with the help of the national expert Paul DiNino and the local, well-connected rainmaker Amy Ayoub. In advance of an Al Gore event in the spring of 1998, Reid listed some of his top prospective donors on his trademark yellow legal pads. Two of the top twelve were media allies—Reid listed the *Las Vegas Sun* owner, Brian Greenspun, as good for $50,000 and NBC affiliate owner Jim Rogers for $100,000. The rest of the high-level fundraising commitments came from casino executives and developer Jim Rhodes ($100,000), who would later build Reid a home in Searchlight.

Reid also had lists of names and phone numbers that amounted to a Who's Who of the Nevada elite—mostly in Las Vegas—and records of when he had called them and what commitments they had made. There also were national names on the lists, including union leaders, and notes about whether contact had been made and what commitments were garnered.

Reid had what seemed like never-ending call lists, hundreds of names of prominent Nevadans with whom he had built relationships, with notations on whether they had maxed out to the campaign and what their previous giving patterns had been.

Reid traveled far and wide to raise money, including to Manhattan, where he met with a wealthy real estate developer named Donald J. Trump. Trump, whose office was a chaotic mess, which irked Reid to no end, handed the senator a check for $1,000 in an envelope "like it was a hundred thousand dollars," as DiNino recalled. Later that cycle, Trump would do a fundraiser for Reid in his gilded penthouse, pulling the senator into the kitchen at one point to rail about the Las Vegas casino mogul Steve Wynn's incursions into the Atlantic City gambling market. (The two developers were at each other's throats for years in Atlantic City, but later became friendly, especially when Trump became president.)

Ensign, though, proved a dedicated fundraiser and by April, his cash-on-hand deficit was not so glaring. Reid had $1.5 million, and Ensign had $1.2 million. Money was clearly not going to be an issue for the challenger, and Reid's irritation began to show a few months later when he called and wrote to Irwin Molasky, arguably the state's best-known developer, expressing disappointment and hurt feelings at his donations to Ensign. Molasky finally wrote a letter to Reid on August 3, invoking their decades of friendship, assuring the senator he had given much less to Ensign than to him, and promising he and his entire family were still voting for Reid. "Harry, I can only attribute your frustration to the heat of the campaign," Molasky wrote.

ONE OF THE critical constituencies in Nevada politics in 1998 was the Mormon vote, which had been divided in 1986 and was even more so now. They were only a single-digit part of the electorate, but their registration and turnout numbers were disproportionately high compared to any other demographic.

Reid's standing with the LDS electorate was not good despite his church membership and efforts through the years to cultivate friendships with high-ranking church officials such as James Faust, the second counselor in the First Presidency, and his son, Marcus, the Capitol Hill lobbyist. Reid rarely talked about his faith, but his office was always receptive to helping the church with problems, be they in the United States or overseas, and Reid would often expedite the requests himself.

Reid's closeness to church leaders came despite a 1992 statement by the council of the presidency and Quorum of the Twelve that opposed gambling "in its various forms. Experience has clearly shown gambling to be harmful to the human spirit, financially destructive of individuals and families and detrimental to the moral climate of communities. The attitude of the church on this matter has been consistent and clear over a period of more than a century."

Reid knew that he had problems with his own church, so he dispatched Megan Jones, a young Mormon staffer who would become deputy political director, from his Capitol Hill office to Las Vegas for the last three months of the campaign. She worked with his son, Rory, and the Mormon activist Sandy Jolley, who had voter lists and strategies from previous campaigns, to mobilize the Mormon vote. It was a real struggle.

"Nobody treated him worse than the Mormons," Rory Reid remembered. "It's really bothered me, it really still bothers me. I think they were just very partisan Republicans. I think it's not that complicated."

The behind-the-scenes campaign was vicious. Letters from angry church members were written to church higher-ups suggesting Reid be excommunicated. Mormon churches were leafleted with "Reid is pro-choice" propaganda.

Rory Reid oversaw the Mormon field campaign, organizing small groups to talk about his father, occasionally with Landra. They had targeted mailers for Mormons "with lists we weren't supposed to have," one operative recalled wryly. They bought ads in a Mormon publication called the *Beehive* and they organized at what were called "Trunk or Treats" on Halloween, shortly before the election. That's where congregants would pull their cars into the church parking lot decorated for the holiday and open their trunks for kids to come and get candy. "They decorated with his [Reid's] face as the devil on the trunks," Jones remembered vividly of one Trunk or Treats event.

Rory Reid remembered another incident at a church when a parishioner told him that all the cars in the parking lot had been leafleted with attacks on his father. "So we ran around, took them off every car, went to every church building in the area, took them off every car, and threw them away," he recalled.

If the election ended up being close, even though the Mormon vote was relatively small, it could make the difference.

AUGUST AND SEPTEMBER brought news that threatened Reid's lead and forced him to adopt new strategies: Monica Lewinsky's affair with President Bill Clinton. Even though Reid expressed disappointment with the president, Ensign pounced on the issue, demanding Clinton resign and accusing Reid of a double standard because he had called for Oregon senator Bob Packwood's expulsion when a sexual harassment scandal broke about the Republican in the mid-1990s.

Right: Harry Reid as infant in Searchlight, Nevada, circa 1940.
Courtesy of Reid family

Left: Reid's home in Searchlight.
Courtesy of Reid family

Left: Young Harry outside his Search-light home.
Courtesy of Reid family

Right: Inez Reid with Harry and Larry Reid.
Courtesy of Reid family

Above: Harry Jr. in Harry Sr.'s arms, with his brothers Dale and Don and their friend beside them.
Courtesy of Reid family

Left: Harry Reid (*center*) prepares to run a marathon.
Courtesy of Reid family

Left: Reid's Basic High School yearbook photo, 1956.
Courtesy of Reid family

Right: Reid strikes a boxing pose.
Courtesy of Reid family

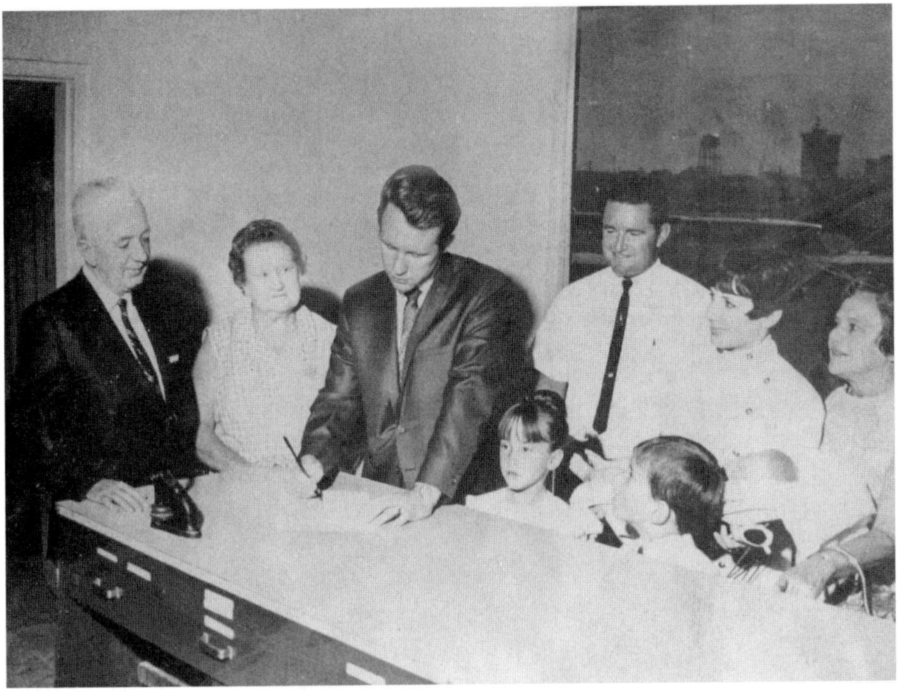

Above: Reid filing for office surrounded by family.
Courtesy of Reid family

Left: Then-Governor Mike O'Callaghan and then–Lieutenant Governor Harry Reid.
Courtesy of Reid family

Left: Wayne Newton, Harry Reid's grandson, and Harry Reid.
Courtesy of Reid family

Below: Harry, Landra, and the children.
Courtesy of Reid family

Above: President Obama signs the health care reform bill.
Win McNamee / Getty Images

Below: Reid's injury.
Brendan Smialowski / Getty Images

Above: President Obama speaks at a Clean Energy Summit in Las Vegas.
Ethan Miller / Getty Images

Below: Congressional Democrats call on Republicans to support American jobs.
Chip Somodevilla / Getty Images

In early September, Reid's staff sent him a memo under the subject line "Presidential Scandal Responses."

"We have disseminated three types of letters for constituents regarding the President's behavior," it began. The three letters were directed at these groups:

- "For Nevadans angry at Clinton and disgusted with his televised 'admission.'"

  In this missive, Reid expressed how "extremely disappointed" he was in Clinton but added he was glad he took "personal responsibility." Reid crossed out a sentence in the proposed letter: "The president has not yet been formally charged with any wrongdoing."

- "For Nevadans angry at Clinton and specifically suggest impeachment."

  This letter was similar to the first, with the same line crossed out, but noted that it was premature to talk about impeachment.

- "For Nevadans disgusted with Special Prosecutor Starr and demand an end to the investigation."

  After a perfunctory nod to his disappointment, this letter expresses Reid's concerns about special counsel Kenneth Starr's tactics. In this one, he left in the line about the president not having been formally charged with wrongdoing.

This was designed to cover all the bases, or so Team Reid hoped.

On September 27, Reid's frustration with his younger foe, who had been in politics for just four years, bubbled over during a town hall–style debate in front of six hundred seniors in a high-propensity voting area in northwest Las Vegas. Reid sneered at Ensign several times, at one point suggesting that a veterinarian had no business "interpreting the Constitution." The crowd booed Reid, and Ensign seized the moment, suggesting people liked veterinarians more than lawyers. The Ensign rapid response operation, which in those days consisted of a fax machine in the back of the room, whirred to life, sending out Reid's comments and Ensign's retort. He had the crowd and the momentum, with the election only five weeks away.

Reid's campaign continued to push the issue of Reid's seniority and argued they shouldn't "trade" him for a junior senator. Reid was carrying around a whip count card in his pocket with the names of all the Democratic senators and crossed off names when he received commitments. He knew he was assured of the number two job in the Senate Democratic leadership. But did voters really care? Ensign, meanwhile, portrayed Reid as "saying one thing in Nevada" and voting differently on Capitol Hill. Painting Reid as being out of touch with his state would be an attack used against him for the rest of his career as he ascended the national leadership ladder.

Ensign's team also was searching for what they thought might be a silver bullet to secure a victory—proving something was shady about all the land deals that had helped make Reid a multimillionaire. For two weeks, the campaign sequestered a couple of expert researchers in a room to try to find a smoking gun—they knew at least one reporter was doing the same. But to no avail.

The message from the researchers, according to one Ensign staffer: "There's nothing here that would allow us to call it illegal, call it unethical to file a complaint. There's nothing. It's perfectly buttoned up."

(Reid's land transactions, the foundation of his wealth—as he had purchased many undeveloped tracts of land in Nevada and Arizona—and the implication by some that he had traded on insider knowledge, would become a public issue about five years later, but no one ever found evidence he did anything illegal, despite rumors and innuendo almost every election cycle.)

Public and internal polling continued to show the race close as Election Day approached. Reid's campaign and its adjuncts showed the incumbent with a small lead outside the margin of error. On October 8, a state Democratic Party poll showed Reid ahead 49–42; on October 14, a Fairbank,

Maslin, poll showed Reid ahead 49–44. A *Review-Journal* poll found Reid up by two percentage points a few days before the balloting.

Reid was not taking anything for granted. On the Friday before the election, in a huge banner headline over a story bearing the byline of the owner of the newspaper, the *Las Vegas Sun* declared, "Clinton: I need Reid." The piece was touted as an exclusive interview the *Sun* owner, Brian Greenspun, a Reid supporter and fundraiser, had secured with the president, whom Greenspun had known since college. "The high-level nuclear waste dump will be on its way to Nevada in 1999 if the voters of Nevada fail to re-elect Sen. Harry Reid," the "story" began, with Clinton telling Greenspun he agreed with his longtime friend's recent column that said Nevada needed Reid to fight Yucca Mountain. Two days later, the *Sun*, not surprisingly, endorsed Reid at the top of its front page: "Rebuff Nuke Dump by Re-electing Reid." It was a full-court press to save the senator. (After the election, the *Washington Post* published a scathing piece about Greenspun's journalistic ethics—i.e., extracting favorable quotes about Reid, whom he was supporting, from his old college pal Clinton, who was happy to oblige.) That same day, the *Review-Journal* endorsed Ensign, but said it was a close call.

THE EARLY RETURNS gave Team Reid reason for optimism. They had banked early votes in Clark County—what would later become a model for the senator's political machine was only nascent in 1998, but Democrats had a substantial advantage among the more than eighty-five thousand ballots cast in Clark County before November 3. Early voting had started in 1994, but was only 3 percent of the overall turnout that year in the Democratic bastion of Southern Nevada. In 1996, it had increased to 11 percent. But in 1998, Clark early turnout was 18 percent, giving Democrats (and presumably Reid) a double-digit lead. "It was easily by a factor of three or four larger than we assumed it would be," the Ensign consultant Mike Slanker would say later.

Ensign was getting on a plane in Reno after giving a rousing speech when he got the call from his Las Vegas headquarters. One of his aides said his face was ashen, and he hung up to say the Clark early voting lead probably could not be overcome.

But an hour or so later when he landed in Las Vegas, the tide had turned as votes from rural Nevada and Washoe County had come pouring in. The race was tightening.

Reid was heading to his victory party at the MGM Grand when the rural numbers started coming, showing the race was too close to call. His wife, Landra, and eldest son, Rory, were in the car, along with close family friend Jay Brown, and Reid's press secretary, Jenny Backus. Reid refused to go to the party with the race undecided, as Backus and Brown calculated the returns on napkins to see what they needed to achieve a win.

By late into the evening, Reid's lead had completely evaporated—it was 48 percent to 48 percent. Ensign was confident he would wake up a senator-elect, a replay of his massive upset of Rep. Jim Bilbray in 1994 when late returns from conservative areas gave him the victory.

But that did not occur. Problems with counting ballots, especially absentees, in Washoe County (Reno and environs) delayed the count until two days after the election, when Reid was declared the victor by 459 votes out of 435,000 cast, a tenth of a percentage point. But Ensign did not concede, and Reid did not declare victory.

Lawsuits and petitions were filed. National experts flew in from both parties—Democratic lawyer Marc Elias and Republican attorney Craig Engel flew to Reno. Both campaigns cranked up their spin machines.

All of the focus was on Washoe County, where an embattled registrar, Laura Dancer, presided over a count that seemed never-ending. Ensign had won the Republican county by 2,162 votes, according to the initial tally. But he had terribly underperformed in a place where Republicans had a sixteen-thousand-voter lead.

When county officials realized that routine postelection testing of ballot integrity had failed because of faulty machines, they went before a district court judge to request hand-counting of sixteen thousand mostly absentee ballots, just under a fifth of the votes cast in Reno and the environs.

"The problems that we noted included a ballot not counted that was clearly there in the test stack and the unexpected vote count for candidates, unexplainable vote counts for candidates and we also encountered machine failures when the machine would just stop working for a period and have to be rebooted and started up again," Registrar Dancer told Judge Janet Berry during a lengthy November 7 hearing that featured lawyers for both campaigns.

Berry granted the request, and then the chaos intensified. About ten thousand ballots were read without an issue. But the Accuracy Certification Board said there were problems with the printing of ballots at Washoe County's print shop. Making matters worse, they were printed in-house to try to save money rather than sent to the usual out-of-state vendor. There were problems of misaligned races on the ballots and others were discovered to have been cut incorrectly, causing one election official to declare that votes would "appear and disappear" in the machines.

By early the week after Election Day, a hand count of those ballots began. County employees worked through the night to count the ballots and by 2:30 a.m. on November 10, one week after the election, Dancer told reporters she believed Reid's victory would stand, pending a final tally to be released later in the day. But the media also painted a picture of disarray, with dozens of election workers overflowing outside Dancer's office and lining the hallway counting ballots. Former Republican governor Bob List, who acted as the Ensign campaign's front man during this time, told the media that the computer problems that forced the hand count raised questions about the reliability of the tabulations.

The results showed Ensign had picked up 58 votes, now losing by 401 votes. The numbers were canvassed and certified by the county, leaving Ensign with only one option: ask for a formal recount.

That's when the Reid campaign quietly decided to open a new front to try to dissuade Ensign from doing so, a quintessential move by the senator's team to leave nothing to chance. They also knew what was self-evident: the Washoe County count was, as newspapers would opine, a disaster and left many wondering whether it was correct. The goal of the new campaign was to make sure only a minimal number of additional ballots were counted.

In a series of internal campaign memos stamped "confidential" and all penned November 13, ten days after the election, Democratic Senatorial Campaign Committee operative Tommy Thompson laid out the public relations and legal strategy to preserve Reid's apparent narrow win. The first memo to Reid began by asserting there were "numerous problems" in the counting results in Washoe County before laying out what the campaign called the second front, which it dubbed "Voters' Choice '98." It was a multipronged approach:

> At this moment we are working a free media strategy to reinforce the former Rep. John Ensign that any moves to contest the election or demand a recount of the results (after they are sent to the Secretary of State on or before November 25th) will damage his political viability and could hinder his chances to seek statewide elected office ever again. This free media campaign includes a strong letter to the editor campaign, a series of visits to op-ed boards and keeping the overall theme of 'we won' alive in the press over the next few weeks.

That is, create the air of inevitability and scare Ensign into surrendering. Thompson went on:

> It is possible that this strategy will fail and that John Ensign will risk his political future by either demanding a statewide recount, pushing for a revote in Washoe County or contest the entire election and ask for a statewide revote . . . If this happens and it is a very real possibility we must be prepared to deal with his challenges just as though it were another campaign. This entails setting up a campaign style organization and hiring a team of people to professionally handle not only the legal challenges we will

face but the field and media battles that will crop up over the next several weeks.

Thompson laid out the budget for the campaign, which he estimated at $244,250–$146,250 for the lawyers, $69,000 for the field program, and $29,000 for the press/research function. The overall budget was the equivalent of close to half a million dollars today—to influence a recount.

Thompson also wrote detailed memos to DC lawyer Elias and the campaign's field general, Paul Worlie, laying out the budget and the plans for the coming campaign. The field team was designed to have an outpost in all seventeen counties in the event of a statewide recount to monitor the counts and report problems.

In a memo to Thompson from Judy Corley, a lawyer brought in with Elias from the DC firm of Perkins Coie, she laid out the "Possible Legal Issues Facing Senator Reid" along with a timeline.

First, on November 25, by law, the state supreme court would make the final canvass, and the governor would issue election certificates to the winners. Corley wrote that she believed the Republicans could try to challenge the canvass, as they had done at Washoe County, but that Secretary of State Dean Heller, a Republican, would likely argue it was purely ministerial.

Second, Corley suggested, quite presciently, that the Republicans might argue for a revote in Washoe County, a do-over where anything might happen and could certainly threaten Reid's apparent victory.

Third, after the high court canvass, Ensign would have three business days (i.e., until December 1) to ask for a recount, which would result in a precinct sampling that could lead to either a machine or hand recount, depending on how large the discrepancy was.

Fourth, Ensign could contest the election in the Senate, which had the power to declare the seat vacant and call a new election. She didn't say it, but this would be potentially problematic for Reid because the Republicans controlled the Senate, 55–45.

The same day Thompson wrote his memo, the *Las Vegas Sun* owner,

Greenspun, wrote a column essentially declaring the race over and urging Ensign to concede and, as the headline said, "Skip Recount This Time." The Reid campaign to win the recount had begun, and it was considerably more disciplined than the one that had been up and running for more than a year.

Eight days later, after a series of scathing editorials, Registrar Dancer resigned, further throwing a pall over the Washoe County balloting. On the day the high court was slated to canvass the results, GOP leaders, as Corley had foretold, called for a Washoe County revote, saying there was too much uncertainty.

In a detailed challenge with statistics and interviews with voters, the Republicans alleged irregularities with people not returning or not recording their ballots that they returned. Hearkening back to the disarray inside the Washoe County's registrar's office, the Republicans argued "ballots were routinely left in unorganized stacks within reach of the general public" and pointed out understaffing for the hand count and the ballot printing errors.

But the state justices certified the results, giving Reid the victory, pending any request for a recount within three days. Reid had tried to dissuade Ensign from doing so, invoking his own sore loser label after his 1974 Senate race loss to Paul Laxalt. His campaign distributed documents to the media showing that recounts rarely change the outcomes of races, and did not in Reid's 1974 loss or Laxalt's even narrower eighty-four-vote loss in 1964 to Howard Cannon.

"If he wants a recount, he can have it," Reid said. "But it's a big waste of money and it won't change the results."

Ensign, having raised the $60,000 to pay for the recount, officially filed for one on December 1, the last possible day. A few thousand miles away, on that same day, the Senate Democratic Caucus elected Reid as the number two Democrat in the US Senate, the highest a Nevadan had ever ascended.

A whip's job, if he could keep it—his Senate seat, that is.

DEAN HELLER MAY have saved Harry Reid.

As the recount progressed, the Republican secretary of state consistently supported the county's decisions, much to the Ensign campaign's frustration.

Heller had brought in a voting machine expert to certify that the Global optical scanning machines had performed properly—Washoe was the only county in Nevada that used them. Two days before the Nevada Supreme Court certified the results, the expert sent a report to the secretary of state that concluded: "I believe that the procedure followed by Global and county personnel was prudent and in the end effective. The procedure should have assured and very likely did assure an accurate count of the election."

After the court certified the results, Heller rejected his own party's complaints, saying that ballots were not missing and uncounted, that there were no improper procedures or numerous legal violations. Heller attested that he and his staff supervised the count and found no issues.

The Republican secretary of state's language became even more strident after Ensign called for the recount. Heller accused his fellow Republican of trying to disenfranchise voters. By the first week of December, the *Reno Gazette-Journal* was praising Heller for putting state over party and urging the GOP to do the same.

Ensign's team was furious with someone they considered an ally. It's not that they necessarily wanted him to cheat, but they certainly hoped that if there was any doubt, he would side with their team. They didn't say much publicly, especially after a private admonition from Senate Majority Leader Mitch McConnell.

"Look, you've got to go through the recount, but nobody really ever wins on a recount," McConnell told one of Ensign's senior aides. "So just watch how you portray yourself. Make sure you are likable, you are fair. And set your image so if you want to run again, you start from a good place and not a bad place."

That is, don't do what Reid did after his 1974 loss.

Team Ensign was seething. They believed that absentee ballots that were arriving late—some of which would certainly be counted under Nevada's current laws—should have been counted, and that Heller could have insisted because of all the manifest problems in the registrar's office. Ensign's team knew they were mostly military ballots and likely to favor their candidate.

Several members of Ensign's team talked to Heller, but to no avail. "Dean Heller couldn't make a ruling in our favor to save his life," one Ensign aide recalled.

Slanker remembered it vividly:

"There was a box in the corner. I'll never forget it because Dean Heller kept walking by it, and he was trying to do a neutral job. And we were wanting him to step in and say these ballots that are coming in late, by no fault of the voter—we need to count them, you can't do this because you've printed the stupid ballots wrong. It's not their fault. And that box kept getting fuller, and fuller, and fuller, because every day we were there more would come in. And so we're staring at enough ballots, we believe, because we won mail ballots in Washoe County by a lot . . . that box makes John Ensign a US senator."

But Heller would not allow those ballots to be counted, arguing they had arrived too late, and by the evening of December 10, the count was finally coming to an end. At one point, as Reid's aide Mary Connelly remembered the scene, the national Republican operatives in the room arose from their seats, shut down their computers, and walked out. They knew. She knew.

Ensign's team told their candidate it wasn't going to happen, so before the count was even finished, the Republican challenger called Reid on his cell phone. Reid was having dinner with his family at Joe's Stone Crab at Caesars Palace when the call came in with Ensign's concession. Ensign then announced to the media that he had lost, shortly before the count ended, with Reid picking up 27 votes to win by 428.

Thirty-six days after Election Day, it was finally over. Harry Reid had been elected to a third term. He could not praise Heller enough. "He deserves a medal for bipartisanship," Reid gushed.

ONE CALL REID had after the election came from his colleague Joe Lieberman, the Democratic senator from Connecticut who had come to Nevada for a day toward the end of the campaign to energize the tens of thousands of Jews in Nevada.

"Harry, I happen to have reliable information, that those four hundred and twenty-eight votes, your margin, they were all Jews," he told Reid. Lieberman was being facetious, but his quip emphasized the point that every little bit helped.

Reid believed for years and said to many people that the governor's race, in which he had encouraged the popular Las Vegas Mayor Jan Jones to run, provided the edge. Jones lost the 1998 race, but in a handwritten note Reid wrote to her about ten months before he died, he repeated a sentiment he had shared many times before: "I owe much of my career to you."

Reid said that if the GOP gubernatorial hopeful Kenny Guinn had run unopposed, he would have lost without Guinn-Reid voters, many of whom were Mormons and pro-choice women. (Reid lost women by only 1 percent to Ensign, exit polls showed.)

For his part, Slanker still wondered decades later what might have been if, for instance, Heller had allowed those ballots to be counted.

"Can you imagine how history would be reshaped if a few hundred votes flipped the other way?" he mused. "Had they counted that box of ballots in Washoe County? I mean: Wow. There is no Harry Reid in the 2000s. Crazy to think about."

CHAPTER FIFTEEN

BUILDING A MACHINE

Harry Reid was convinced he should have lost in 1998.

He was not happy with his staff, his campaign, his prospects. He believed he needed to make wholesale changes to be successful as the number two Democrat in the US Senate and to ensure he never had another race like that again. The first thing he had to do was fire his best friend from high school.

Reid already had nudged Rey Martinez out of his role as campaign manager after national Democrats had told him to make a change during the campaign, perhaps in the nick of time. But now he had to finish the job. He called Martinez into his Washington, DC, office.

"It was short and to the point," Reid said about firing the man he played baseball with in high school, the man who helped him become student body president, the man whom he had picked for the high-level post of chief of staff more out of friendship than anything else. Reid would later say that no other conversation he ever had with an employee was "even a close second" in terms of difficulty as that one with Martinez, who died in 2022.

Some close to Reid thought the Martinez saga exemplified how his loyalty blinded him to incompetence, while others saw it as a sign that his loyalty had an expiration date when someone became expendable.

Yet Martinez's departure heralded a new era and the beginning of the formation of what would become known inside and outside the office as Team Reid. It began with his choice of a chief of staff, a young former employee who had only recently left to take a job as a spokeswoman for the Department of Housing and Urban Development. Susan McCue had been Reid's communications director from 1992 to 1997 and had indirectly helped him in the 1998 campaign by going to Nevada to consult on Jan Jones's gubernatorial bid.

McCue, only thirty-three and six feet tall, would become a towering presence in Reid's life, helping to professionalize his staff as he cemented his place on the leadership ladder. McCue would become one of the most important people in both his personal and professional life, evidenced by his co-dedication to her of his autobiography, *The Good Fight*, along with his beloved mentor, Mike O'Callaghan.

Reid rhapsodized about McCue a few months before he died.

"She always had more confidence in my abilities than I did," Reid said. "She always pushed me very hard . . . She is an impressive person, one of ten children and she put herself through school, working as a waitress. And she was just my kind of person."

McCue not only marshaled a terrific staff to help Reid with policy, she also had a firm hand on the political side. Shortly after the new Congress began on January 27, McCue recommended that Reid have his data expert, Chris Brown, conduct a survey explaining, "What happened?" It would be "a thorough analysis of voter tendencies and demographic trends in order to help guide the direction of Senator Reid's legislative, political, communications and state operations in the upcoming six years." It was a move to integrate Reid's legislative agenda with his political operation, in conjunction with the state Democratic Party.

Reid also had learned well from Robert Byrd that knowing the rules inside and out was knowledge that could be transformed into power on Capitol Hill. He had one goal: "I was going to be the best whip they ever had."

Reid had decided on his own that he would be the whip morning, noon, and night on the floor, which often left him alone with his staffers. He would not leave, talking to as many people, senators and staffers, as he could, akin to what one person who worked with him described as playing a game of human pinball.

Reid's onetime legislative director Jimmy Ryan said being ubiquitous on the floor enabled the new whip to develop relationships with key behind-the-scenes players, too. "You got to know the bill clerk, the enrollment clerk, you got to know the parliamentarian, you got to know the sergeant at arms, you got to know the secretary of the Senate, you got to know the secretary for the minority, secretary for the majority, all of the cloakroom, all of the sort of back office functions of the Senate, which are boring and archaic. You got involved in process, precedent, politics, personality, you've got to know that just from sitting on the floor, stuff that you'd never learned reading."

What Reid also intuitively understood was that most senators, be they committee chairs or ranking members, relished coming to the floor to present a bill but didn't want to do the grunt work of shepherding it through the floor process, complete with amendments and other procedures. That was where Reid came in.

"Reid saw that as an opportunity to basically play a strong role," Ryan said. "And so early on, the chair would basically let us take over the bill once they gave their opening remarks. And Reid played traffic cop on all of the flow of amendments that would come up on everything and any given bill."

Even if there were a hundred amendments to a complex bill such as the National Defense Authorization Act, Reid would take on the role of a committee chair and negotiate the list until it was pared for passage. As he did so, he was able to aggregate favors from senators of both parties who were happy to let the new assistant leader do the trench work.

Said Eddie Ayoob, a key staffer for many years: "There were so many times when it was Harry Reid who went to Senator so-and-so and said, 'Senator, we've got to get this bill done and your amendment just doesn't work, but I'll find some way to make it up to you.' The other senator would acquiesce and withdraw the amendment because they trusted him. And then one of us Reid staff would get a call from the other senator's staff saying, 'Damn it, I worked for nine months on that issue. Your boss just talked my boss out of doing the amendment.' That's just one example of how Harry Reid was able to help get legislation through. You always heard about him being the consummate dealmaker. Those kinds of things behind the scenes without any fanfare are what allowed many bills to become law, because he would pull senators aside by the elbow, and have one-on-one conversations in the cloakroom or on the Senate floor. Then he'd come back to us and say, 'All right, I took care of that amendment. Let's move on to the next one.'"

Little did his colleagues know, Reid was faking it until he made it.

"We would go into meetings in the Capitol with Daschle and the [committee] chair," Ryan recalled. "We've been involved in the highest level of meetings, solving issues important to getting bills through word problems that would come up . . . that you had to get resolved. And we'd have the meeting, figure out some solution, and then we'd walk out and Reid would say, 'Well, we bluffed our way through that one pretty well.'"

After a fashion, of course, Reid was not just pretending to be authoritative; he was.

"You just have to have some sense of what it is that somebody needs for this problem to go away," Ryan said. "It's not something you learn. Or you can be taught; it's just something you have a sense of, and I've never seen anybody like this since. And we've had plenty of other whips. He really had this unusually exceptional instinct for what it is that a politician needs to do something or not do something."

As Gary Myrick, another key Reid aide and a master of the floor, put it: "He knew his way to power was to get to know everybody's problems and help them. And it was a different time. We did a lot more stuff back then. We weren't nearly as polarized and there were deals to be made. Everything was sixty votes, but there were moderates in both parties that still worked together on stuff."

One of the reasons Reid was able to build all those relationships was that Daschle, who had little interest in the floor, allowed Reid to be his eyes and ears.

"It was invaluable, it really gave me an opportunity to do other things as leader that were important as well," Daschle remembered. "He came to me frequently throughout virtually every day we were in session to give me his candid assessment of circumstances. And that is such an important tool for any leader, if you can't be there yourself, you need a surrogate, who can be there, and who can assess things."

His colleagues would later marvel at the method to his madness that put him on the path to succeeding Daschle when the opportunity presented itself a few years later.

Maryland's Barbara Mikulski observed: "He spent a lot of time on the floor. He learned the process, he mastered the process. There are so many rules—Rule Twenty-One, Rule Twenty-Three: You can't have a Kleenex. Rule Twenty-Seven: You can have a Kleenex if it's raining. I mean, there's so many parsings and whatever. I'm making fun of it, but it does run the Senate."

Perhaps the most revealing testament to Reid's job as whip came from the man who succeeded him, Illinois senator Dick Durbin. "He said to me, 'You've got to do what I did. My recommendation is sit on the floor every minute the Senate is in session.' And I thought to myself, 'I wouldn't want the job if I had to sit on the floor every minute. I want to be there when something's happening. But most of the time, it is deadly boring, and nothing's happening."

Nothing, that is, unless you're the human pinball machine.

SOME POLITICIANS ACQUIRE power and don't use it to the fullest. Harry Reid was not that kind of politician.

After ascending to the number two position in the Senate Democratic Caucus, he wasted no time in using his clout, as he had in the past, to help gaming and mining.

Reid corresponded with the president about mining, raising questions about the administration's commitment to reforming the industry and changing how royalties were paid. Bill Clinton had reassured him in a March 16, 1995, letter that he did not include any projections from increased mining royalties in his budget "because the future of mining law reform remains uncertain."

Reid would make it one of his career goals to ensure it remained in limbo, and four years later, having accumulated more influence, he was in a position to do even more. In early 1999, he expressed opposition to new regulations that would make it more difficult to obtain open-pit mining permits, saying it could hurt smaller mining operations who did not have the wherewithal to build underground operations. Later that year, when Vice President Gore suggested that as president he would raise $2 billion to expand the national park system by charging a new royalty on the mining industry, Reid was blunt. "It's not going anywhere," the whip told the *Las Vegas Review-Journal.*

Reid's fealty to the Las Vegas Strip was no less fervent. The senior senator and the rest of Nevada's delegation were constantly fending off attempts to tax the industry either with a frontal approach or back-door methods such as taxing employee tips. As Reid amassed power, he was able to more decisively entomb what he saw as antigaming proposals, whether it was a Clinton administration move to tax gaming or a Babbitt-led effort to help Indian tribes getting into the casino business, which at the time the Nevada enterprises considered a mortal threat. (Later, the state-based gambling companies would see Indian reservations, as they did Atlantic City and elsewhere, as revenue opportunities.)

Reid, as he did with mining, saw no need to justify his advocacy for the state's largest industry, insisting that protecting gaming was protecting Nevada jobs.

MCCUE, THE NEW chief of staff, also was much more sophisticated than Martinez had been about building a better political foundation for the senator. Despite just having cast his Hispanic chief of staff into the wilderness, Reid understood that he had to court that voting cohort to survive. His staff prepared a fifteen-page document in January 1999 entitled "Hispanic Outreach Mission Statement."

This was about laying the groundwork for a Hispanic vote that would prolong his career in 2010 and help Democratic presidential candidates have a chance. The document had updated data to make the case: Nevada's Hispanic population was projected to grow from 192,000 in 1995 to 538,000 in 2025—nearly threefold. It turns out that was a gross underestimation, though. The current Hispanic population of the state is estimated to be nearly 30 percent, or more than nine hundred thousand, making their potential impact even greater.

That 1999 blueprint envisioned a congressional Hispanic task force with key Nevada leaders, north and south, and an annual, three-day Hispanic conference in Washington, DC, hosted by Reid. Similar documents would be generated as the year went on, and by year's end, Reid had four staffers on board dedicated to Hispanic outreach. Reid would also become hyperfocused on finding Hispanic candidates for office, too.

BEFORE HE COULD dive fully into his new senatorial and political roles, Reid, like his colleagues, had to deal with the president's impeachment trial, which took place in January and February of 1999. Reid had been quite critical of Clinton after the affair with Monica Lewinsky surfaced, going so far as to accuse Clinton of betraying legislative Democrats.

"Bill Clinton has been a friend of the state of Nevada," Reid said in a speech on the Senate floor. "He's been a friend to me, but he has committed grievous wrongs against his family and his friends. He has dishonored his high office and lowered the standard of public behavior."

He was even more unfiltered when he explained, not long before he died, what the dynamic was at the time: "He was as we all know his own worst enemy. All those things he did. He had a reputation that preceded him . . . no woman was ever safe in his presence."

REID WOULD SOON be joined in the Senate by a former nemesis when John Ensign decided to make a comeback after Reid's old friend Richard Bryan abruptly decided to retire in 2000. Reid insisted he would do everything he could for the Democratic candidate, the personal injury attorney Ed Bernstein, but he knew Ensign would win. In one television interview, Reid said the state would be well served by either candidate. Some Ensign supporters would later say Reid even opened fundraising doors for the Republican. A far cry from the open disdain he showed toward Ensign just a short cycle ago, Reid's attack-dog bite was reduced to a muffled bark.

Ensign won in a landslide, and Reid would play "if you can't beat them, co-opt them": the pair would eventually develop a productive working relationship (Reid even got Ensign to allow him to pick some judges) and a genuine friendship. When Ensign resigned in disgrace in 2011 after a sensational sex scandal, Reid, as he might have done with others, did not join in the public scorn.

If 1999 was the beginning of Reid's unchallenged role as Nevada's Democratic gatekeeper, it also began the era of the senator as a force in national politics. McCue pushed Reid to do meetings with various key players, to upgrade his political team, to leverage his position to gain more influence in national political affairs.

As Gore's presidential run ramped up in 2000, Reid maneuvered to quietly become an insider. They had known each other since they served in the House together, when Gore mentored Reid on a subcommittee. At one point, McCue set up a meeting with the Teamsters president, Jimmy Hoffa Jr., for Reid to broker disagreements over trade between the labor union and the incipient presidential nominee.

Gore, of course, would go on to lose, but Reid, with the aid of his loyal lieutenant, was just getting started as a national figure. McCue knew Reid needed to step up his game a notch or two, so by 2002, she was trying to put the best people around him—or in front of him. She arranged meetings with key capital influencers, from the pollster Mark Mellman to the media maven Bill Knapp. This, she knew, would help him not just on Capitol Hill but as he prepared for reelection in 2004, hoping not to have a repeat of the Ensign close call.

McCue already had set up a meeting earlier that month with Frank Luntz, the GOP pollster and messaging expert who had done work with the gaming mogul Steve Wynn and a major Democratic donor from Nevada, Stephen Cloobeck. Reid was receiving advice from the top Republican and Democratic operatives in the country, thanks to his chief of staff.

IN 2001, THE Senate was fifty-fifty, but Vice President Dick Cheney gave the Republicans a de facto majority.

"I made up my mind I was going to change that," Reid recalled. So he began to ruminate about who might be willing to switch parties. His staff was in the dark—"He worked the whole deal himself," one said—as Reid set out to find a Republican he could persuade.

He talked to Maine's Olympia Snowe, whose husband, John McKernan, had served with Reid in the House. She was a progressive Republican, and Reid thought she was a good possibility. But "she didn't want to do it," he recalled.

Reid also considered Lincoln Chafee of Rhode Island, another moderate Republican, but "he couldn't do it because of the family situation." The Chafee family was part of the New England Republican aristocracy—his father had been governor—and so Chafee balked. (Years later, Chafee got over his qualms and became a Democrat.)

Meanwhile, Vermont Republican Jim Jeffords, constantly at odds with his colleagues and the White House over funding of programs that would benefit children with disabilities, seemed ripe for a pitch. Reid didn't tell Daschle or anyone else. He simply and quietly made his move in the spring of 2001.

At first, there were casual conversations on the Senate floor, seemingly innocuous to the other senators there. Jeffords seemed open to the idea right away, but he was concerned about the consequences, including the loss of his seniority. So Reid, ever the strategist and political godfather, went to Jeffords and made him an enticing offer. "I said, 'Jim, you're fighting with the Republican president all the time. Here's the deal. I will let you be the chairman of the Environment and Public Works committee [Reid was the ranking member]. You can have my 18 staff members, my beautiful suite of offices. All you have to do is change parties. I can get my caucus to approve this."

The committee was enormously powerful and had broad jurisdiction. It would have been the first committee chairmanship of Reid's career, but he knew it was the prize that would seal the deal with Jeffords.

By early May, Reid had brought in Daschle and the deal was done. By then, word had leaked, and Jeffords's Republican colleagues, Vice President Cheney, and even President Bush tried to talk him out of it. But Reid had him.

On May 24, Jeffords announced he would become an independent and caucus with the Democrats, thus giving them the majority. Reid would not become the chairman of the Environment and Public Works Committee, but he was now the majority whip, not the minority whip, and Daschle was the majority leader.

Some thought it was remarkably unselfish of Reid to give up a chairmanship that he could have used to funnel money and projects to Nevada. But Reid knew that Jeffords would be so grateful that he could get anything he wanted for Nevada from the newly minted chairman. And he was also playing the long game, giving the Democrats the power to change the Senate's agenda and the direction of the country and putting him in line to become the most powerful Democrat in the country should Daschle, as some speculated, run for president.

This was the consummation of all of Reid's skills: his ability to make one-on-one connections with colleagues and his strategic vision to think several steps ahead.

BY THE END of 2002, Reid made it clear that if Daschle decided to run for president, he would be the new leader, especially after there were murmurs that Connecticut's Chris Dodd might be interested. "Reid Counts Enough Votes to Win Senate Post," read the front-page headline in the *Reno Gazette-*

Journal. McCue, rarely quoted in the media, told the newspaper that Reid had thirty-five of the forty-eight Senate Democrats locked up.

McCue talked to the newspaper after three days of making calls to all of the Democratic senatorial chiefs of staff. She kept a detailed log. Some of her colleagues were not around, but most were and many said "told Dodd, totally with Reid" (Barbara Boxer) or "absolutely w/Reid and told Dodd" (Herb Kohl) or "will help in any way; surprised at Dodd" (Chuck Schumer). But the most effervescent endorsement came from Susan Russ, who indicated to McCue that her boss, Jim Jeffords, remained grateful: "Jim doesn't care if God is running against Reid, he's w/Reid."

BEFORE 2002 ENDED, Reid would cast one of the more consequential votes of his career and one he would later claim was not only his biggest regret but his *only* regret: supporting the resolution to go to war with Iraq after Saddam Hussein's invasion of Kuwait.

By the time Reid voted for the use of force resolution on October 11, he had repeatedly signaled he would support President George W. Bush's plan to invade Iraq and topple Saddam Hussein. Reid had been one of his father's most ardent supporters in 1991 before the first Iraq War.

More than a decade later, even though he expressed slightly more reluctance for the son's war, Reid nevertheless voted for the invasion, emphasizing that the United States should not go it alone and should only use force as "a last resort." Reid was among an overwhelming majority of senators, seventy-seven, who voted for the use of force.

Reid said in both cases, and in other votes involving sending troops into harm's way, he followed the lead of experts and those who served, whether they were in the Senate such as John McCain or Bob Dole, or in the military, such as Colin Powell.

"I think the reason [for the vote] was my lack of military experience," Reid said years later. "I didn't feel I had the credentials to go against the military."

Few were as publicly regretful as Reid, who eventually would call the war "the worst foreign policy mistake" in American history.

Landra Reid agreed years later that the 2002 vote was her husband's biggest regret: "That was so colossal when it brought about just a chain reaction that affected our country for twenty years," she said.

CHAPTER SIXTEEN

A LEADER IS BORN

Harry Reid was known for his dedication to his wife, Landra. But what was not as well-known was how fiercely protective he was of his children.

This would become an issue for him by 2003 when his sons all had professions that potentially intersected with his—as lawyers or lobbyists—and his daughter, Lana, was married to a capital advocate, Steve Barringer. It was only a matter of time, now that Reid had ascended so high in the Democratic leadership, that the national media would take notice. In 2003, the *Los Angeles Times* did so, and the Team Reid pushback was vociferous. This was a product of many forces: a small state with (at that time) one large law firm that had most of the political juice, his sons and son-in-law who were making their living advocating for the state's major interests, and Reid's reflexive defense of his relatives, buttressed by Landra's own protectiveness, no matter how questionable it might look to outsiders.

Reid had seen the issue of his relatives coming for some time. In 2001, he had gone to the Ethics Committee after talking to his relatives and on September 27, he wrote a memo to his chief of staff, Susan McCue:

> I've been advised that there is no law or Senate rule specifically restricting lobbying activity by a relative of a member of the Senate," Reid wrote. "The issue is really one of discretion and common sense. My relatives are very aware that their lobbying activities could reflect upon me and the Senate. Further, they appreciate that any appearance of favoritism, unfair advantage or special access could potentially be created by their activities . . . To the extent that any of their activities necessitate their working with my staff I would expect that they be treated no better and no worse than any other lobbyist who calls upon this office.

The directive lasted until the *Los Angeles Times* began nosing around about his relatives the following year. After Reid submitted to an interview late in the year, McCue wrote an "All Staff" memo on October 22, 2002, to notify the team of "a change in policy with regard to Sen. Reid's family members lobbying our office." McCue cited the *Times* interview and said that "after thoughtful review, I am issuing a new directive effective immediately establishing a firewall between Sen. Reid's children and his Senate staff."

She went on to talk about two specific members of the Reid family: his youngest son, Key, who was working for Lionel, Sawyer & Collins, then the most powerful firm in the state, which also employed Reid's three other sons and former senator Richard Bryan; and Barringer, the senator's son-in-law and an experienced environmental attorney with mining expertise:

> Indeed, their limited work with our office was made more productive because, like us, they are dedicated to doing what is right for the State. Nevada is well-served by both of them, and it is unfortunate that we will no longer benefit from their considerable expertise to advance our shared priorities. But Sen. Reid has long held that elected leaders must take steps to prevent even the appearance of impropriety, and it has become clear this ban is necessary for that reason.

The story was finally published on June 23, 2003. The piece by the reporters Chuck Neubauer and Richard T. Cooper was damning, a nearly five-thousand-word story that detailed how Reid's sons and son-in-law had been involved in legislation that the senator had advocated for as the second most powerful Democrat in the Senate. The headline was searing: "In Nevada, the Name to Know Is Reid."

The piece was published the day after a *Los Angeles Times* article laid the groundwork by reporting that seventeen senators had relatives who lobbied Congress:

> But Harry Reid is in a class by himself. One of his sons and his son-in-law lobby in Washington for companies, trade groups and municipalities seeking Reid's help in the Senate. A second son has lobbied in Nevada for some of those same interests, and a third has represented a couple of them as a litigator.
>
> In the last four years alone, their firms have collected more than $2 million in lobbying fees from special interests that were represented by the kids and helped by the senator in Washington.
>
> So pervasive are the ties among Reid, members of his family and Nevada's leading industries and institutions that it's difficult to find a significant field in which such a relationship does not exist.

The pushback to the story by McCue was focused on how the various bills benefited Nevada and how the relatives' influence was relatively irrelevant. Reid, though, sounded almost flippant or unconcerned about the appearance in his responses, as was his wont. To wit:

"Have they said something? I am sure they have," he said. "I don't have meetings with my children to go over business things."

"Steve Barringer has been a lawyer for more than 20 years," Reid said. "They are not hiring some doofus."

His staff, though, knew the potential damage the story could cause, coming as it did only six months before Reid's reelection year. Top legislative aide Kai Anderson sent the article to the staff, with a note saying, "The article is slanted to try to create a controversy where none exists." He attached the McCue lobbying memo and added, "Simply put, they are not allowed to lobby our office."

A letter was drafted to Dean Baquet, then the managing editor of the *Los Angeles Times* and later the executive editor of the *New York Times*. It began by referring to the "highly misleading parts" of the story, trying to parse that only Barringer and Key Reid lobby the federal government, even though the firm had many clients affected by federal matters:

> Rory, Josh and Leif are highly accomplished attorneys that do no federal lobbying what-so-ever. They all work at the largest, most influential law firm in Nevada. But to hold them accountable for contracts at the entire firm would be like holding you accountable for what occurs within the *Los Angeles Times*' advertising and sales departments. It is patently wrong.

The missive also argued that the Clark County Lands Bill, a focal point of the story and one supported by environmentalists and developers, had already passed the House with bipartisan support, so no extra help was needed.

Meanwhile, the staff was busily preparing a "Harry Reid Response Packet," which envisioned a joint statement from both Nevada senators that would say: "Irresponsible, inaccurate journalism, proud of work for gaming, mining etc. Lands bill passed unanimously w/ [Republican congressman Jim] Gibbons. Most significant piece of legislation to protect Nevada's future. Story intentionally misleading. Agenda journalism."

They also planned to solicit a letter of support from the Republican governor Kenny Guinn, as well as statements from the American Gaming Association, which had hired Key from Lionel, Sawyer and Collins, the Nevada Mining Association, and the Howard Hughes Corporation, to decry factual errors. The team also hoped to get quotes from various environmental groups supporting the lands bill to counter the perception that it was a favor to developers.

None of this eventually proved necessary, though, as the story petered out, and there were few follow-ups. At home, the ever-friendly *Las Vegas Sun* ran a short story with this headline: "Reid: L.A. Times' Story on Sons' Lobbying 'Misleading.'" The *Review-Journal* headline was also anodyne, "LOBBYING CONGRESS: Senator Downplays Family Ties," but also had this tart Reid quote: "If that's the best they can find, they've got nothing."

This would become a pattern for Reid, whose relationships with lobbyists and friends would occasionally spark news coverage and perhaps even incrementally added to his critics in Nevada, but not much ever came of the stories. His family members would continue to lobby or be tangentially or directly involved with Reid's legislative duties, much to the consternation of ethics experts and some in the media, but nowhere else.

In 2006, McCue issued a more blunt directive under the rubric "Updated Office Policy on Lobbying":

> No family member of the Senator or staff may lobby anyone in the office on any matter pending before or involving Congressional action. For the purposes of this policy a relative will be defined as a parent, spouse, sibling, or child. This policy also covers the spouses of relatives as herein defined. Everyone should always use common sense in these matters and we always need to be mindful of appearances.

The Reid family's activities would occasionally pop into public view—for instance, he would lobby in 2011 for his son Josh to become the city of Henderson's attorney, the same position he once held. But rarely did these stories have much staying power.

AFTER THE *LOS ANGELES TIMES* scare, Team Reid began to focus on 2004, when the senator would be running for his fourth term, and had accumulated baggage over twenty-two years on Capitol Hill that would burden any member. They knew that the *Los Angeles Times* story would be used by national Republicans to sell potential candidates on the viability of a race against a man who had won by only 428 votes in 1998. McCue and her boss also knew that they had to make changes in the Nevada Democratic Party, which badly needed to be modernized into an efficient vehicle to assist candidates. Reid didn't know it at the time, but a personnel move he agreed to earlier in 2003 would change the party and his life and plant the seeds for what would flower into the best state party in America. The ascension of Rebecca Lambe, who would become part of a troika of influential women in Reid's life along with his wife and McCue, would change the direction of a state that had been red since the mid-1960s.

Lambe had moved to Nevada at the end of 2002 after a career in Missouri politics, taking a job in Reid's Las Vegas office. But she was a campaign operative, a lawyer who understood finance and field operations, and she longed to be back in the fray. So she approached McCue and Reid about helming the state party, pegging her qualifications on her coordinating campaigns in Missouri for the top elected officials in that state, most notably Sen. Mel Carnahan. Lambe also was familiar with the flexibility of state parties to raise unlimited funds, which would eventually allow Reid to raise millions of dollars to be funneled into party-building activities.

The state party needed help as Reid's reelection campaign loomed. The last two cycles had been ominous harbingers for him. President George W. Bush had won the state in 2000, and the Republicans also had elected their first senator, John Ensign, since 1982. In 2002, the Democrats lost a newly created congressional seat, and saw the Republicans easily reelect Governor Guinn and sweep all the other statewide offices. Not only did the Republicans have a voter registration edge, but at least two of the recently elected constitutional officers, Secretary of State Dean Heller and Treasurer Brian Krolicki, were known to be ambitious and possibly considering a run against Reid. What's more, the Democratic Party was in the red.

If all of that weren't stacking the deck against Reid, the scene Lambe walked into when she assumed the executive director duties of the state party did not bode well. "There were two longtime activists as staff, a bunch of broken-down desks and chairs and cardboard boxes," she recalled. "Oh, and an intern." (That intern, Justin Gilbert, later became a key cog in the Reid Machine, a data analytics expert and one of the first hires to build the data file.)

Considering what the organization eventually became, its beginnings were about as humble as Reid's in Searchlight. "We didn't actually have a voter file," Lambe recalled.

This was the moment that would change Reid's fortunes, transmogrify the state party into an electoral monster, and begin the trajectory of Nevada from a reliably red state to a bluish-purple one while also electing dozens of Democratic candidates at the highest and lowest levels of the ballot. In so doing, Lambe and Reid would forge an effective political partnership unrivaled in the state's history.

Reid said he and Lambe shared a laconic style that made them a great match. "I get along well with her because I don't talk a lot and she doesn't, either," he said shortly before he died.

(Eventually, Lambe would be one of the few non–family members—the others were close friends Jay Brown and Dr. Ike Khan—on a VIP list for front-office staff in Reid's Capitol Hill suite; if anyone on this list called, staff was to immediately notify the senator.)

One of the first things Lambe did when she arrived was to commission a poll to gauge Reid's vulnerability in his reelection. She wanted to see how Reid would match up against the most likely Republican candidate, Congressman Jim Gibbons, an Iraq War veteran in his third term. The survey by The Southwest Group found Reid ahead of Gibbons by nine points, 40–31, but in a July 4 memo to Lambe, the pollster Billy Rogers saw softness in the numbers and suggested Reid was very vulnerable, especially because his lead was nearly halved among likely voters. "An incumbent senator who polls at 40 percent and holds a 5-point lead among the most likely voters is clearly in trouble," Rogers wrote.

Gibbons would flirt with the race in the media for a few weeks as Reid amassed a war chest of more than $3 million, but announced in late August he would not run.

Only three days after Gibbons's announcement, Richard Ziser, an anti-abortion activist who had helmed a successful effort the previous cycle to ban gay marriage in Nevada, announced he would run for Reid's Senate seat. Team Reid did not consider him a formidable candidate, but they were still wary of Heller and Krolicki. Heller, who had won reelection with 60 percent of the vote, was the most dangerous, a former lawmaker and maverick secretary of state who could appeal to moderate voters.

This was the same secretary of state who had stopped the Washoe County recount in 1998 and had been credited by Reid and others for putting partisanship aside. That was now forgotten, and Heller became a target. By now Reid had developed a reputation for doing what he needed to do to survive. So it was no surprise that on October 14, 2003, his son Leif met with the ambitious secretary of state in his Carson City law office. Leif Reid memorialized the meeting in a dictated memo, which showed the apple hadn't fallen far from the tree. It read, in part:

> Leif explained that, on paper, we want there to be a Republican primary because it's better for Sen. Reid. Leif said we don't care if Krolicki runs, but we do care if Heller runs because, with Heller, "it's personal." Leif then went through a litany of things Sen Reid has done for Heller . . . Heller asked about the Reid-Ensign relationship and asked why he [Heller] and Reid couldn't be friends when it was all over, like Reid is with Ensign. Leif explained there was no prior relationship with Ensign, and the current friendship works well for both Reid and Ensign. "If you run unsuccessfully and survive, the same would not be true," Leif warned. "To get anything done, you need to go through Sen. Reid and he'd have no interest in helping you. He would work against you."
>
> Heller said that over the years he has run into former Reid employees, members of the LDS Church and others who tell him you can't trust Sen Reid. "If he doesn't need you, he'll throw you out with the trash," Heller

said. "He has no interest in you." Leif said the stories are unfounded, questioned the source(s) and assured him [Heller] that he can trust his Dad. "But if you cross him, you'll regret it," Leif said. "He's tough. He hasn't achieved what he's achieved without being tough and astute politically. I think you'd find if you ran against him, it'd be the worst career decision you ever made."

Leif said he needs to get out now to avoid permanent damage . . .

Leif's gut tells him it was a very effective meeting today, and Heller is not going to run.

Leif Reid's gut was right: it took a while, but Heller announced in February 2004, not long before candidate filing opened, that he would not run, two weeks after Krolicki had bowed out, saying Reid, who had now amassed a more than $6 million war chest, could not be beaten.

ELECTION NIGHT 2004 changed Harry Reid's life. With his race never in doubt on November 2—he would win in a 61–35 landslide—Reid watched from a ballroom at the Rio Hotel off the Strip as George W. Bush's reelection became inevitable, and Democratic losses (four seats that would bring the GOP majority to 55–45) in the Senate, too. He had known his friend and Democratic leader Tom Daschle was locked in a close race with John Thune, but as it became clear the race would be in doubt for hours, he and his family retired to a suite upstairs at the hotel. McCue was there, too, as was Jay Brown.

About midnight in Las Vegas, the word came from South Dakota that Daschle had lost. McCue understood what this meant right away and talked to Reid, who was sitting on the hotel bed with Landra. "You've got a big decision to make, a consequential one," she told him, referring to running to succeed Daschle. "Do you need time to think it through?"

Reid looked up at his chief of staff, that trademark wry half smile on his face, and said in his usual deadpan: "I don't need to think it through."

The room erupted in laughter, but the joviality soon gave way to singularity of purpose. Landra recalled that her husband realized he would never know whether he could become leader until he tested the waters.

In his pajamas and slippers, Reid had made his way to the small hotel desk and began calling members, slowly checking off names. It started slowly, but after his Senate floor maven, Gary Myrick, smartly advised him to call the more conservative members first, those who would prefer him over the liberal Chris Dodd (if he chose to run, too), he began to gain confidence and support.

By early morning, Reid had received the required twenty-three commitments—a majority of the Democratic caucus—to become leader. The long hours spent on the floor as whip, getting to know senators, helping them with amendments or talking about their kids, had paid off.

The outcome, Dick Durbin of Illinois said, was never in doubt. "Harry would work the phones completely and faster than anyone," said Durbin, who would soon be tapped by Reid to be his number two. "He knew everybody's favorite issue and he probably helped [the senator] with it. He called in all the favors and in no time at all, it was clear that Harry had lined it up."

After a brief conversation with the Republican president who had just been reelected, in which Reid said they discussed "the need for reconciliation," he appeared in front of the media at the downtown Las Vegas federal building for the first time as the presumptive Democratic leader. He announced that he had the support of most of the caucus and was ready to lead after a formal vote on November 16.

Before that caucus meeting, Reid and his aides prepared remarks he would deliver after he ascended. The text is quite extraordinary and read in part:

> We are faced with a wartime President who claims a popular mandate for his programs, and his appointments . . . with a uniquely partisan majority in

> this body . . . and with the other House of Congress controlled by individuals willing to go to quite extraordinary lengths in their quest for political power.
>
> We do indeed face a wartime President . . . but in a war brought on by his own stubborn hubris . . . and unwillingness or inability to face reality. We must all realize that the war in Iraq has not united us . . . but we are united in the war against international terror.
>
> We face a President who can claim a popular mandate only in the sense that this time, unlike four years ago, he actually won the election.

That is, Gore had been denied what was rightfully his.

Then Reid really unloaded:

> Both in the popular and electoral vote, however, he could claim victory by only the slimmest of margins. Had the vote only slightly differed in just one state . . . had his party not spawned and sponsored purveyors of outright lies and calumnies about our Presidential candidate . . . the current occupant of the White House would at this moment be considering how to pack his bags, rather than how to pack the Supreme Court.
>
> Of such a slim and gossamer tissue is not a mandate made.

Of such words are not reconciliations made.

Embracing his new role as a national leader, Reid also did not mince words about the overall picture for Democrats, including a 30 percent loss in the white rural vote. Reid then spent some time on Democratic gains in lower-ticket battles for state legislatures before quoting a man who lived in Nevada for a time:

> The report of our death is, as Mark Twain would have said, an exaggeration. Indeed, I think we may look forward with some confidence rather than a miracle of resurrection, merely a return to sanity. It is toward making that return to common sense and what used to be common virtues, that I pledge to you to toil unceasingly.

From Searchlight to the center of American political power, be it opportunism or calculation, or a combination thereof, Harry Mason Reid, the unprepossessing son of a hard rock miner, the pro-life, pro-gun senator whose political career had been declared over in the mid-1970s and almost ended in 1998, and who had been the target of death threats and the FBI, was now the leader of the Democrats in the US Senate.

CHAPTER SEVENTEEN

CREATING A WAR ROOM AND DEFENDING THE FILIBUSTER

One week after the 2004 election, and in anticipation of Reid becoming the Democratic leader, Susan McCue wrote an extensive memo to the senator after two days of conversations about the coming term. It was clear she was becoming his alter ego, channeling what she knew he needed to make him successful. She would set the table for a Capitol Hill operation and political machine for the rest of his public life.

In the memo, McCue made mention of an idea that had been percolating on Capitol Hill for some time but one that she insisted Reid needed to implement: a Democratic "war room"—a place where the party could do rapid response to a Republican president and his initiatives.

There was more, too. McCue wanted Reid to go on a red state tour, to begin thinking already about 2006 Senate candidates ("Must be priority. Repubs new mantra is '60' [votes]. Ours should be 50+"), celebrity thank-you letters (Sheryl Crow, Ed Norton, Leonardo DiCaprio, Sean Penn), and an NRA endorsement statement for him ("Libs won't like . . . we need red state credibility and should take it when we can").

A week later, McCue fleshed out the war room idea, aka the Democratic Communications Center. Its mission would be a perfect reflection of Reid's personality:

> Develop core themes and a salient message overlay and aggressively put forth those messages to media in a consistent, coordinated way for you as leader and the Democratic caucus; provide rapid response and aggressively seize opportunities to expose Republican failings; pioneer Internet communications between blogs and direct mail; leverage current outreach with key interest groups and policy initiatives.

"We were coming into the digital age, and it was super-clear to me that Harry Reid was way behind," McCue said.

The operation was broad and deep. Reid hired young, relentless staffers who were eager to do what the Democrats had failed to do since the days of James Carville in 1992: take on the Republicans at every turn in a coordinated way. This was how Reid was, too—a perpetual brawler, a counterpuncher who loved to be in the ring.

Jim Manley, an experienced Hill veteran who worked for Ted Kennedy, was brought on as staff director. Manley was a natural partisan fighter and perfect for the job.

"This was something that had never been done before," said Rebecca Katz, one of the early war room conscripts. "And it was a very hard moment in Democratic politics. There was licking of the wounds, a lot of dysfunction."

Another early recruit was Ari Rabin-Havt, who described McCue's pitch thusly: "We need to set up an online program to communicate with blogs, with the online left, with this world, and we have no idea how to do it."

Rabin-Havt had been deputy director of online communications for the John Kerry presidential campaign, so he was looking for a job. This time, he would be the top dog, and the challenge appealed to him. Reid essentially was a tech-resistant guy who still used an old AOL address, but Rabin-Havt realized the Democratic leader was serious about two things: taking on the president and, as he put it, "treating this online world as a serious political universe."

Rabin-Havt had relationships with the burgeoning leftist blogosphere, people such as Markos Moulitsas of Daily Kos and Josh Marshall of Talking Points Memo as well as MoveOn, a progressive outfit that would eventually give tens of millions of dollars to help Democrats. Reid, through Rabin-Havt and his willingness to listen to these bloggers, some of whom he invited to a Senate retreat at the Kennedy Center, harnessed their power to his and the Democrats' advantage.

There were other aspects, too, including a robust Hispanic outreach operation before anyone else had one. The war room eventually had about thirty operatives churning out anti-Bush and anti-GOP propaganda and organizing news conferences after White House announcements.

Reid also had decided that as much as he and Daschle had been—and would remain—close friends, he wanted to have a different style. "One of the first things I did is recognize that Byrd, Mitchell, Dole, all the leaders I've served with, they were one-man teams," Reid recalled. "They didn't have anybody else help them. They were on their own. I thought I wanted to change that. I thought I could do better with some help."

Reid, unlike some leaders who were insular, decided he would decentralize power, believing that would benefit him in the long run. He wanted to reempower committee chairs, some of whom had been irked when their jurisdiction was usurped by ad hoc task forces Daschle approved.

Reid also created a kitchen cabinet to help him make decisions and to ensure he could maintain broad support within the caucus. The first person the new leader reached out to was New York's Chuck Schumer, whom he asked to head up the Democratic Senatorial Campaign Committee, the outfit that would be responsible for trying to put the Senate back in Democratic hands.

It was an offer the ambitious Schumer could not turn down. Reid wanted a three-person leadership team, and he had already told his friend from his House days, Illinois' Dick Durbin, that he wanted him there, too. Durbin, the new whip, immediately agreed.

Reid wanted a third member, and he thought he needed a woman. His choice was Washington state's Patty Murray, who had just been reelected to a third term. Murray still remembered in 2021 how it came about:

"I was actually in my state driving and it was a usual Harry Reid conversation of 'Patty, okay, here's what I need you to do. And you're going, 'Can I think about this? Oh, no, I can't, I actually have to answer you right now? Because you're gonna hang up on me kind of moment.' But it was an easy answer, because I knew that we agreed on most things."

Even though it was clear Reid wanted a woman to blunt criticism of his stances on social issues, especially abortion, Murray said she never felt like a token. "He never, ever conveyed that or portrayed that," she said. "But he was right in his understanding that if he wanted his leadership to be successful, he needed all voices at the table."

Reid's strategy was simple and the execution would show how he held on to power until he retired. He would meet with the three members of his team at five o'clock every Monday evening, so as to head off any potential problems when the full caucus met the next day. There would be no ambushes, no surprises. During the day, he would occasionally call his trio into his office to ask for counsel on a decision he had to make—sometimes that happened three or four times a day.

Durbin said he "never expected" Reid to be as collaborative as he was. "I knew that each leader has his own style. But when Harry said, 'It's a team effort,' he really meant it. He really was inclusive, and we were in it together."

The new team and the war room would almost immediately be faced with a challenge to the approach that would test their cohesion and aggressiveness.

SHORTLY AFTER HE was reelected in 2004, President Bush made what seemed like a boastful declaration: "I earned capital in this campaign, political capital, and now I intend to spend it." Bush had both houses of Congress, so the check he wanted to write was to privatize Social Security, something he had talked about for decades. Reid was determined to stop him.

Reid and Nancy Pelosi, the House Democratic leader who had ascended in 2002, decided they would go all out to derail Bush's efforts, further outlined in his 2005 State of the Union. This was the beginning of what would become—to both of them at least—a beautiful partnership, one that would result in his repeating to anyone who would listen decades later that Pelosi was the best Speaker in history.

Pelosi saw Bush as having given Democrats a gift. "We had to bring his numbers down," Pelosi recalled. "So we had to make a plan. Now this took real strength and collaboration and friendship and the trust of our members."

It also took the full force of the recently created Democratic war room under Reid's stewardship. The House, despite Pelosi's rhetorical clout, could not stop the Bush plan, as Republicans controlled it 232–201. The Republicans controlled the Senate, too, 55–45, but Reid had the filibuster so all he had to do was count to forty-one. If he could gather that many senators, he could by Senate rules prevent votes on any issue.

That, however, might not be so easy as it seemed.

"In the Senate, Reid had a significant problem," Rabin-Havt said. "Now [in 2022], we have [Joe] Manchin and [Kyrsten] Sinema [who could bolt the caucus]. Then he had [Mark] Pryor, [Blanche] Lincoln, [Mary] Landrieu, [Ben] Nelson, [Joe] Lieberman, [Kent] Conrad. He had at least eight to ten Democrats who could abandon him on this issue" and vote with the Republicans.

Reid's strategic insight on his possible mutineers was that if one went rogue and tried to negotiate a deal with the White House, the dominoes would start to fall. "All these geniuses out there were saying, 'How can the Democrats expect to win this fight if they don't have their own plan?'" Pelosi recalled. "Well, we do because our plan is Social Security."

Rabin-Havt remembered that Reid directed the war room to "just fight on this, like every day, wake up in the morning and say, 'How do I prevent Social Security from being privatized today?' "

So they had events and photo ops, but they also were working behind the scenes with bloggers, with Reid occasionally directing Rabin-Havt to have his friends in the blogosphere publicly go after a wobbly Democratic member. And then he would inform his besieged colleague that Rabin-Havt could soothe the bloggers so long as that Democratic senator would reaffirm his or her opposition to privatization.

This was "Reid to his core, because it was this very tactical thing where he knew we had to hold these people, and he would just trade whatever he wanted to hold these people," Rabin-Havt said.

This was a preview of the transactional Reid to come, especially four years later during the fight to pass the Affordable Care Act, but it was also very personal to him. "My mom wouldn't have survived without Social Security," Reid said to Rabin-Havt. "My mom would have died. This was his mother and George W. Bush, a rich kid from Connecticut, was playing with his mom's life. It was that. And I think that's why he basically risked his entire leadership on that. Because if it had gone wrong in those six months, he wouldn't have been leader next time."

It also may help explain, along with Reid's inability to edit himself, one of the most enduring and telling of all his gaffes that threatened their entire campaign on Social Security.

IT CAME ALMOST two months to the day after his celebrated Reidism of 2005, when he lambasted Federal Reserve Chairman Alan Greenspan as a "political hack" for supporting private investment accounts for Social Security.

But the Greenspan comments, while enduring, did not have nearly the resonance or indelible impact on Reid's reputation as something he said in Las Vegas on May 6. The senator was speaking to about sixty students in a civics class at Del Sol High School late that morning when he was asked about the president's policies. "The man's father is a wonderful human being," Reid said quietly. "I think this guy is a loser."

Erin Neff of the *Las Vegas Review-Journal* was the only journalist in the room, and she would later report, "A few students chuckled. One teacher smiled. A few kids looked surprised, while others looked bored. An aide to the senator sat down and began typing on her Blackberry."

That aide, spokeswoman Tessa Hafen, still remembered the scene vividly years later.

"They were such smart kids, totally engaged," Hafen said. "It was really a nice event. And then he just dropped that 'this guy is a loser.'"

When they returned to the car after the event, Hafen told her boss, "You know, you just called the president a loser. I think he said, 'Well, that's what I said, right?'"

Hafen also remembered how lucky they were that this was before the era when someone—or multiple people—in a room would be creating videos on their cell phones and immediately posting them to social media. But word nevertheless spread relatively quickly. Hafen made a half-hearted attempt to kill the story by calling Neff, but she knew. "I was not going to suppress that story. No way," she said.

Indeed, Neff had already begun to do what any reporter would; she was seeking comment on Reid's remarks. By three o'clock, the Republican National Committee was expressing the requisite outrage, and the widely read blogger Matt Drudge displayed a banner headline. To make matters worse, the president was out of the country, traveling in Europe and not immediately reachable. So Reid called Bush adviser Karl Rove, with whom he was consistently sparring over Social Security, and apologized.

But it was too late. The Drudge link ensured the comment would go viral and would cement in some people's minds—almost certainly Bush's—that the new leader could say anything, no matter how crass or nasty, at any time.

Reid, as was his wont, did not dwell on it for very long. He was in a battle he was determined to win, and he would not be sidetracked. When he was asked about the incident in an interview with *Rolling Stone* a few weeks later, he was blunt:

Q: You've called Bush a loser.
Reid: And a liar.
Q: You apologized for the loser comment.
Reid: But never for the liar, have I?

UNDETERRED DESPITE THE media constantly asking Reid about his intemperance vis à vis the president, Reid and Pelosi stayed on their Social Security privatization message, and the war room staffers executed a relentless, day-in-and-day-out strategy that included putting the Democratic leaders on cross-country tours. They weren't sure it was working. After a few stops on the tour, Rebecca Katz picked up the *New York Times* and started perusing to find some coverage. She couldn't find it until another aide told her to flip back to the front page. "There on the front page was a picture of Reid and Hillary [Clinton] and everybody talking about Social Security," she recalled. "It was right there on the front page next to a picture of Bush making his case. We were on equal footing and ready for the fight."

There were constant media events, including outreach directly to Hispanics through a group the war room created called "Latinos for a Secure Retirement." They had unveiled a report at a roundtable led by Reid on the impact privatization would have on Hispanic families.

Even though the president embarked on his own national tour early in the year to sell the privatization plan, the Democratic message was overwhelming Bush's. They also had an easier sell, and one at which Reid would excel: scaring seniors that their accounts could be jeopardized. By late summer, the Bush plan was barely alive; by the end of 2005, House Republican leaders did not even have it on a list of priorities for the next year.

But the impact of what Reid and Pelosi had accomplished in scuttling the president's plan extended well beyond its entombment. The failure damaged Bush's numbers—by the time of the 2006 election his approval rating was under 40 percent. Reid and Pelosi smelled blood and were able to recruit quality candidates who saw weakness in the White House. On Election

Night 2006, the Democrats took back both houses. Reid had come to the House party and just as he was walking in, Paul Pelosi, Nancy's husband, told him the news: "Harry, you just won Virginia [Jim Webb had defeated George Allen], you're in the majority."

Reid smiled as broadly as he could.

THE SOCIAL SECURITY fight had crystallized in many minds what kind of leader Reid would be and what his alliance with Pelosi would look like. That may have been the most significant policy battle of 2005, but it was followed closely by a parallel, internal Senate game of brinkmanship that Reid engaged in almost every day, too.

The issue was judicial confirmations, and Senate Majority Leader Bill Frist had signaled he might invoke what was called the "nuclear option" to evade the filibuster and instead only require a majority vote to confirm judges, except for Supreme Court justices. Instead of needing sixty votes, which would require at least five Democratic defections, Frist would only have to hold fifty-one of his fifty-five Republicans, a simple majority. Frist, who reportedly was mulling a presidential run, had the support of social conservatives, including Pat Robertson and James Dobson, and their army of followers.

Reid brought all the armaments at his disposal to block Frist from eliminating the filibuster to confirm ten judges that had been held up for confirmation. He shrugged off the "obstructionist" label affixed to him by the White House and the Republican National Committee and plowed ahead to protect the filibuster—nay, as he framed it, the institution of the Senate itself and the rights of the minority. He was prepared to shut down the Senate if Frist proceeded—that's how strongly he said he felt about preserving the filibuster.

Reid knew he needed half a dozen Republicans to stop Frist, and that was assuming he didn't lose any of his own caucus. His staff prepared a "target list," a matrix showing where they thought all the senators were and who could possibly be swayed. A March 4 version of the document had only twenty-nine of the Democrats as certain to oppose the nuclear option, with fifteen of his caucus (including the independent Jim Jeffords) along with Maine Republican Olympia Snowe and Rhode Island Republican Lincoln Chafee listed as "+?" in a second column. Forty-nine Republicans were listed as either supportive of Frist or "+?," or likely to be supportive. That left Nebraska Democrat Ben Nelson and four Republicans Reid could work on in a middle column with a question mark: Arizona's John McCain, Maine's Susan Collins, Oregon's Gordon Smith, and Virginia's John Warner.

Reid knew he would have trouble holding those in his own caucus who did not believe the filibuster was an immutable part of the institution. If Robertson and Dobson were convinced to oppose the move, the Democrats had to mobilize their own special interests to provide grass-roots cover and pressure. They would eventually spend millions of dollars on ads and a coordinated campaign to get the votes to stop the nuclear option. The war room was whirring.

Team Reid also prepared internal documents with quotes from the likes of the conservative columnist George Will and *National Review* supporting the filibuster as an essential tool for the minority, and they produced previous statements from Republican senators that helped make their case.

Reid warned on April 8 that if Frist succeeded, it would be the beginning of the end of all types of filibusters. By the time the minority leader made one of his relatively rare appearances on a Sunday news program on April 10, talking about the issue on *Face the Nation*, Reid and the war room had been harping on "radical Republicans" and insisting that Democrats were only blocking ten judges and had approved more than two hundred. (The ten, though, were about a fifth of all appellate judges.)

Reid told host Bob Schieffer about the slippery slope of eliminating the filibuster for lower court judges and where it might lead: "It's judges today, it's Cabinet officers tomorrow, and pretty soon we're nothing, just an extension of the House of Representatives, and it will change our basic form of government that's been in existence for more than 200 years."

With assistance from unlikely quarters—former Senate majority leader Bob Dole cautioning Republicans about the danger of such a move—and the national GOP moving too slowly to counteract the avalanche of ads from leftist groups such as MoveOn and People for the American Way, the odds began to tilt in Reid's favor. Frist, it seemed, did not have Reid's cutthroat instincts.

"Bill Frist was just such a nice man," Reid would say before he died. "But he was not politically savvy . . . and I messed with him."

As a May 24 vote loomed on Priscilla Owens, one of the nominees the Democrats had blocked, the renowned *Washington Post* columnist David Broder wrote about the significance of the battle and suggested the high stakes for Frist (his supposed presidential bid) and Reid: "In his first months as leader, the Nevadan has compiled a spotty record of verbal gaffes and parliamentary gambles. But if he is able to turn back Bush and Frist on this giant issue, his stature among his fellow Democrats would be vastly enlarged."

Broder's column came four days before the scheduled vote on Owens, and he also suggested the nuclear option could boomerang on Republicans if they were to become a minority again. That echoed Dole's fears and that of others in the GOP caucus, some of whom agreed to become part of a bipartisan Gang of 14 to find a middle ground to head off what some saw as a constitutional crisis. Eventually they would do so—just in time for the Owens vote—ensuring the Democrats would only filibuster judges in "extraordinary circumstances" and Republicans would not invoke the nuclear option. The logjam was broken. Owens and others would be confirmed.

After the Owens vote, during a joint press conference with Reid, Frist tried to put the best face on not using the nuclear option, while Reid, trying hard to suppress a smile, seemed to ignore that the agreement was only for the 109th Congress. "The nuclear option is gone for our lifetime," Reid declared, words that would eventually prove untrue because of Harry Reid.

JUST A FEW months later, after midnight on August 16, Reid's head of security, Brian McGinty, was sound asleep in his Maryland home when his phone rang. He went into the bathroom so as not to wake his wife, but he knew it couldn't be good news. A frantic Landra Reid was on the phone. She told him that they were settling into bed in Searchlight—Reid had sent the security detail back to their hotel—when the sixty-five-year-old senator suddenly tumbled onto the floor.

"I could see that half of his face was droopy," Landra remembered. "And of course, he did not want to go into Vegas, didn't want to go to the doctor. I called the volunteer ambulance service there. And they came, took them about twenty minutes or so. And by that time, you couldn't see the difference on the side of his face. And he marched out and said, 'I'm not going.'"

That's when she called McGinty, who had elicited a promise from Reid when he started on his detail that he would always listen to him in fraught situations. "Mrs. Reid had told me that when she talked to him as it was happening he was slurring and he was incoherent," McGinty recalled. Reid was furious. McGinty said his speech wasn't slurred by then, and he "was denying anything had happened." But McGinty called the security detail and told them to return to the house to get Reid to the hospital. By now, Landra called family members, and two doctors who were close friends of the family, Ike Khan and Javaid Anwar, who asked her about Reid's symptoms. They in turn called Reid, who assured them he was fine. But the doctors were not so sure, and they told Landra to bring him into the city. Reid was recalcitrant, but by then Rory, his eldest son, had gotten involved, and McGinty was firm: "It was difficult to convince him, and when the team showed up and were basically manhandling him, he knew I was serious and he wasn't being given a choice."

The doctors were concerned because if Reid had had even a small stroke, or a transient ischemic attack (more commonly known as a TIA), it could be a forewarning of a larger one to come. They needed to see how he was doing, whether his speech was impaired, whether any part of his body was paralyzed. Time was of the essence, and it took about an hour, with calls to his sons, too, to persuade Reid to go to Sunrise Hospital for observation.

Reid was very private about his health, and he did not want anyone to know he had had a serious episode.

The next day, his staff began to weigh in, and they were hyperconscious about how it would look for the relatively new Democratic leader to be hospitalized with what appeared to be a stroke. So there was a blackout for a few days—some close to Reid didn't want to have any public disclosure at all—something that would be much harder to accomplish today. The doctors also wanted to be cautious, even though those who saw Reid said he looked and sounded fine.

It was not until three days later, after there was no recurrence of the original symptoms, that his staff put out a statement saying he was recovering from a ministroke but was doing well. He had to be convinced to stay in the hospital even for a few days, and he was on his phone much of the time.

The lapse of time between the incident and the disclosure fueled rumors, probably amplified by hospital scuttlebutt, that his condition was much worse than it was. He had been advised by his doctors to cancel all public appearances, and the timing was fortuitous because Congress was in recess.

Reid did not appear in public until August 24, eight days after the incident, in North Las Vegas for an event at Nevada Partners, a job-training facility affiliated with the Culinary Union. The ex-boxer deadpanned that he was ready to go a few rounds with the assembled media and was excited to return to work. Reid never again showed any symptoms from the TIA, although he developed balance issues a few years later of unknown origin.

When he returned to Washington, DC, after the recess, Reid went to Walter Reed hospital to get checked out, Landra said. It is, perhaps, because he was so fit that the TIA did not do any more than evanescent damage.

CHAPTER EIGHTEEN

MEDDLING AT HOME AND IN A PRESIDENTIAL RACE

A year into his tenure as the leader of the Senate Democrats, Reid found himself more of a target for Republicans, but it did not make him more cautious or more temperate. Quite the contrary.

By late 2005, he had put his assets in a blind trust—his wealth would be a constant source of scrutiny and attack from Republican groups who would imply, sans evidence, that he had enriched himself in the Senate. But in all other areas, Reid was only too content to meddle in national politics, affecting a presidential race and history, and state elections, too, relishing his role as a gatekeeper for who ran and didn't run for office. He also would try to take Nevada from a speck on the political map to a key state deciding Democratic presidential nominees and then a critical swing state in the general election—again, a history-making endeavor. Never one just to fight a one-front war, Reid also took on major policy fights at home—intensifying his criticism of the electric monopoly in Nevada—and on Capitol Hill, becoming a darling of the environmental movement. Reid meddled everywhere and anywhere he could—and for the Senate Democratic leader, that was a wide field. He not only did not shy away from trouble, he asked for it. Reid defiantly refused to return about $61,000 in contributions from clients of the disgraced lobbyist Jack Abramoff, convicted in a corruption probe. When the *Washington Times* reported in January 2006 that Reid could be under federal investigation related to Abramoff, he sneered, "You have to really stretch things to call it a newspaper."

A few months later, Reid scoffed at revelations he had accepted free ring-side seats to boxing matches, claiming he was on the job. But he almost immediately reversed himself, saying he would no longer accept the comped tickets.

Reid's staff saw the danger—polls showed his numbers dropping as he became more like a partisan buzzsaw than "independent like Nevada." A spring poll from the *Las Vegas Review-Journal* showed his approval ratings had plummeted since his 2004 reelection. He was at 53 percent approval and 25 percent disapproval when he won his fourth term; two years later, he was at 43–39.

McCue asked her top team for an assessment, writing, "It's arising from Sen Reid's perceived positioning—and a few verbal bombs—in DC. But let us know how better to present his image from DC to Nevada and the country. But Nevada first."

Rebecca Lambe, who was quietly becoming more of a force inside the office, responded at length. The gist: Reid needed to do more local media to affect his numbers; he should have surrogates praise him at events; he should offer moderate messages whenever he can, maybe even in rural Nevada; his team should build lists for mailings to the state; and he had to strike a balance between his national role and his Nevada role.

Reid also had to contend with an increasingly hostile and influential news outlet, the *Las Vegas Review-Journal*, by far the state's largest newspaper, which was unrelentingly critical. So much so that publisher Sherman Frederick, in May 2006, wrote a pre–political obituary for Reid, who was not up until 2010, saying he was no longer electable in Nevada because he had become too liberal.

Even that far out from an election, Team Reid knew he was vulnerable, and they would let no attack go unanswered, so they prepared letters to the editor, often with scathing attacks against Frederick and the newspaper. They also knew—as did the senator—that part of protecting him was erasing potential foes from the political map and making the state more Democratic. They had plans to do both.

HARRY REID AND his team viewed the 2006 election the way they viewed most elections: how would it affect his political future? So they went to work recruiting candidates to protect his flank, especially from the possibility of Rep. Jim Gibbons (R), an Iraq War veteran, becoming governor, and Rep. Jon Porter (R), a well-liked former state lawmaker, getting reelected. Both were possible 2010 foes who would have legitimate prospects to defeat Reid.

Porter had been elected in 2002 and was a moderate Republican, an amiable insurance salesman who had ascended from local politics to the state legislature, where he led a move during reapportionment to have a new congressional district drawn for him. He was ambitious, and Team Reid had been looking for a candidate for some time. But Reid could not find anyone who was interested in taking on Porter in the new district, which was built for a Republican, as the southern Las Vegas suburbs were expanding and becoming redder.

Then Reid had an idea—perhaps his Capitol Hill spokeswoman, Tessa Hafen, a member of a longtime Henderson Mormon family, could do it. Some were skeptical. "'Well, we've talked to everybody else, no one else will do it,'" he told Megan Jones, one of his aides. "'Why can't Tessa do it? The Hafen name [a venerable Nevada family] is good . . . she can win.'"

The only person he hadn't told was Hafen. Then, on January 3, 2006, Reid was driving to a Democratic strategy meeting to talk with other elected officials about potential candidates for November and Hafen was with him.

He turned to Hafen and out of the blue suggested she run against Porter. She was stunned and didn't say much. "I thought he was kidding," she recalled.

About twenty minutes later, sitting with the others, Reid told them, "I have the perfect candidate right here in this room. Tessa Hafen." Calls followed, a meeting with Harry and Landra at the senator's house, and Hafen was in, knowing full well what Reid's motivation might have been.

"Senator Reid was a chess player," she would say later. "Even if he couldn't beat Porter, he had to weaken him."

Most observers thought Hafen was a sacrificial lamb, simply a placeholder so Porter would not get a free ride. But Reid was right—or almost right. She came within two points of defeating Porter, who emerged victorious but banged up.

By contrast, Reid's attempt to eradicate the threat of Gibbons was disastrous. Dina Titus, the Democratic leader of the state senate, had announced her intention to run for governor. But Reid was convinced she was too liberal to win a statewide race. Titus also had never kowtowed to Reid as some other Democrats had, and the two were not close. Even though he tried to leave no fingerprints, Reid clearly searched for an alternative and alighted on Jim Gibson, the much more conservative Democratic mayor of Henderson. Gibson had almost everything Reid liked in a candidate: he was Mormon, he could raise a lot of money, and he was a moderate. Reid—and others—believed he had the best chance to defeat Gibbons in the general election. Gibson also assembled a formidable campaign team, including David Plouffe, who would soon become renowned for his role in electing Barack Obama president one cycle later.

Early polling showed Gibson and Titus in a close race. But it would not last. Titus was relentless in solidifying the Democratic base and Gibson stumbled on abortion, opening him up for attacks from the left. In the end, it wasn't close. Titus prevailed by seventeen points. But, as Reid feared, she lost in the general election to Gibbons, leaving the newly elected governor in a great position to run for the Senate if he chose to in 2010.

The results of balloting across the country, though, had a large impact on

Nevada and national political life. The Democrats had captured the Senate majority, thus changing Reid's title. On November 13, 2006, Harry Mason Reid was unanimously elected as the US Senate majority leader; the man from Searchlight was now the most powerful Democrat in the country.

Reid called the majority leader's post "the opportunity of a lifetime for me" and vowed to work with Republicans and President Bush in the "spirit of bipartisanship" and to "fight for the sparsely populated state of Nevada."

That was Susan McCue's cue to do a mic drop, which she did by announcing her departure to become the first president and CEO of ONE, a campaign started by U2's helmsman, Bono, and the billionaires Bill Gates and Warren Buffett to combat worldwide poverty. McCue would remain close to Reid until his death, but he had a new consigliere: Rebecca Lambe became his chief lieutenant.

AS THE DEMOCRATIC leader, Reid saw that a handful of his caucus members were considering running for president in 2008, most notably Hillary Clinton. But he had concluded that Barack Obama was the strongest candidate. Reid had been taken with Obama from the moment he got to the Senate, marveling at his oratorical gifts. Reid, without telling his staff or anyone, decided to act on his belief in mid-2006. He summoned the freshman senator and was his usual blunt self.

"I called him into my office, and I said, 'You should run for president,'" Reid recalled.

The conversation clearly had an influence on Obama, who had been musing about the idea. "Harry is not a romantic, but instead a very hard-nosed politician," Obama said in 2022. "For him to say, this is something that you really need to think about, was impactful, because what that indicated to me was that he actually thought I might be able to get the nomination. And number two, it meant that he thought that I could be a help, rather than a hindrance to what I assumed was his primary goal, which was keeping the

Senate. Yeah, and I think it was a wake-up call. It indicated that I had to look at it more seriously than I might otherwise."

Soon afterward, Obama talked to David Axelrod, his political guru. "Maybe he would have run anyway," Axelrod said. "But when the leader asks you to run, that event added an element of seriousness to it, internally."

When Clinton read the story about the Obama meeting much later, she said she "didn't know what to believe. Because Harry also encouraged me. I haven't publicly talked about that because obviously, Harry could have encouraged both of us. We were both in his caucus. I knew that he respected me. And I had no reason to doubt that he was going to stay out of it since he was in an awkward position with [others in the caucus running or thinking about it]."

Clinton also pointed out that Reid's eldest son, Rory, helmed her campaign in Nevada, and she scoffed at the notion that Obama needed Reid's nudge.

"I don't think Barack needed much encouragement," Clinton deadpanned. "I think he was going to run from the moment he got elected senator. So I take that with kind of a grain of salt."

Reid, remembering his motivations in 2006 a decade and a half later, was blunt: "Of course, I love the Clintons. But I just felt that the country was ready for Obama."

REID ALSO SET the wheels in motion during 2006 for a dramatic change in Nevada's national influence when the Democratic National Committee decided to change which states would have an early say in nominating a presidential candidate.

Rebecca Lambe immediately saw what this could mean for Nevada. "So I went to Reid, I briefed him on the situation, I asked him if he'd be willing to be a part of a coalition of Western leaders," she said. "He would obviously be the most prominent because he was high in leadership."

Reid grasped how important this could be for Nevada—and clearly he and Lambe understood that it could help be a springboard to 2010, when he could face the most difficult reelection of his career.

The proposal eventually evolved into a matrix of four early states—two primaries and two caucuses. New Hampshire and South Carolina had primaries, so the Western entrant would have to be a caucus state along with Iowa. Nevada already was a caucus state—albeit a previously meaningless and poorly attended one—and it checked other boxes, too: a vibrant labor population and a burgeoning Hispanic population seen as critical to future Democratic wins.

In the spring of 2006, Nevada made its pitch to the DNC. Behind the scenes, Reid was as active as he could be, calling DNC members, labor leaders, and others to bolster Nevada's case. The state needed all his juice because establishment supporters of the status quo were caricaturing Nevada as a land of sex workers that would sully the party's image. But the man who learned to swim in a brothel and whose mother washed the prostitutes' clothes was undaunted.

The public and private efforts paid off in August when the DNC approved Nevada as the second nominating contest on January 19, only five days after Iowa. South Carolina would be fourth a week after New Hampshire's January 22 date.

IT DID NOT take long for the new majority leader to utter another one of his infamous Reidisms, one that caused his staff the most problems. It came in the spring of 2007 as the debate had intensified about the war in Iraq. Reid had voted for the war and, unlike others in his caucus, refused to apologize for it—at least not yet. The current conversation was whether the so-called surge was working, with criticism, especially on the Left, about continuing to have American troops in harm's way. Reid had become increasingly convinced that having troops in Iraq was a mistake. The House had just passed legislation to mandate troops withdraw within a year when Reid faced reporters and delivered his blunt assessment: "I believe myself [pointing to himself with his right hand] that the secretary of state, the secretary of defense—and you have to make your own decision as to what the president knows—that this war is lost, and that the surge is not accomplishing anything . . . I believe the war at this stage can only be won diplomatically, politically and economically."

Reid's distillation of his message to the president, however, became headlines around the world. Most media outlets led with his "war is lost" quote, generating instant GOP opprobrium.

Reid would later say he was only relying on what he had been told by General David Petraeus and others, that the war could not be won militarily. But it was too late. Newspaper commentators nationally and at home were savage.

The usually sedate and sober David Broder began his *Washington Post* column a week after Reid's comments with scathing words: "Here's a Washington political riddle where you fill in the blanks: As [former attorney general] Alberto Gonzales is to the Republicans, Blank Blank is to the Democrats—a continuing embarrassment thanks to his amateurish performance. If you answered 'Harry Reid' give yourself an A." Broder concluded: "The Democrats deserve better, and the country needs more, than Harry Reid has offered as Senate majority leader."

Schumer attempted damage control for Reid after the column, getting the entire caucus to sign a letter to the editor headlined "Sen. Reid's Fine Leadership." It read in part:

> In this age of scripted politicians speaking only to their base or claiming that they "don't recall" anything, the fact that Mr. Reid speaks his mind should be applauded, not derided. His brand of straight talk is honest, comes from the heart and speaks directly to the people.

Reid's candor or inability to self-edit or a combination thereof was unique in Capitol Hill political life, but it also took its toll on his standing with voters in Nevada. Now that he was the face of the Democrats in Washington, Reidisms were not just the focus of local newspapers but were highlighted nationally by Republican spinmeisters, who ensured the national media underscored Reid's remarks.

By October, Reid's numbers had dropped significantly, according to a *Review-Journal* poll. His favorable rating was only 32 percent and his unfavorable rating had risen above 51 percent, a potential death knell for any politician even three years away from an election.

REID MAY HAVE had his potentially problematic 2010 reelection in the back of his mind, but for most of 2007, he was thinking about 2008, the first early Nevada presidential caucus. The chance to influence a presidential race. The imperative of retaining the Senate.

Reid knew his relatively new title could easily disappear if he did not ensure that the Democrats did well in 2008. There was no Senate race in Nevada, but there was a target-rich environment elsewhere as twenty-three GOP seats were up. One region where the Democrats could do well was in the West, as the left-wing publication *Mother Jones* pointed out in its last issue of 2007. A piece headlined "How the West Might Be Won" focused on Nevada and argued that changing demographics in Reid's home state and elsewhere in the West—including Oregon, New Mexico, and Colorado, where Republican Senate seats were on the ballot—were an opportunity for Democrats to expand the Senate majority and win the White House.

Reid's number two, Dick Durbin, sent him the article, and Reid wrote back after reading it on October 26 in one of his handwritten missives:

> *Dear Dick,*
>
> *I do not subscribe to Mother Jones, a little to [sic] far left for someone who is as cautious as I am. But I do appreciate your sending me a copy of "How the West Might be Won." Even tho the magazine is really "way out" I thot that piece was informative and well written.*
>
> *P.S. I am more of a Wall Street Journal guy.*

By the time the calendar turned, Reid was being incautious—or so it seemed—about the Nevada presidential caucus. His prediction of a six-figure turnout seemed pie in the sky, especially since only a few thousand regularly voted in the caucus. But Reid's confidence would be borne out. By the time of the caucus, after Nevada had also secured its first-ever presidential debate, 114,000 Nevada Democrats turned out. Thirty thousand new Democratic voters registered that day in early 2008, the catalyst for an advantage that would inure to the Democrats' benefit for many years to come in Nevada and especially for Reid in 2010. It would change the nature of national politics, forcing presidential candidates to campaign in Nevada, where races would be indelibly affected by the result. It would also dramatically shift state politics, where Reid's Democratic machine would become a dominant force that would use that winter day in 2008 to begin to erect a voter firewall in populous Clark County that would serve the party—and him—very well.

The first early caucus also had a profound impact on the presidential race, a sign of cycles to come. Despite Barack Obama being endorsed by the powerful Culinary Union, Hillary Clinton won the balloting by five points after her husband helped her campaign and blunted the impact of union-dominated caucuses on the Las Vegas Strip. But in what would become an emblem for the contest, Obama's team understood the complex caucus delegate apportionment better and the Illinois senator took the most delegates from Nevada, erasing Clinton's momentum that had been the narrative since she won New Hampshire. Obama would build toward the nomination after Nevada, and by June, after he had secured it, Reid would endorse him and what he called his "historic campaign for president."

Few political acts Reid oversaw had as much long-lasting impact as his drive to make Nevada a player in presidential politics and to help Democrats cement a registration edge they would only relinquish to the Republicans, and only briefly, four years after his death. It also transformed Nevada from a reliably red state, nearly uninterrupted for forty years, to a blue one, no small feat and one with wide-ranging consequences. Reid didn't just change how the game was played in the race for the White House and up and down the state's ballot; he created an entirely new game with an unlevel playing field that he knew would favor his party and himself.

THE FRUITS OF the Reid-Lambe labors became clear in November 2008 when the Democrats swept to victory in Nevada. Obama won the state in a landslide, by thirteen points. Obama's victory was a statement for the machine Lambe had built for Reid, with the registration change now giving the Democrats a hundred-thousand-voter lead. The Democrats won the state's only swing congressional seat, took control of the state senate, and gained a supermajority in the assembly. The effect down the ticket was a blue wave that would be repeated, to varying degrees, in every subsequent presidential cycle until Donald Trump's three-percentage-point win in 2024, the first presidential cycle after Reid's death.

Nationally, Obama's victory over John McCain also helped the Democrats expand their majority in the Senate to a much more comfortable margin as they won virtually every contested seat, including those Western ones. The Democrats picked up eight seats, giving them a 58–41 edge with an unresolved election in Minnesota.

Reid was in a powerful position now in the Senate, with a near filibuster-proof majority to help the new president. His own numbers were still not good, but the only statewide Republican who seemed interested in challenging him was Brian Krolicki, the ambitious lieutenant governor.

Then, shortly after the 2008 election, news surfaced that the attorney general, Democrat Catherine Cortez Masto, was seeking to indict Krolicki for misusing funds to promote a college savings program when he was state treasurer. A legislative audit had found he flouted state laws, but the news of a possible indictment surprised almost everyone.

Krolicki immediately went on the offensive, saying his interest in the Senate race had prompted Cortez Masto to convene the grand jury, which was almost certain to indict him. "In Nevada, all Democratic partisan roads lead to Harry Reid," Krolicki said at a late November news conference. On

December 3, the indictment came, accusing Krolicki of four felonies. (They would eventually be dropped.)

Reid denied any involvement with the case. But the notion that he might have erased a potential foe by using an ally in the attorney general's office was a testament to his reputation as a Machiavellian politician.

Despite Reid's vulnerability, no major opponents were on the horizon as he prepared to run for a fifth term. His son Rory was thinking of running, too, against the now scandal-plagued Republican governor, Gibbons. A Reid-Reid top of the ticket seemed quite possible, with both of them potentially being favorites.

Reid also was basking in his relationship with the president-elect. He urged Obama to choose the vanquished Clinton as secretary of state, and when he did so and Clinton initially balked, Reid called her and encouraged her to do it, telling her she needed to fix what Dick Cheney had broken around the world. "Harry was very, very supportive, very, very encouraging," Clinton recalled.

Before he could completely focus on his campaign, Reid was about to enter the most eventful year of his career as the country teetered on the brink of a depression, the gaming industry faced potential collapse, and Obama decided to pursue two legislative initiatives—one to save the economy and one to change the health care system—that would test the majority leader's resolve and skills.

CHAPTER NINETEEN

THE YEAR OF LIVING DANGEROUSLY

On the Thursday after the 2008 election, Reid met with Connecticut senator Joe Lieberman, who had backed Republican John McCain's presidential candidacy and was now the object of the Democratic caucus's ire.

"'Joe, you know people are upset with you about the fact that you supported McCain and spoke at the Republican Convention,'" Reid began, as Lieberman recalled. "He said, 'Some of them want me to deny your seniority . . . I have to ask you to give up your chairmanship of Homeland Security.'"

Lieberman told Reid that he would not relinquish the chairmanship, nor would he take a substitute such as the Small Business Committee. "So he put his head down in that classic Harry way that to me, it felt like five minutes, it was probably ten seconds," Lieberman said. "And he looked up, and he said, 'Yeah, that's what I thought you would say. Okay, let's talk now about how we're going to defeat a motion in the caucus.'"

Reid made the calls to the caucus members, then he spoke against the motion to deny Lieberman's seniority. The vote was overwhelming, 42–13, to allow Lieberman to keep his status.

Kai Anderson, one of Reid's key staffers, remembered that the majority leader was willing to take short-term heat from the left for saving the sometimes pious senator from Connecticut because he was playing the long game: "[Reid] hated sanctimonious speeches, too, like it made him nuts. But he would not lay a glove on Joe Lieberman. And when you need sixty votes, he had sixty votes, just a career of like little chips being pushed into the bank, right? And then, and then what did he choose to spend it on? He spent it on Obamacare."

Before health care, though, Reid and the president would focus on saving the economy. During a series of private meetings over the next month with elected colleagues and cabinet officials, Reid helped negotiate a solution, albeit a controversial one. The meetings are outlined in a series of notes taken by one participant.

Reid would bring Obama's designated chief of staff, Rahm Emanuel, and the incoming president's chief economic adviser, Lawrence Summers, in with Democratic senators to talk to them about threading the needle between staving off a depression and not spending like drunken sailors, as Summers would put it.

Obama, according to meeting notes, was thinking at that time of a stimulus in the $675–$775 million range. Jason Furman, the chair of the new administration's council of economic advisers, told the caucus the total needed could be as much as $800 million to $1 trillion. The sticker shock on his caucus was obvious, but Reid believed that Furman's number was right. The majority leader knew he had to keep the number below $800 million to get Republican votes. He needed two. This was one of those times when he and the GOP leader Mitch McConnell would work together; the stakes were too high.

Obama attended one of the private gatherings and made the case: absent a recovery plan, three to four million more Americans would lose their jobs, the president-elect said.

McConnell assured the group that the Republicans wanted to be part of the process. House Minority Leader John Boehner emphasized a commitment to transparency. He said that the Troubled Asset Relief Program (TARP) passed in late 2008 to buttress the economy was done too quickly, that members should be allowed to offer amendments.

In another meeting, David Axelrod, who had helped Obama win the White House, presented a slide show designed to provide political cover. One of the slides showed that voter confidence in the incoming president was at 67 percent, the highest since Ronald Reagan. Some of Reid's members were still suffering from the TARP hangover and wanted to ensure that they didn't take a vote they would regret, especially if it did not pass.

On January 11, Reid called another special caucus and told the group, in a nutshell, according to notes from a participant: "Unchartered [*sic*] territory . . . new sheriff in town, have privilege to criticize but at least do so privately."

Just over a week later, on January 19, Reid had a conference call with Treasury Secretary Hank Paulson and Federal Reserve Chairman Ben Bernanke, both of whom reiterated to the majority leader the urgency of the situation. Paulson told Reid the credit markets were freezing up, while Bernanke said this was the worst financial crisis since World War II. Reid told the pair that he was generally supportive of what the administration was trying to do, but that plans had to be presented for Wall Street and Main Street.

On January 28, the House passed its version of the stimulus, an $819 billion bill, without one Republican vote. The next day, in another Senate Democratic caucus meeting, Max Baucus, the Democratic Finance Committee chair, expressed angst that health care reform was not being tackled first, that it would be diluted, wrapped up in other issues.

Emanuel, the incoming White House chief, came to admire Reid's method through many of these meetings trying to corral a few Republican votes, with the focus on Susan Collins, Olympia Snowe, and Arlen Specter. "I was locked up there with him, three consecutive days, countless hours," Emanuel recalled. "He would sit there, let everybody have their space to work, get to the bottom line."

That bottom line was $787 billion. Maine's Collins was the last domino to fall. Reid had wrangled the sixty votes necessary for passage and on February 13, the Senate did so. Obama signed the measure into law four days later.

The first crisis of 2009 was behind Reid, but the next one, much closer to home, was just around the corner.

IN EARLY 2009, the emirate of Dubai decided to stop contributing to the construction of a joint venture with MGM Resorts on the Las Vegas Strip called CityCenter. Before the recession, a group of international banks had committed $7 billion to the funding of the sprawling development. But with Queen Elizabeth ordering United Kingdom banks to stop lending outside her domain and Asian banks following similar policies, the project suddenly was in jeopardy—and with it, the future of Nevada's economic engine, the Las Vegas Strip.

The MGM Resorts chairman, Jim Murren, had tasked one man to help with the US banks who could give them a waiver to make a $200 million payment to the contractor, Perini Corporation.

"I went to Senator Reid," he recalled. "I explained the situation . . . There were [thousands of] construction workers working on site. We're the largest employer in the state, largest taxpayer in the state. And if MGM went under, you know, where would Nevada be? Where would the Las Vegas Strip be? Fifty thousand employees, representing over a hundred and fifty thousand lives if you think about their families. And so I gave him a list of the banks that were in our credit facility, JPMorgan, Bank of America. And he called every one of them, he called the CEOs. And when Senator Reid calls, people take that call."

Reid went to work soon after Murren approached him. Later his staff would try to whitewash what he did, saying he just asked the banks to give MGM a "fair shake," that Nevada's other senator, John Ensign, had also made calls. But Reid would later acknowledge exactly what he had done.

"No one in their right mind would have done what I did," he said. "I called presidents of banks, threatened them any way I could."

In one call Reid made to a midlevel executive at one of the banks, the bank staffer relayed the message he wanted passed up the chain: "He said, I want you to tell him that, for all the years of his life, [his company] has been the screwer. If he reverses himself on this decision and doesn't fund this project, I will spend the rest of my life making sure that [the company] is forever the screwee." Shortly thereafter, Reid hung up.

Murren had given Reid talking points about the importance of MGM to the Nevada economy, but he had no idea how far he had gone. "And then I got very annoying, very annoying messages from the banks," Murren said. "'We don't need some politician to call us to tell us what to do. You don't have to sic the dogs on us. You know, this is not constructive.' And I loved every bit of it, because he was clearly having an impact, whether it was annoying them, or shaming them, or at least bringing it to their attention, and it was a turning point."

Reid did more than just call the banks. He called the emir of Dubai. "I told him it would be very bad for his country to let this go, and he should do everything he can to move the project forward," Reid recalled. "He was very nice, but he didn't tell me if he would do it or not do it."

By March, it still didn't look good. MGM had purchased construction fencing to put around what was about to become a defunct project. Rumors about the end of the line were rife among the thousands of workers, and they were starting to percolate to the media. CityCenter would have to go into bankruptcy, with the parent company soon to follow. The end seemed near.

Murren was in his office on the Las Vegas Strip on the phone with one of the banks on the day the financial institutions were scheduled to vote on whether to help MGM make the $200 million payment. As he talked, Murren heard the noise above him. "I could hear the helicopters overhead, like vultures," he recalled. They were television station helicopters, providing video for the story that had dominated the news.

That day, the lenders—Morgan Stanley, Bank of America, Wells Fargo, JPMorgan, and Citibank—narrowly voted not to force the payments. The vote came in for MGM at 50.43 percent, about as close as a Harry Reid race, to keep the project alive.

"That moment was the moment that we saved CityCenter," Murren said.

In April, MGM and Dubai World announced a renewed commitment to the project. Reid had no regrets, no hesitation that he was just doing his job.

"Reid's view was this: If MGM doesn't get to finish this project, this is going to be a permanent scar on the Las Vegas Strip," recalled Jimmy Ryan, a top Reid aide for many years.

Today, CityCenter is a thriving Strip jewel, thanks to a US senator who did what no one else would have done.

DESPITE THE PAINFUL struggle to pass the stimulus bill, President Obama still wanted to press forward on health care. He had talked about it during his campaign, and the president thought that with the large majorities in both houses, it could be done. Reid, for whom the issue remained important after his terrible childhood health care experiences, was on board. He was eager to be the president's foot soldier and, along with Speaker Nancy Pelosi, pass a comprehensive bill.

Reid's top lieutenant, Chuck Schumer, was not sure the Democrats should proceed so quickly to health care. "My view was that there were things that maybe we could have done that might have been done easier," Schumer recalled. "Immigration reform we might have had, then it would have changed America, labor reform, getting unions better ability to vote, all of those things, when we had sixty or fifty-nine votes, we had real chances for. I thought health care would take a very long time. So I wanted us to do a few more things earlier, and then go to health care. But Harry said health care, and that was it."

Emanuel, Obama's chief of staff, also was skeptical after going through the health care wars during the Clinton era. He thought that those who had put the country in an economic tailspin needed to be held accountable. "I wanted to do financial reform first," Emanuel recalled. "I wanted some Old

Testament justice for bankers. It was about sequencing, show the public we were holding one of these interest groups accountable."

It was clear early on that getting the votes for health care reform would be more difficult than with the stimulus measure. The Republicans seemed dead-set and unified against voting for a health care bill, even long before it was introduced in July. Reid knew he would need sixty votes, and he only had fifty-eight. The Minnesota Senate race was still in limbo, and even if that one broke in favor of the Democrats, Reid would only have fifty-nine votes—one short of a filibuster-proof majority. That all changed in late April when Republican Arlen Specter of Pennsylvania switched parties. The Democrats now had enough votes to ward off a Republican filibuster, but the long road to passage was just beginning.

With almost no chance of Republican support, Reid had no margin for error. The majority leader also knew two things: First, some of his members were hardly sure votes and he would have to find a way to woo them. Second, Max Baucus, the Democratic Finance Committee chair, would take his time and potentially obstruct what the president and Reid wanted to do.

"Max could be very hard to deal with," Reid said. "He was temperamental. I knew I couldn't jam him. So I made the decision to give him all the time I needed for him to believe that he had some hand in passing it, which he did. But he kept thinking he could do a deal with [Chuck] Grassley [the ranking GOP member] from Iowa, but Grassley never would have agreed. But they had meeting after meeting after meeting. I knew they couldn't get together on it, but I gave him all that time to make sure he felt invested in the program."

Durbin remembered how frustrating it was for Reid and the leadership team, as Baucus held more than thirty meetings on the bill to try to get consensus. "Everybody wanted to get on with the business of the new president and get this bill passed," Durbin recalled. "And we're waiting, patiently waiting . . . maybe too patiently."

It was frustrating for the White House, too, but as a Reid staffer pointed out, the majority leader was trying to hold together a fragile coalition.

"There was no choice because the only way you could keep all the Democrats together was to run every bipartisan [idea] to the ground," the aide said. "And that took time . . . We had to keep all of our moderates in the wheelbarrow."

But it was not just the moderates or conservatives whom Reid needed to get to sixty votes. He had to make sure that left-wing Democrats, especially Bernie Sanders, were on board and that a group of pro-choice female senators thought that abortion was attended to in the final package. His cobbling together of votes also was complicated by the absence of Ted Kennedy, who had been diagnosed with a brain tumor in 2008. Reid asked Connecticut's Chris Dodd, Kennedy's good friend, to oversee the bill's passage through a committee that the ailing Massachusetts senator usually chaired, the Committee on Health, Education, Labor, and Pensions.

By summer, with bills introduced in the House and Senate, progress was slow and Reid had to deal with impatience on Pennsylvania Avenue. But the president also realized that once he handed off the measure to Reid, he had to let the majority leader do what he couldn't—or wouldn't—do, and that was get the votes.

"In order for us to get the votes we needed, Harry had to be able to corral a number of Democrats who—how can I say this artfully?—thought in fairly transactional terms, and who were not going to be persuaded by a bunch of policy arguments from me or my health care team," Obama said shortly after Reid died.

This was when all the relationships Reid had carefully cultivated through the years and cemented during those long hours on the Senate floor as whip paid dividends—literally for some of his colleagues, as Reid essentially tried to buy their votes. He understood what his colleagues wanted and needed better than anyone.

A case in point, as Reid recalled, was Sanders, the obstreperous independent senator from Vermont.

"I knew to get the Affordable Care Act passed, I had to have Bernie because even back then he controlled a lot of the progressive movement in the country," Reid said. So the majority leader summoned Sanders to his office and said, "Bernie, I need you to pass the Affordable Care Act, so tell me what you need." Sanders returned a few days later and told Reid about something "I had never heard of before. Community health centers . . . It was a place where the poor can go to get health care. And I really was impressed with the presentation [by a community health care expert Sanders brought to the meeting]. So my staff did some work on this. And I called him back. And I told Bernie to come on over. I said, Bernie, I'm going to get some community health centers. I'm gonna give you $25 billion for it." (The final number actually was $10 billion.)

But that was just the beginning of the transactions Reid would have to negotiate to get the bill passed, and the hardest part was yet to come because the public was hardly on the Democrats' side.

AS THE SUMMER wore on, the Democrats increasingly were losing the public relations battle. Baucus had the bill bottled up in his committee as the Republicans and their allies used their platforms and ad campaigns to try to persuade Americans that the bill was a dangerous government takeover of health care policy. Reid was not cowed and by midsummer, he was saying a bill was coming before Labor Day and would include a public option. He told a meeting of Nevada's chapter of AARP, "The American people support a public plan, and before this is over, we'll have one." Reid also told the group, echoing Obama, that the bill would be through both houses by the August recess.

Reid's bravado to a friendly group notwithstanding, the majority leader knew he did not have the necessary sixty votes. By the time the August break loomed, public support diminished even more, partly because former Republican vice presidential candidate Sarah Palin had pushed the notion that the bill provided "death panels" that would decide whether a person is worthy of health care. The term immediately caught the attention of the American public, or at least a significant portion of it.

The Democrats were dealt an emotional and mathematical blow on August 25 when Kennedy succumbed to his brain tumor, leaving them a vote short. An interim senator, Paul Kirk, would eventually be appointed, but a special election would decide Kennedy's successor in January 2010. It was hard to imagine a Democrat would lose in Massachusetts, but Kennedy's death shook the caucus.

By the time senators returned after Labor Day, the climb had become much steeper after members had been pummeled at town halls by voters worried about not just the death panels but other aspects of the legislation, too. The public option, which would allow the government to compete with private companies, was especially nettlesome.

With too many voters persuaded that the bill was "government-run health care" and little chance any Republican would support a measure with a public option component, Baucus supported excising the government-run plan Reid had sounded so confident about a few months earlier. The committee, with some Democrats voting against the public option, rejected two proposals, one by West Virginia's Jay Rockefeller and the other by Schumer. Baucus voted against both amendments on September 29.

Two weeks later, on October 13, the Senate Finance Committee, after months of deliberations and dozens of meetings, finally passed the health care bill without a public option by a 14–9 vote. Olympia Snowe, the moderate Republican from Maine, voted for the measure. But Reid knew that Snowe's vote had not increased his margin for error because she declared that she reserved the right to change her vote on final passage.

Just two days after the measure moved out of the finance panel, Reid was scheduled to meet with Schumer when he received a startling email from his deputy chief of staff, David Krone, with instructions not to show it to anyone:

> I know Senator Schumer is your close friend but he is not helping your re-election. What he has done over and over again is undermine you with the progressive community. His comments concerning how you could put

> a public option in the merged bill and force 60 votes to remove it leads the progressive community to believe that anything short of that is weakness on your part . . . Chuck Schumer has turned himself into the hero of the left at your expense . . . By undermining you with the progressives Schumer is forcing you to move to the left. We shouldn't have to do that. The left should be our base as we head into 2010. Instead we now have to pacify them simply to keep them on board. . . .
>
> Now, if we include a public option in the merged bill it looks like we did so only to appease the left (at Schumer's urging). When we fail to get 60 votes to proceed then you look weak and everybody will not give us any credit for trying.

Reid, ever terse, responded four minutes later to his chief of staff: "With friends like him do I need enemies?"

REID KNEW HE had to keep momentum building for the bill, so he decided to schedule a vote on amendments for early December, right after the Thanksgiving recess. Barbara Mikulski, who had been working on a women's health amendment to the Affordable Care Act, was sipping her coffee the morning after the holiday, savoring her previous day's dinner with her family, when the phone rang. It was Reid.

"'Well, you got to get ready,'" Mikulski remembered Reid began. "'You're going to be the lead-off speaker' . . . I said, 'Harry, it's Monday, I've got to get it together . . . Harry says, 'You're as ready as you'll ever be. Just do it. I'm counting on you to take the floor . . . bang!' He had hung up. And with Harry, you never got to finish a thought, a sentence, and forget about a paragraph."

Mikulski gathered her staff together and worked feverishly the rest of the holiday weekend to put together her presentation. On Monday, she was ready to present her plan to eliminate copays and deductibles on preventative screenings, among other provisions to make health care more affordable and accessible for women seeking mammograms and other procedures.

Mikulski insisted to Reid that only women in the caucus speak for the amendment and that the men who supported her should wear pink ties to show solidarity. "We were a sea of pink, we were armed and ready to go," Mikulski recalled. "And that's how the debate began. And Harry placed every resource of his office at my disposal to move that amendment."

Reid had predicted correctly that Alaska's Republican senator, Lisa Murkowski, would offer an alternative to the Mikulski amendment, and the debate went on for a few days before the Democratic version prevailed, 61–39.

News reports pointed out that the sixty-one votes included at least three members who might not vote for the final legislation, naming Lieberman and Louisiana's Mary Landrieu on the Democratic side and Olympia Snowe on the Republican side. Reid believed he had Landrieu's vote after offering her hundreds of millions of dollars in Medicaid funding for her impoverished state, a deal later derisively nicknamed the "Louisiana Purchase." Landrieu would fiercely defend the decision and the need for the money while Reid, when questioned and accused of bribing a colleague, would recite some shibboleth about compromise being the coin of the realm.

He was still not at a certain sixty votes for final passage, especially with the public option back on the table.

ON DECEMBER 13, Lieberman almost made Reid regret letting him back into the caucus after his McCain '08 transgression. The Connecticut senator, who had privately expressed grave concerns about having a public option in the final bill, was slated to be on *Face the Nation*. Before he went on the program, he made up his mind to go public: "I finally decided that the hell with it, I'm going on *Face the Nation* one Sunday morning . . . and I'm just going to say that I'm not gonna vote for the bill if the public option is in."

As Lieberman left the CBS studio, the phone in his car rang; it was Reid.

"He said, 'Did you just say you wouldn't vote for cloture if the public option is in?'" Lieberman recalled. "I said, 'Harry. That's what I've been telling you and Schumer for the last two or three months. I mean, I wrote it in an op-ed piece.'"

The majority leader asked Lieberman whether he would meet him in his office later, and Lieberman agreed. Reid then called his whip, Dick Durbin, who was putting up wallpaper at his home and had not been watching television. "He [Reid] said, 'Joe Lieberman just came out against the public option,'" Durbin said. "'We have exactly sixty votes,' he said, 'it's [the public option] gone. We're not gonna waste any more time on it.'"

When Lieberman arrived in Reid's office on that mid-December Sunday, Emanuel and Durbin were there, too. Reid began, as Lieberman remembered it.

"So Harry said, 'Knowing you really feel strongly about this, you won't vote for the cloture if the public option is in. And I told him why. And then Rahm said, 'If we take it out, will you support the bill?' I said, 'Enthusiastically. I've been for it from the beginning.'"

The public option died at that meeting. Reid had showed Emanuel the president would have to accept it, lest they lose Lieberman's vote. They were not going to get any Republicans, so the public option would go.

Reid had to tell his caucus the bad news, and he knew it couldn't wait. He called Lieberman the next day. "So Harry calls me on the Monday, the day after, and says, 'I gotta call a caucus this afternoon to deal with this, because the liberals are so upset,'" Lieberman recalled. "'I want you to come and it's not gonna be comfortable for you. You don't have to speak. I just want you to be there.'"

Lieberman told the majority leader, "It's okay. Of course, I owe it to you. I'll be there."

At that meeting, Reid, who had loved to brag about having won a hundred jury trials, brought all of his skills to bear. "They all say he wasn't Cicero, he wasn't William Jennings Bryan," Lieberman said. "But he was a litigator, he knew how to make a case to a judge or a jury. And he said, 'I know you're upset with our friend, Joe Lieberman, about the public option. And I don't agree with him on this myself. But we need his vote to get the rest of this bill done. And the president and I feel that we have got to just delay the public option for another day, because we have an opportunity to get something really important done . . . And he was brilliant. And it ended. I can't say a lot of colleagues came over and hugged me and said, 'We love you.' But really, that was the end of the rebellion."

It was not, however, the end of the climb to sixty votes for the majority leader.

REID, WHO WANTED to pass a bill by Christmas, still had not secured the vote of Ben Nelson, the conservative Democratic senator from Nebraska. That state's governor, Dave Heineman, had said publicly the Medicaid expansion would bust his budget. Nelson went to Reid, who eventually agreed to include a waiver in the bill for the federal government to pick up the cost of Nebraska's share. This, of course, was not granted to other states and became known as "the Cornhusker Kickback."

But that was not all Nelson wanted in exchange for his vote for Obamacare. He wanted to make sure that there was strict language in the bill, as there was in the House version, that prevented any federal funds from being used to subsidize abortions.

This was an issue Reid tried to thread his entire career as a pro-life Mormon who nevertheless had to support the pro-choice women in his caucus, so he decided not to handle this negotiation himself. As a snowstorm descended on the capital, he let Barbara Boxer and Patty Murray negotiate with Nelson, with Schumer as the emissary. Boxer and Murray were stationed for a couple of days in Reid's majority leader suite, coming up with proposals to mollify Nelson.

Recalled Murray: "Once more, we come down to some of the most important issues of the day and choice is the last issue to be decided and you got people in the room on both sides and, Harry, to his credit, was not going to make the decision for our caucus. He was going to allow Barbara Boxer and I to negotiate a deal with that."

Pro-choice groups were upset about the bargaining with Nelson, but Boxer brushed them back because of the overall importance of health care reform. "They didn't like any of this," Boxer said. "But I said, this bill is not going down because of abortion. We have to come up with something."

The negotiations were protracted as the storm raged outside, and Schumer occasionally had to shovel snow to pave the way to Nelson's office.

"We were in his office late at night, long hours exchanging information, tough conversations," Murray recalled. "And he [Reid] didn't get in the middle of it. But he certainly knew what was going on and was really pushing us to come to a solution. And what I respected about him was he was going to back whatever we came up with, but he was not going to allow us to walk out of that room without coming up with this solution."

When they finally agreed to a workaround—an evasion of the ban to allow a woman to make a separate payment for abortion on a credit card and allow the states to decide whether they wanted to offer abortion coverage under Obamacare—Nelson came over to Reid's suite of offices. "We hugged and it was so amazing," Boxer said. "And what if Harry had given up, okay? Or if Harry said, 'Look, take it or leave it, women, you just can't get it. Period, give it up?' You know, I don't know what would have happened."

Reid now had enough votes committed to shut down a Republican filibuster, and the legislation finally came to a vote on December 24, 2009. Reid would point out that it was the first time in 150 years that the Senate had convened on Christmas Eve.

The vote, as expected, was along party lines.

In a handwritten note he penned that evening to Reid, Chris Dodd recognized the enormity of the moment and paid homage to his late friend Teddy Kennedy, who had said "health care was the cause of my life" and whose widow was on hand:

> Thank you for having the confidence in me to assist in this journey. We are about to alter the way in which America treats her people in ways unimaginable. Nothing will ever be the same again. To lift a financial or physical

burden from one's shoulder is one thing. To lift fear—rational fear—from one's burden is historic. With Teddy's passing in mind, I thank you for including me in this monumental result.

Not all considered it so monumental. *The Post*'s David Broder, who had already expressed a lack of respect for how Reid conducted himself as leader, wrote a blistering column.

"Forced to bargain for every vote among the 60 in his caucus, Majority Leader Harry Reid did what he usually does: He reduced the negotiations to his own level of transactional morality. Incapable of summoning his colleagues to statesmanship, he made the deals look as crass and parochial as many of them were—encasing a historic achievement in a wrapping of payoff and patronage."

Reid didn't much care. He was going to celebrate Christmas and then return to work out differences between the Senate legislation and a House bill that had passed with one Republican vote a month earlier. But first, the road to passage would get bumpy again in a surprising way.

ON JANUARY 19, 2010, as House and Senate negotiators were trying to find common ground on their health care bills, an electoral temblor in Massachusetts changed the calculus. In a stunning upset to fill Ted Kennedy's seat, a Republican, Scott Brown, who had campaigned against the Democrats' health care reform, defeated Democrat Martha Coakley. Suddenly, Harry Reid was one vote short of passing a merged bill out of the Senate.

To make matters worse, Speaker Nancy Pelosi was appalled with what the Senate had passed, the Frankensteinian cobbling together of parts so they could get to sixty. Despite pressure from the White House, Pelosi wasn't simply going to roll over and pass the Senate bill.

"The bill was terrible," she said in late 2021. "I wouldn't have even voted for it, much less asked my members to vote for it . . . Harry may think it was better than it was. Terrible. The president said, 'This is all we can get in the Senate.' I said, 'I didn't come here for that, all we can get from the Senate.'"

Pelosi and some of her members were upset about various aspects of the measure, and she had a long-earned disdain for how the Senate conducted its business. She thought her members knew much more about the actual policy than the preening members of the Club of 100, who were eager to make deals to pass the bill, thus polluting its contents. As much as she respected, even liked, Reid, she had no regard for the process by which the bill had passed on Christmas Eve. The negotiations over how to pass the measure after Brown was elected caused the only time that Reid and Pelosi had what she called "a moment." Pelosi told Reid that she could not support billions of dollars in the Senate bill paid for with a tax on medical devices, which she insisted on removing.

"Harry flipped his lid," she recalled. "'How dare you take this out?' The only time I ever had words with Harry."

Because Reid only had fifty-nine votes, he and Pelosi decided to use a process called reconciliation to change the Senate bill. That method, which had been used many times over the years by both parties, would only require a majority vote and could not be filibustered, so Reid had plenty of breathing room. By late February, it became clear that was what the Democrats planned to do, much to the consternation of Republicans and other foes who had been celebrating Obamacare's death after Brown's victory.

Pelosi had secured an agreement from Reid that he would have fifty-one votes to pass the changes her members wanted, and he went the extra mile and prepared a letter with the fifty-one names. "He brought it to me," Pelosi said of the letter. "And for some reason, it must have been being a Catholic or something, I said, 'I trust you, Harry, you don't have to give it to me.'"

By the time the House voted on the amended bill on March 21, Ben Nelson's so-called Cornhusker Kickback had been removed. He did not vote for the final package—and Reid no longer needed his vote. The House and the Senate passed the new bill within days of each other in late March, without a single Republican vote, and Obama signed the legislation on March 23 after a raucous celebration with House members and senators in which he heaped praise on Reid and Pelosi.

Reid was elated, even though polling showed the new law was far from popular, nor was he back home. His nemesis Sherman Frederick, the *Review-Journal* publisher, who regularly pummeled Reid in his weekly column, already had predicted Reid would lose. "The end's a-comin', Harry, one way or another," he had written in January 2010, suggesting the majority leader would not file because he knew he could not win.

Two weeks before he took a victory lap on the Affordable Care Act, though, Reid filed his candidacy for reelection.

CHAPTER TWENTY

THE RIGHT ANGLE

At the beginning of 2010, Reid was a dead man walking. His poll numbers were in the tank. The president's approval rating also had fallen from the high of his inaugural to 50 percent and was on its way to the forties. The Affordable Care Act, which Reid and Obama considered a spectacular legislative triumph, was not seen so favorably by the American public. Brandon Hall, who had been hired by Rebecca Lambe to manage the reelection campaign in early 2009 after he helped elect Sen. Mark Begich in Alaska, had spent the first six months of his tenure trying to keep people out of the race. A top-tier candidate would almost surely be a favorite, even a prohibitive one against a senator damaged from years on the legislative battlefield.

They were most worried about Dean Heller, who had replaced Jim Gibbons in Congress, so Hall and others put out the word that any money given to Heller would be considered a donation against Reid. They also made it clear, through Freedom of Information requests to Heller's office, that they were going to play hardball. Ultimately, Heller would not run, perhaps partly because of a Republicans for Reid group that had marquee names from Wayne Newton to Republican kingmaker Sig Rogich to the first lady of Nevada, Dawn Gibbons.

Reid, though, had a likely foe in Sue Lowden, a former anchorwoman and state senator, who was ahead of Reid in some late 2009 polls and whose husband's casino career Reid had made possible when he was a regulator. Rep. Mark Amodei also had announced; there was blood in the water, although the congressman would soon decide discretion was the better part of going up against the Reid buzzsaw. The senator's campaign knew Lowden could be formidable; some Democrats even thought she would probably win.

What's more, the state's largest and theoretically most influential newspaper was on a mission to defeat Reid. The senator had, in his inimitable way, poked the bear in late August 2009 by saying to the *Review-Journal*'s advertising director, Bob Brown, at a public event: "I hope you go out of business." That allowed Frederick to ignore the obvious, albeit clumsy, Reid attempt at humor and put himself on the cross in one of his many anti-Reid columns, headlined "Enough Is Enough, Harry."

Thus would begin a nonstop blizzard of columns, blog posts, and editorials from the *Review-Journal*, with the editor Tom Mitchell occasionally chiming in with his own anti-Reid screeds, as the newspaper further stacked the long odds against a Reid fifth term. Reid's friend, fundraiser, and ally Brian Greenspun at the *Sun* intermittently defended the senator from the *Review-Journal* attacks, but his paper was not nearly as well read. The Great Las Vegas Newspaper War was not just a sidelight to the 2010 US Senate race; it was in the foreground, constant.

If nothing else, Team Reid was going to be prepared. Greenspun had hosted a campaign meeting the previous August at his media group's headquarters in Henderson, a four-hour conclave in which fundraisers, pollsters, opposition research experts, field operatives, and consultants weighed in. They had changed the registration dynamic with the early caucus in 2008 and an eye toward Reid's reelection—the Democratic lead was above eighty thousand at the end of 2009. Also, Reid's lieutenant Rebecca Lambe had overseen a move in the legislative session to push back the primary from September to June, so Reid's team would have more time to improve their chances and try to destroy whomever the Republicans nominated. The

Republicans for Reid group was also a useful hammer whose membership would continue to swell, a product of Reid's decades of cultivating unlikely friendships and quietly accumulating due bills. He would eventually woo arguably the most powerful Republican in Nevada, the state senate majority leader, Bill Raggio, onto that list (and Raggio would lose his leadership position because of the endorsement). Reid also tried to get Paul Laxalt to join, but that was a nonstarter. The number, though, would move into the dozens and send a powerful message.

But all of this seemed to many observers in Nevada and in Washington as piling up sandbags against a midterm red wave that would surely wash over Nevada.

One of the first things Hall had done when he came on board was to build a research team, one designed to not just delve into Lowden and any other possible opponent but also track their every public appearance for possible fodder. Heading it up was Matt Fuehrmeyer, who had worked for the Democratic Senatorial Campaign Committee and Tom Daschle. Reid himself was a de facto member of the research team, whispering to the campaign, inveterate gossip that he was, every rumor he had heard about a potential foe. He wanted no stone left unturned, no blade of grass left uncut.

Reid's aides knew the election had to be a choice between him and someone the campaign beat to a pulp, not a referendum on his record. That frustrated the senator to no end, bothered him to his core that voters did not give him credit for what he had done for Nevada. But he understood and accepted the political realities. The staff would show him polling that, even after voters were informed of all he had done, the numbers did not move. Some inside the campaign wanted to use the slogan "Harry Reid, a powerful voice for Nevada," but he nixed that, saying his soft-spoken demeanor would be dissonant with the idea.

Danny Tarkanian, the son of the legendary UNLV basketball coach Jerry Tarkanian, Sharron Angle, an ultraconservative former assemblywoman, and Lowden, the state Republican Party chair, were all in by year's end. Lowden was generally considered the best candidate on paper, and a

Review-Journal poll in December 2009 showed her with a ten-percentage-point lead in the primary. There was possibly a clue she was better in theory when she went on a right-wing radio talk show in November and cavalierly implied, along with the host, that the attempt to rig Reid's car with a bomb thirty years earlier had never occurred. The Reid campaign immediately released the police report from 1981. This was both a sign of Lowden's potential weakness as a candidate and the smashmouth Reid rapid response campaign.

Going into 2010, Reid also had to deal with another albatross, which was that his son Rory had decided to run for governor.

Some of the senator's political advisers thought this would be a large impediment to the majority leader's reelection. Having two Reids on the ballot would spark talk of dynasties, another straw that could break the camel's back. Rory Reid told people he believed that his father was not going to run again, perhaps hearing what he wanted to hear when his father and mother encouraged him to run for governor if he wanted to.

Landra Reid would later say her husband never considered not seeking a fifth term despite his approval ratings and what looked like a Sisyphean endeavor. Neither Reid nor Landra tried to dissuade Rory from running—"He would never tell him not to run," Landra said—and later the senator would tell an aide he understood why his team tried (unsuccessfully) to nudge the younger Reid out of the race.

AS IF REID didn't have enough problems as he entered his reelection year, the hole became deeper early in 2010. Late on January 9, a Friday evening, the revelation appeared on the *Atlantic* website that in a conversation with the authors Mark Halperin and John Heilemann for their forthcoming book, *Game Change*, Reid explained why he had encouraged Barack Obama to run for president. The Illinois senator was a "light-skinned" African American who had "no Negro dialect, unless he wanted to have one," Reid had told the authors in an interview for their just-published book.

Years later, Reid staffers would insist the senator made the comments off the record, that he never would have said that for publication, as if that mitigated it. But this was a Reidism for the ages, and the senator would not deny he had said it. Over that weekend it would become a media sensation.

Reid almost immediately called the president to apologize. But, Obama would say in 2022, he had "very little reaction" when Reid came on the line.

"I immediately when he called said, 'Harry, don't worry about it. We got bigger things to worry about,'" Obama remembered. "Look, Harry was a man of his generation, born in a particular place in time . . . Harry was twenty years older than me, born in Searchlight. And for me to expect that somehow his entire life experience up until then, it was no longer politically acceptable to say 'Negro,' that, to me, that would be missing the big picture."

Reid, too, would cite his Searchlight upbringing, the town without any residents of color, to explain what he called an "impulsive" remark. "Remember, I wasn't raised in a cosmopolitan area. I was raised in Searchlight, Nevada. I married my wife (who was Jewish . . . but if I hadn't), I hope I wouldn't have been an anti-Semite. But people in Searchlight were anti-everything."

That explanation notwithstanding, Reid knew that damage control would be necessary by Saturday morning. It could not have been lost on either man that Obamacare was still hanging in the balance—it would not pass for another two months—and they could ill afford any fissure to widen. So Reid immediately assembled some of his closest advisers on a conference call.

"He said, 'It's a 9-1-1,'" recalled Megan Jones, a top confidant. "He said, 'This is coming out in the book. I already talked to Obama and he's fine. I said it. You're gonna have to do all the damage control.' Then he said goodbye without saying goodbye," the usual abrupt Reid click-off.

What Jones remembered, too, was that it was "one of the only times I can remember him saying, 'I made a mistake. I didn't remember. I'm really sorry.'"

For the next twenty-four hours, Jones and two other Reid aides, Darrel Thompson and Mary Connelly, split up the contacts list and delivered a message that varied a little but essentially was: "He didn't really mean to say it. He has talked to the president. He's willing to sit down with you and talk about things but remember his list of accomplishments within your community. His history is long, and his loyalty is demonstrated."

Reid himself called a slew of people, too, mostly civil rights leaders such as Al Sharpton and congressional colleagues such as South Carolina representative James Clyburn. His staff also had a Reid statement ready for the deluge of media inquiries: "I deeply regret using such a poor choice of words. I sincerely apologize for offending any and all Americans, especially African Americans, with my improper comments."

They coordinated with the White House for an Obama statement as well: "I accepted Harry's apology without question because I've known him for years, I've seen the passionate leadership he's shown on issues of social justice and I know what's in his heart. As far as I am concerned, the book is closed."

Of course, the book was just opening on an already difficult campaign. Republicans immediately called for Reid to step down as leader. Lowden said the comment was another in a long line of embarrassing comments Reid had made. "It's time to stop making excuses for Harry Reid," Frederick, the *Review-Journal* publisher, agreed.

The newspaper's latest poll showed Reid with an approval rating of only 33 percent and forecast he would lose to all Republicans mentioned as foes. Even some inside the campaign thought the revelation might be fatal. But Reid would not abandon his campaign for a fifth term in the Senate.

DESPITE REID RAISING more money than any candidate in Nevada history—$15 million pledged and $9 million on hand—most national oddsmakers rated the Nevada Senate seat as a toss-up.

The Reid campaign was almost singularly focused on Lowden. The Reidites saw on paper a nearly perfect candidate to end the senator's career, so they began going after her and tracking her every public move. In early January 2010, at a campaign meeting, the message was clear, as Fuehrmeyer remembered it: "The general election starts today, we're gonna open up the book on Sue Lowden, and we're just gonna start unloading on her. And we did."

The campaign dumped some opposition research to the media, including that Paul Lowden had taken a large bonus while laying off casino employees—but Reid's numbers were not moving, even after President Obama came to visit. Soon afterward, the *Review-Journal* published a poll that showed Reid losing by thirteen percentage points to Lowden and eleven percentage points to Tarkanian. No one was paying attention to Angle, who languished at 8 percent in the survey for the primary, with Lowden ahead of Tarkanian by eighteen points, 47–29. The election in June was still months away, but it was difficult to see Lowden, who had begun buying TV time, as anything but a solid favorite to become a US senator. The Republican establishment in Nevada and Washington, DC, was giddy.

National and local Republicans, though, were concerned with a potential third-party candidate, Scott Ashjian, who was carrying the banner for the newly filed Tea Party of Nevada—they believed he was a Reid plant to siphon votes from the nominee, something Team Reid would never confirm or deny.

Reid's annus horribilis got even worse on March 12 when Landra and his only daughter, Lana Barringer, were involved in a horrific car accident on a Virginia highway. Barringer suffered relatively minor injuries but her mother broke her neck and back. A week later, she would have surgery to stabilize her spine, with speculation percolating anew that Reid would not run again because of his wife's injuries.

"The only time I ever saw Harry cry was when he told me Landra had an awful car accident and had broken so many bones," Chuck Schumer recalled. "He said over and over again, as tears streamed down his cheeks, 'My poor little Landra. My poor little Landra.'"

Landra would, as always, be resilient. She was released from the hospital only a few days after the accident, and Reid declared that she would make a full recovery, quelling any rumor-milling about his retirement.

ON APRIL 6, a Reid campaign aide, Paul Smith, was sent to Mesquite, a small community about eighty miles northeast of Las Vegas, to tape a Lowden event with a group called Friends of the Founding Fathers. The gathering was relatively small, and Smith feared he might get booted by the Lowden campaign or the organizers. But no one approached him, and he captured the Republican frontrunner's interactions with the crowd without interruption.

Not surprisingly, Lowden had been using Obamacare, which was still unpopular a month after it was signed into law, as a bludgeon against Reid. (Reid, unlike most Democrats, was airing ads touting his support for the health care reform.)

After hyping health savings accounts as an alternative, Lowden raised another possibility if the Affordable Care Act were repealed: "Those doctors who you pay cash, you can barter, and that would get prices down in a hurry. And I would say go out, go ahead out and pay cash for whatever your medical needs are, and go ahead and barter with your doctor."

Smith thought the snippet would make for a nice "out of touch" hit on the wealthy Lowden, and he called Reid's research director, Fuehrmeyer, to tell him what he had. The research director thought it was worth transcribing—he wanted to see the video—but he didn't think it was game-changing. "We knew we had something good when we got that; we didn't realize how much better she was going to make it," Fuehrmeyer recalled.

There wasn't much local interest in the video, so on April 12, the campaign's press secretary, Kelly Steele, reached out to Eric Kleefeld, a reporter with the liberal site Talking Points Memo, to gauge his interest in what he slugged his email as: "Nutty NV Sen clip."

Kleefeld published the video and two days later, Jay Leno mocked the idea of bartering on *The Tonight Show*, mentioning (and misspelling) Lowden's name but wondering how that would work "if your doctor is not

Amish." Still, though, there was not much pickup anywhere else; the story's legs seemed broken.

Then, a week after Kleefeld first published the video, the entire campaign changed. The Republican frontrunner went on a Reno-based television program called *Nevada Newsmakers* that was cohosted by Marlene Lockard, a lobbyist and former top aide to Reid's old friend Richard Bryan. Lockard asked Lowden about the bartering comment, and the candidate not only reaffirmed her support for bartering but used an unfortunate analogy that would soon become known far and wide:

"You know, before we all started having health care, in the olden days our grandparents, they would bring a chicken to the doctor, they would say I'll paint your house. I mean, that's the old days of what people would do to get health care with your doctors. Doctors are very sympathetic people. I'm not backing down from that system."

A few feet away in the studio, a couple of Lowden campaign aides looked at the floor. They knew.

Meanwhile, Team Reid watched from campaign headquarters. "[We] were just dumbfounded, utterly dumbfounded," Smith said. They also knew what they had, which was a chance to make Lowden the object of ridicule, which is often much worse for electoral prospects than being the object of criticism. "Seriously, Has Sue Lowden Lost Her Mind?" was the headline on a Reid campaign release the next morning.

If the issue had just been about bartering, which is not uncommon in rural America, Lowden might have survived it. Or if she had simply said she was using the chicken analogy as an example and it was not viable today, she might have survived. But out of stubbornness or arrogance, she refused to back down and the Reid campaign squeezed every ounce of free media they could get while a third-party group run by a former Reid aide, Patriot Majority, began running ads. National newspapers and cable shows ran pieces on "chickens for checkups." The Nevada Democratic Party, controlled by Lambe, brought a goat to Lowden's headquarters to trade—having tipped a TV station it was coming. The party also began having a person dressed as a chicken attend various events to keep the issue alive. The mockery was everywhere.

Later that year, when the staff celebrated campaign manager Brandon Hall's birthday, they presented him a cake with icing decorated from a cartoon by the *Review-Journal*'s Jim Day that featured Sue Lowden with a thought bubble not emanating from her mouth but, like a knife, piercing her torso: ". . . bring a chicken to the doctor."

REID'S CAMPAIGN DID not think "chickens for checkups" had ended Lowden's chances in the primary, but because it happened less than two months before the June 8 balloting, they thought it might have weakened her. What their ads and free media had not accomplished, Lowden had done to herself. The internal instructions to Reid staffers were simple: don't lay a glove on Angle. They believed if the far-right assemblywoman were to somehow win, her extremism could save Reid.

Polling began to show Lowden coming back to the field and Angle surging, partly thanks to a seven-figure influx of money from the Club for Growth, an influential and moneyed conservative organization. A *Review-Journal* poll in mid-May, only a couple of weeks before the June 8 primary, showed Lowden at 30 percent, Angle at 25 percent, and Tarkanian at 22 percent. The pollster for the newspaper also showed Reid now running within the margin of error against any of the Republicans.

On June 2, First Lady Michelle Obama went to Las Vegas to do an event for Reid, who caught sight of *Nevada Newsmakers* cohost Marlene Lockard at the event. "All of a sudden, I had a tap on my shoulder, and it was Harry," she recalled. "And he looked at me and he had this big old grin, and he stuck out his hand and gave me a big old handshake."

That same day, the *Review-Journal* poll showed Angle had taken the lead—32 percent to 24 percent for Tarkanian and 23 percent for Lowden. By then, the Reid folks knew Angle was going to win. With the names of all who had voted downloadable, the campaign was robocalling and asking whom they had voted for. The results showed Angle was ahead by thirteen percentage points. They had planned on a rural Nevada digital effort to hurt Lowden that weekend, but after seeing those numbers, they demurred. Hall told Reid that Angle had it locked up. "He thought I was crazy," Hall recalled. "He didn't believe it."

Two days later, Angle celebrated a smashing victory, garnering 40 percent of the vote. Lowden was second with 26 percent, a precipitous and stunning fall from frontrunner status, and Tarkanian finished with 23 percent.

Team Reid was nothing short of jubilant. "We all prayed and hoped it would be Sharron Angle," Fuehrmeyer said. Their prayers had been answered.

REID'S CAMPAIGN HAD the candidate he wanted, but fueling their drive, as one put it, "All of us knew that if we were responsible for Senator Sharron Angle, we'd never work in politics again. Like we just knew that we were just done, we'd all just go open a Dairy Queen franchise."

Angle's multifarious weaknesses notwithstanding, the hatred for Harry Reid, inside and outside Nevada, was peaking in 2010. Inside Nevada, he was seen by some on the right and even some in the middle as having lost touch with the state, no longer independent like Nevada but partisan like a Democrat. Outside Nevada, he was the symbol of an out-of-touch partisan warrior, making Congress more dysfunctional, a win-at-any-costs politician, bad for the country.

Reid was especially disliked in Nevada's fifteen rural counties, where they had been socked with high unemployment and where Obamacare was terribly unpopular. The rural vote was not large enough to win the race for Angle—it was barely more than 10 percent—but if she could drive up the margins enough, it could make the difference. The loathing was palpable.

Reid's staff knew this, the polling showed it, even Reid knew it, although he was exasperated that Angle was polling within the margin of error. (It was so bad that when they tested their negative ads against Angle, the focus groups' dials went up for the incumbent during the attacks on Angle but dropped precipitously when participants heard "I'm Harry Reid and I approve this message.")

The Reid campaign set out to define the little-known Angle before she could define herself, using their huge money advantage over a campaign that was being run by amateurs out of Angle's Reno living room.

Within forty-eight hours of the primary, Reid was using his financial advantage to put up attack ads on television portraying Angle as well outside the mainstream—and she embraced her far-right status—using her comments about phasing out Medicare and Social Security during a primary debate. They knew they had to drive up her negatives, to take the opportunity to define her as someone unpalatable to swing voters. The Reid campaign wanted her to be perceived as extreme and dangerous, their most frequent adjectives to describe her, so that moderate voters would either hold their noses and vote for Reid or not vote at all. They even had a research document detailing various positions headlined "Sharron Angle—Dangerous and Extreme."

This was a numbers game for Team Reid. They knew he was underwater and had sunk even further since the race began. But Angle was not yet that well-known by the broader electorate, so they had to change that before she could raise any money. The Democrats had a fifty-eight-thousand-voter edge over the Republicans in Nevada in June 2010, or about 5 percent. If he could hold the Democratic base, if the Reid Machine could turn them out, and if they could stop independent voters and middle-of-the-road Republicans from going for Angle, they had a chance.

National Republicans saw what Reid was doing, but they did not funnel money to Angle to counteract the ad campaign. They also were being stymied by Angle's close friend and campaign manager from her state senate days, Terry Campbell, who like the candidate did not trust the establishment. Campbell, along with far-right activists with little campaign experience at this level, were in Angle's ear all the time. They would advise her on strategy, even shoot a television ad for her at one point, and eventually came to be known inside the campaign as the denizens of the Island of Misfit Toys, an allusion to the place where defective gifts were tossed in *Rudolph the Red-Nosed Reindeer.*

They seemed to think accepting cash from people who walked in the door would be a good idea; it's illegal except in very small amounts. (It apparently did not happen.) When they heard John McCain was willing to come do an event, they tried to stop it because they called him a RINO (Republican in name only); McCain came anyway and raised money for her.

Angle wasn't helping her cause, either, talking about "Second Amendment remedies" as a possible necessity if Reid were reelected. The comment received a lot of attention in local and national media outlets.

The national Republicans knew their only hope was to professionalize the campaign. Jordan Gehrke, who had been advising Angle from afar and had worked in Republican campaigns, came out to Nevada on a rescue mission and soon two other experienced Republican campaign hands, Jarrod Agen and Amanda Kornegay, joined the team.

Meanwhile, the clock was ticking, Angle was getting thrashed on television, and as would become a pattern, it was with the interviewers with whom she felt most comfortable that she made her most damaging mistakes. Reid aides also made a habit of calling into right-wing radio shows to ask questions they thought might trip her up. It worked. Women could take "a lemon situation [unwanted pregnancy after rape or incest] and turn it into lemonade [through adoption]," she told one radio host in late June.

Angle began to slip in public and private polls, hemorrhaging so much that any advantage the Republican nominee had was erased and Reid was ahead or close to it. The Reid campaign plan since May—get Angle through the primary, then define her while her bank account was empty and she couldn't respond—had worked so far. Their internal polling showed Reid ahead, with the pollster Mark Mellman assuring the campaign the other public surveys that showed Reid losing were flawed. ("In Mellman we trust" was the drinking toast Reid staffers routinely had at the Hammer, a bar near the campaign headquarters.) Nearly every public poll showed Angle winning, which was nerve-wracking for Reid, who thought he should be ahead of her by twenty percentage points. Hall believed in Mellman but would later concede, "There was never a moment where I felt comfortable."

ABOUT THIS TIME, word began to circulate that the National Rifle Association was seriously considering endorsing Reid for reelection, which sent outrage through the right-wing blogosphere. Long forgotten were the days in Carson City in 1968 when Reid pushed for a handgun waiting period. Reid, knowing the power that the NRA had and knowing how gun-happy his Western state was, had courted the NRA for years. This had caused him headaches with progressives—and some on his own staff who despised the group—but as with other issues such as abortion, he had managed to thread the needle. Considering the NRA's clout in a federal race, though, with all of its members and so many in Nevada, Reid wanted the endorsement. He thought he would get it. Just a year earlier, the NRA had sent a missive to its Nevada members thanking Reid for opposing a proposed assault weapons ban after Barack Obama became president. The letter could hardly have been more gushing, talking of his "consistent" opposition to gun bans. "For many years now, Harry Reid has been supporting our Second Amendment rights in the U.S. Senate," the letter read. The group said Reid had been "instrumental" in preventing gun manufacturers from being sued in certain cases and that he had voted against gun confiscation attempts. Reid had also voted, the letter noted, to allow "law-abiding citizens to carry firearms for self-defense in national parks and wildlife refuges."

More recently, at the dedication of a Las Vegas shooting park in late August 2009, a project Reid had shepherded through Congress, the NRA CEO at the time, Wayne LaPierre, declared, "He is a true champion of the Second Amendment." The Reid campaign had a lengthy document prepared, titled "Reid Stands Up for Nevadans' Second Amendment Rights," that had a long list of advocacy that the NRA liked. Indeed, Chris Cox, the head of the NRA's PAC, came to Nevada in mid-2010 and indicated to Hall during a meeting at the Mandalay Bay Resort and Casino that the group was going to endorse Reid. Hall and others were giddy, knowing how important it was for a Democrat to get this nod in a Western state.

"We knew the NRA was going to endorse Reid and we went apeshit," recalled one Republican insider. "We pulled every door in Washington we could. I mean, everybody called [the NRA], every Republican senator. We had anybody who could call, we got to call."

Angle's campaign also launched a website that hyped her bona fides for gun rights and asked people to sign a petition. They amassed tens of thousands of signatures and delivered boxes of petitions to the NRA office in Washington, DC.

By late August, the Angle campaign had done its job. RedState's Erick Erickson floated the possibility of the NRA going Switzerland in the race. It lit up social media, so Hall called Cox. He wouldn't take the call.

National Review's Jim Geraghty had the news on August 27: "The NRA will not be endorsing Harry Reid," his piece began. The NRA statement on its site rationalized the decision by saying many factors went into their decision, but Reid's votes to confirm the Supreme Court justices Elena Kagan and Sonia Sotomayor essentially were disqualifying. Even though she did not get the endorsement, either, this was a victory for Sharron Angle that saved her campaign for the moment.

Hall was apoplectic, as were others inside the Reid campaign who had bitten their tongues—or not—to accept Reid's pro-gun advocacy out of political expediency. Now that was all for naught. Hall called the NRA's Cox and lit him up in a voicemail. As one staffer who witnessed the call remembered: "We are going to win," Hall told Cox. "And when we win, I'm going to spend the next six years reminding Harry Reid that you, Chris Cox, fucked him."

THE GREAT LAS Vegas Newspaper War intensified after the primary, with Sherman Frederick and the *Review-Journal* having a distinct advantage over the much less well-read *Las Vegas Sun* and Brian Greenspun.

After the publisher revived Reid's "war is lost" fiasco on July 4, Reid's communications chief, Jon Summers, sent a memo to the campaign: "I spoke to Reid about Sherm's column. He has policy folks pulling facts together so Greenspun can write a column taking Sherm to the woodshed."

Sure enough, on July 11, Greenspun obliged with a Sunday column that began, "Shame on Sherm." After defending Reid and accusing the *Review-Journal*'s parent company of a jihad, Greenspun concluded his column thusly: "That's why Sherm has stopped at nothing and stooped so low by attacking our senator's patriotism. Sherm, have you no shame?"

That same day, the Reid campaign attacked the *Review-Journal* for its propensity to use its news pages to defend Angle, while quoting from Greenspun's column. The coordination was unmistakable and unsurprising.

By mid-July, the newspaper war was making national headlines. In a July 17 piece, the *Los Angeles Times* media columnist James Rainey highlighted the to and fro in a piece headlined "Las Vegas Papers Take Sides on Harry Reid-Sharron Angle Race."

Rainey tried to have a conversation with Frederick's accomplice, Mitchell, but the editor hung up on him.

THE SUMMER WAS characterized by a gaffe-off between the candidates, with each one seemingly trying to outdo the other in damaging public statements.

Reid came under fire in mid-July when he was asked by a local television reporter about a Pew Hispanic Center report that found 17 percent of the nation's construction workers were undocumented. Reid's response: "That may be some place, but it's not here in Nevada."

This was a strange thing to say, considering it was long known that Nevada had one of the higher percentages of undocumented workers in the country, many of them working in construction, which was ever present in the country's fastest-growing state.

"Harry's so dumb," Frederick wrote.

A few days later, David Drucker of Roll Call put into writing what many Republicans in DC were whispering: "Republicans are growing increasingly frustrated with Sharron Angle and her lackluster campaign to unseat Senate Majority Leader Harry Reid (D-Nev.), fearing she is jeopardizing what they had long viewed as a sure pickup and costing them a chance to reclaim the majority."

National Republicans, though, had not given up and believed the race was still winnable. Angle was keeping pace with Reid in fundraising—they each raised a little more than $2 million in the second quarter.

By the end of July, all of the public polling, including the *Review-Journal*'s, showed the race had reverted to a dead heat. On August 10, the campaign's rapid response director, Justin Barasky, sent an email to the team:

> At the official event today Sen. Reid responded to a question from a reporter and said "I don't understand how anyone of Hispanic heritage could be Republican."
>
> Needless to say, this could cause some problems . . .

A statement was drafted after exchanges under the header "draft non-apology Hispanic issues hit." The expected criticism rained down, including the exhumation of those 1993 anti–birthright citizenship comments.

BY SEPTEMBER, ANGLE'S campaign was hoping to use immigration combined with the economic doldrums to push her over the top. She released an ad with ominous images of Hispanics trying to cross the border to label Reid as "the best friend an illegal alien ever had." The ad immediately received national attention.

What followed was one of the sharpest disagreements inside the Reid campaign on whether the senator should bring up the DREAM Act, which would have given young undocumented residents a pathway to citizenship.

"There was a real split in the campaign on whether to do that," said one Reid staffer who was there at the time. "Some of the longtime Reid folks did not want that to happen. [They believed] it would bring the backlash from white voters, rural voters, basically what is now a lot of the Trump people, and generate that level of turnout from those places. And so that was the downside, and you weren't going to have the upside of Latino voters actually turning out."

Mellman had informed Reid in 2010 that, according to his numbers, if the senator pushed the DREAM Act, he would hemorrhage so many white independents and conservative Democrats that Hispanics would not be able to make up the difference. Still, Reid announced he was going to bring the DREAM Act to the floor. It was a gamble that easily could have cost him the election.

MEANWHILE, THE GAFFES kept coming. Reid was at New York mayor Michael Bloomberg's town house at a fundraiser for his Democratic colleague, Kirsten Gillibrand. In praising her, Reid said, "We in the Senate refer to Sen. Gillibrand as the 'hottest' member." The remark published by *Politico* soon went viral. Gillibrand said she was "flattered" and Reid supporters were mortified. The *Las Vegas Review-Journal* boss, Sherman Frederick, accused Reid of sexual harassment.

Soon thereafter, the influential FiveThirtyEight website increased its odds of Angle winning to 57 percent from 52 percent. By the end of September, as Frederick resorted to implying Reid was addled from his 2005 ministroke, the *Review-Journal* had the race tied, but Mellman had found Angle no closer than four percentage points since mid-August.

On the first Sunday of October, a month before the election, the *Review-Journal* endorsed Angle. It was not subtle:

> The good senator is 70 years old now, his gait a bit slower, his countenance slightly weary. He's become prone to verbal gaffes and sometimes loses his

> place while delivering the campaign stemwinder. As he has climbed higher and higher in the Democratic hierarchy, he has veered further and further to the left, becoming politically disconnected from Nevada and its residents.

On October 7, a field director in the Reid campaign, Steven Montoya, sent an internal message that didn't seem to mean a lot at the time but showed just how far Team Reid's tentacles reached:

> Mr Barone, of Rancho High, came by the office today in order to confirm that Angle's campaign has accepted their request that she visit the school. Her visit is set for next Friday, Oct 15th. Mr Barone has planned a strategy session for next Wednesday, Oct 13th in order to determine what questions they will ask of her, as well as what manner of reception she is to receive.

It was nice to have a heads-up about the event and to be asked to provide questions, but it was unlikely to be of much use. Or so they thought.

ON THE EVENING of October 14, Reid and Angle met in their only debate of the election at the Public Broadcasting System studio in Las Vegas. The Angle campaign was feeling pretty good coming into the matchup. Angle had just posted a record $14 million haul in the third quarter, less a product of voters across the country falling in love with her than their abiding hatred for Harry Reid. It was a stunning number, nearly five times what Reid raised during the same period, with Frederick greeting the news by declaring: "Meet your new senator, Nevada."

Angle had been holed up in the off-Strip Trump Hotel with her team for a week—ironic perhaps for a MAGA candidate before MAGA existed—practicing for the debate, and her team was confident she would be disciplined and on message. She was as ready as she would ever be.

The day of the debate, Mellman had the race at 44–40 in a head-to-head and 47–40 in a six-way vote with minor party candidates included. Reid was ahead, perhaps not comfortably, but he was ahead. His confidence would perhaps explain what was about to happen, especially since his team was so pleased with his rehearsal on the last day of preparation. However, Reid's performance turned out to be one of the worst ever by a sitting senator, one that was roundly lambasted in the local and national media. He was lackluster and lethargic, occasionally lost in his papers and syntax, clearly not wanting to be standing next to Angle. She was steady, despite some occasional nervousness, and delivered the money lines she had been given, including at one point telling Reid to "man up" and take responsibility for Nevada's problems.

The silver lining for Reid was that few people watch a PBS debate on a Thursday evening. The media coverage was not especially damaging for him, and Mellman's tracking on Friday showed a dip but no precipitous dive. Just in case, though, the Reid campaign prepared a document to answer a previously whispered charge that Angle had shouted at the debate, one that had percolated for years: that Reid had become rich during his Senate tenure. The document detailed his wealth accumulated before he became a senator, mostly from real estate, and how it had fluctuated very little over the last decade. It appeared that *Politico* had access to the document when it penned a story headlined "Reid's Riches Are a Campaign Issue." The story detailed how Angle had raised the issue in the debate and Reid had called it "really kind of a low blow." But, Manu Raju wrote: "In 1996, for example, Reid's assets ranged from $2.6 million to $5.7 million—but in 2008, his net worth ranged between $2.9 million and $5.9 million."

There had never been any evidence that Reid had gotten rich off his public service. But it was a potentially resonant avenue of criticism, especially when combined with the fact that he lived at the Ritz-Carlton in Washington, not in a penthouse as the attack was usually framed but on the second floor. The second floor at the Ritz-Carlton, though, was still . . . the Ritz-Carlton.

The Reid campaign was so concerned about his debate performance that David Krone, Reid's DC aide, wrote an email to the campaign about getting a negative Angle story highlighted on the *Sun* site: "Sorry it took so long to get the Angle story up on the Sun website. Brian [Greenspun] is in Northern California and he doesn't have the best cell service. As soon as I told him he started working on getting the stupid debate story down and the Angle story on her idiotic comments about her ad."

The latter story resulted from Angle's visit the day after the debate to the Hispanic Student Union at Rancho High School. Reid's campaign knew she was there, thanks to the tip the previous week; Angle's campaign staff had begged her not to go—they didn't believe it was going to be nonpartisan and they feared she would veer off message, but she insisted, saying she would repeat her debate lines to the students.

That's not what happened.

First, Angle was quoted as saying "I'm not sure those are Latinos" in reference to her ads, which featured dark-skinned, thuggish-looking Hispanics, posing as menacing marauders crossing the border illegally. Then, she continued by telling the Hispanic Student Union, "Some of you look a little more Asian to me."

Angle's staff called an emergency meeting to discuss damage control. It took some time to persuade Angle this was terrible for her campaign. Some of her local sycophants insisted it was not that bad. But Angle finally agreed that she had to stop doing events, her face ashen over what she had done.

Could they fix it? They weren't sure. Would they pray with her? Agen and Gehrke, who were standing, agreed and they joined hands with a still-sitting Angle imploring God to forgive her, to get her out of the jackpot. And then: "Please, Lord, give Jarrod the words to get me out of this mess."

EARLY VOTING ALSO had started that weekend. In Nevada, this two-week period had proven to be very popular. In 2008, two-thirds of voters had cast their ballots early.

This is where the Reid campaign separated itself from the Angle team. The Reid folks had been building a ground game since 2008, and it was now a well-oiled machine. The Angle campaign could not compete. The Reid campaign's goal was to offset any usual Republican turnout advantage, especially in a midterm, by turning out their base voters—Democrats still had a 5 percent registration edge—and moderates.

After every day of voting, Justin Gilbert, a numbers maven and strategist for the campaign, would send the team a report. His message after the first weekend of early voting: "All in all, things on track."

In his ninth update on October 25, Gilbert wrote to the campaign: "Overall, we are in solid position and remain as always cautiously optimistic."

The next day, the GOP-leaning firm Rasmussen released a poll showing Angle ahead, 49–48. Angle penned a "Dear Loyal Supporter" letter that cast doubt on the legality of Reid's get-out-the-vote tactics and risibly said a local television station had reported machines were preset to select Reid.

By now, the national numbers guru Nate Silver was saying that there was a 73 percent chance of Angle winning, with an average of all polls showing her up by three percentage points. Two new national polls had shown Angle ahead.

The final early vote numbers looked favorable for Reid:

Total votes—422,620
Democrats—182,587
Republicans—173,829
Independents—66,204

On Election Day, the head of the Nevada Mining Association, Tim Crowley, reported to the Reid campaign in an email that he had done the best he could to tamp down rural hostility to the senator by pitching his candidacy this way: "I focused on the point that mining needs Reid as majority leader to look after our industry. I also mentioned that, should Reid lose, mining issues could be controlled by Chuck Schumer. That's something that should scare conservative Elko voters."

Reid was never going to win Elko County. But reducing the margins in rural Nevada could make the difference if the race were very close.

The first numbers in urban Nevada posted about an hour and fifteen minutes after the polls closed, showing Reid with a huge lead in populous Clark County and a sizable edge in Washoe County. By 8:17 p.m., Gilbert was reporting that most of the rural counties were in and Reid still led statewide by thirty thousand votes. At 9:43 p.m., Gilbert informed the team that AP, Fox News, and NBC had called the race for Reid. It was over. The final margin would be forty thousand votes, or nearly 6 percent, hardly a nail-biter.

Over at the Venetian on the Las Vegas Strip, where the Angle campaign party was being held, reality was starting to settle in. (Her Clark County phone bank had shut down hours before the polls closed because her staffers wanted to get good seats at the victory party. So she had no one calling voters on Election Day after five o'clock or so, a fitting emblem for her amateur-hour campaign staff and a contrast to the no-stone-unturned Reid campaign.)

Angle was inconsolable, holed up in a bathroom in the suite. She would not come out even after Sheldon Adelson, the chairman of the company that owned the hotel and a Republican megadonor, knocked on the door and wanted to see her. She refused.

Angle finally emerged after being coaxed to concede. In another room next to the ballroom where the main party was being held, some of Angle's most rabid local supporters were having their own gathering. Angle insisted on stopping at the door, and one of the supporters buttonholed her, said he was a gunmaker, and handed her a gun inscribed "Take this to DC and blow them away," or words to that effect. Angle thanked him and entered the room and a chant immediately rang out: "Don't concede. Don't concede." They insisted she had won and that the election was rigged. Angle pointed the gun up in the air and said she would not concede. One person witnessing this looked at Agen, her spokesman, and said, "That's the craziest shit I've ever seen."

Angle eventually conceded. On November 7, five days after the election, Frederick wrote a postmortem blog post, suffused with bitterness and brimming with near conspiracy theories about how Reid won. It ended this way: "And finally, dear readers, do you think I'll get a holiday card from Sen. Reid this year? If I do, are there any volunteers out there who would open it for me?"

Reid had an early Christmas gift for Frederick, all right. A few days after the election, he was out of the *Review-Journal* as publisher, shunted to a role as a "consultant," and his lieutenant, Mitchell, soon left the paper. Reid, when asked many years later about Frederick's departure, had a simple boast: "Don't think I didn't have something to do with that."

When you come for the king, you'd best kill him.

CHAPTER TWENTY-ONE

DOING WHAT NO ONE ELSE WOULD DO

Reid's 2010 victory was in stark contrast to Democratic carnage across the country, where Republicans gained six Senate seats (still short of a majority) and took the House with a net gain of sixty-three seats. (Reid's eldest son, Rory, lost the governor's race, in a Shakespearean twist, to Brian Sandoval, whom Harry Reid had helped install on the federal bench to take him out of the political game but who gave up the lifetime appointment to run for governor.)

The Affordable Care Act, which Reid had shepherded through Congress for Obama, was assigned much of the blame for the Democratic losses, as was the economy. The shellacking, as President Obama himself called it, made the lame-duck session of Congress even more important. In the Senate, where Reid still had fifty-nine Democrats until January, the majority leader oversaw one of the more productive interim sessions in modern history. By the time the calendar turned, the Democrats had passed a new nuclear treaty, repealed the "Don't Ask, Don't Tell" policy for gays in the military, and enacted other significant laws, including a food safety bill and a 9/11 responders' measure. What's more, the Senate confirmed nineteen of Obama's judicial picks.

Obama told Reid shortly after the election that he hoped to pass the gays in the military bill, the START treaty, a child nutrition bill near and dear to First Lady Michelle Obama, and several other measures, too, before John Boehner took the gavel from Nancy Pelosi and the Democrats' maneuverability all but evaporated in the Senate. "[Reid] grumbled and complained and he muttered, and he hung up on me after saying he couldn't do it," the former president said. "And then you know what? He did it. All of them got done. So there are repeated instances like that, that maybe are less high-profile than the ACA, but I think are in some ways more indicative of his focus, both his legislative skill and his willingness to do hard stuff that was not politically convenient."

(As the journalist Ryan Grim reported, Obama and Reid disagreed over tactics, causing the senator at one point to hang up on the president after saying, "Well, Mr. President, sometimes you just gotta roll the dice.")

It was not an entirely successful lame duck for Reid, though. After several casino companies, most notably MGM Resorts and Caesars Entertainment, supported his reelection effort, Reid tried during the postelection session to push through an online poker legalization bill. Caesars had drawn controversy as the election ended for appearing to push its employees to vote for Reid, but he denied that played a role in what for the senator was a policy reversal. Web poker had been an issue that divided the industry, with many of the companies seeing an opportunity to make more money despite potential pitfalls, and others, most notably Sheldon Adelson, already a major Republican Party donor, opposing it on moral grounds. Reid would maintain a back-channel relationship with Adelson throughout his career, even when they disagreed on politics and policies. (One of his top aides, David Krone, also frequently corresponded with Adelson's right-hand man, Andy Abboud, on issues such as web poker and Israel.) They had a grudging respect for each other and were always candid with one another, including during lunches the Las Vegas Sands chairman hosted for the two in his Strip office. Reid never used any of the harsh rhetoric for Adelson—he rarely talked about him at all—that he used for the Koch brothers, insisting that his home-state billionaire was principled, and the out-of-state brothers were not.

REID'S REELECTION ALSO heralded a new era in his office as Gary Myrick, the Senate rules savant who had taken over out of necessity for Susan McCue as chief of staff, stepped aside to take over floor operations for the Democratic majority while David Krone, a deputy chief, took his place. Krone would become a fixture in Reid's professional and personal worlds for the next five years, as influential and effective at times as McCue was, but with a combative and loyal nature that Reid would both love and occasionally wince at because his new chief would grow to loathe the White House. Reid referred to Krone as his "fifth son," but he also described him as "quirky" and "temperamental."

Krone had come from an unusual background to the pinnacle of appointive Hill posts, having been an executive and lobbyist for Comcast before joining Reid. He and Reid met in Colorado when the cable television executive drove the senator from the airport to a campaign fundraiser in 1992. They kept in touch and by 2003, Krone was the lead lobbyist for the National Cable and Telecommunications Association in Washington, eventually earning a reported $5 million a year plus benefits. He also was a large donor to Reid, contributing $35,000 to the senator and his PAC.

In 2008, Krone took a gigantic pay cut to $165,000 a year to become a senior adviser to Reid, eventually becoming a deputy chief.

When he became chief of staff, Krone had more freedom than most chiefs because he was independently wealthy, which apparently freed him from any diplomatic niceties. He frequently called people "idiots" and worse in emails—including his own staffers—but saved much of his vitriol for the White House and Obama, whom Reid loved and admired.

Reid would occasionally be frustrated by what he saw as the White House meddling in his arena, but Krone took it to another level, at various times writing in internal emails to Reid and others, "Fuck this White House. You can tell them to go to hell or I can. They are idiots," and "I hate this White House." (This was all the more unusual because his girlfriend and future wife, Alyssa Mastromonaco, was a top White House aide.)

This clearly made Reid uncomfortable and his relationship with Krone almost disintegrated over the Obama tensions later that year.

It was about this time, too, that Reid was pressing on with a mostly sub rosa but occasionally public war with NV Energy, the state's electric utility monopoly, which had been purchased by Warren Buffett. Reid, who had gradually become a renewables evangelist, had insisted the company shut down its coal plants, even bragging that he had scuttled financing for a planned new one by calling a hedge fund manager hoping to finance it. "I called the guy and I told him, 'You don't know me, but you're going to know me because you try to build that coal plant in Nevada and I will do everything I can to screw up your business, everything. You understand that?' So he backed out of that. And I was able to bluff my way through all that."

In 2012, Reid wrote to the NV Energy CEO, Michael Yackira, and criticized the company's plans to build transmission lines while not accelerating renewable energy development. When the utility monopoly tried to pass legislation in Carson City that Reid did not like, he did not hesitate to interfere, calling lawmakers to hector them. He publicly assailed the utility for its coal plants polluting the air, especially near an Indian reservation, whose residents complained.

Reid invited—nay, conscripted—NV Energy to come to his Clean Energy Summits in Las Vegas, where he, without hesitation, would insist that the utility give up coal. When the utility did not move fast enough, he would get on the phone with Yackira. The company eventually agreed to shut down or not build any proposed coal plants—and Reid was an important reason.

IN JUNE 2012, the developer/lobbyist Harvey Whittemore was indicted for violating campaign finance laws based on contributions he was alleged to have illegally funneled to the Democratic leader. For Reid's inner circle, it was a five-alarm fire. Whittemore was not some tangential figure in Reid's orbit; he was all but an honorary member of Team Reid.

Whittemore, who lives in Reno, was a lobbyist who had raised a fortune for Reid in the past, was friends with and/or law firm colleagues with his sons, and had asked the senator for help with a massive development he was building outside Las Vegas. Reid had been instrumental in helping Whittemore with Coyote Springs, a master-planned community that occasionally needed a boost, including a dramatic realignment of a right of way that Reid helped facilitate and became a focus of a *Los Angeles Times* exposé on the developer's influence with Reid.

The senator's staff was keenly aware of Whittemore's closeness to Reid. In 2004, the developer needed a provision of a controversial water bill to help Coyote Springs and also wanted some environmental laws waived, which sparked some discussion among staffers. At one point, Kai Anderson, Reid's well-respected legislative director, wrote to fellow staffers, "The Harvey component of the bill is time sensitive to Harvey but without us he is in a really tough spot so I think he can wait. Problem is, I expect, that Reid has told him he will do it now."

"From a political perspective we should strip Harvey's deal out," Chief of Staff Susan McCue had written back. "Let's talk to boss about holding off on Harvey's deal 'til next year." But the warnings were too late to stop the *L.A. Times* piece, which was immensely unflattering and raised, again, the issue of Reid's sons being Whittemore law partners and involved in lobbying. The *Times* would continue pursuing this angle, doing a third story in 2006 that showed the interlocking relationships and how Reid advocated for Whittemore's interests while accepting tens of thousands of contributions raised by the lobbyist.

The coziness all ended, though, when Whittemore became a liability in a scandal that involved his fundraising for Reid. The allegations against Whittemore were that in 2007 he had acted as a conduit for contributions to Reid—by reimbursing employees who donated, a violation of campaign finance laws.

Court testimony would later show that Whittemore met with Reid at the Four Seasons in Las Vegas, where the developer agreed to raise $150,000 for the senator. Just as the third quarter ended, Whittemore had nearly $150,000 in checks delivered to the campaign, making good on his promise. Shortly thereafter, Reid sent a note to him: "Dear Harvey, you are a man of your word. You are my friend today and for all tomorrows."

But those tomorrows would end after Whittemore was convicted in 2013. So-called conduit contributions, including in two previous high-profile cases in Nevada, generally had resulted in large fines. But in Whittemore's case, the government was seeking prison time, leading to speculation that the real target was Reid. The Department of Justice subpoenaed records from Reid during the investigation in early 2012.

The senator did not wait for Whittemore's indictment to distance himself from his forever friend. Months earlier, when word surfaced in the media that Whittemore was being investigated, Reid shed the donations, including five figures from his family members as well. After the indictment, the senator, through a spokesman, denied any knowledge of how Whittemore raised the money.

A year later, after a two-week trial, Whittemore was convicted of making excessive campaign contributions, making contributions in the name of another, and causing a false statement to be made to the Federal Election Commission. That false document was filed by Reid's campaign, but the Department of Justice said he was not culpable. "On April 15, 2007, the senator's campaign then unknowingly filed a false report with the FEC stating that the conduits had made the contributions, when in fact, Whittemore had made them," a DOJ release said after the conviction.

Whittemore served nearly two years in prison and emerged in 2016 a broken man, his law license revoked, with no relationship with Reid or the sons with whom he had also been close.

BY 2012, REID already had established a lengthy record of diversifying Nevada's representatives on the federal judiciary, and he was proud of the rainbow on the bench. Later that year, Miranda Du would be confirmed as the first Asian American to become a so-called Article III judge, seated on a specific kind of federal tribunal. But when another seat opened, he wanted the spectrum to be even wider. "I had put on the federal bench a couple Blacks, a few Hispanics, lots and lots of women," Reid said. "Frankly, I didn't have a Jew . . . I wanted to put a Jew on the federal bench."

By February, he had found her. When President Obama nominated a district court judge named Elissa Cadish in February, some speculated, including Reid, that she would be swiftly confirmed, even in an election year. Her pedigree was impeccable. She had been appointed in 2007 to the district bench by a Republican governor, had two decades of legal experience, and had received stellar ratings in annual surveys of lawyers conducted by the *Las Vegas Review-Journal*. She also was young, forty-seven, so she would be there for some time, if confirmed.

Reid had a call with Cadish toward the end of 2011, and neither anticipated any issue with the nomination, especially considering Reid's close relationship with Obama. The process can be quick. Once senators from a state sign a so-called blue slip, the Judiciary Committee usually proceeds apace. Up until this nomination, Reid had enjoyed a cordial relationship with his Republican counterpart, Dean Heller, who had been appointed to replace John Ensign after a tawdry scandal that ended his career. Reid had never forgotten that Heller, as secretary of state, had short-circuited that Washoe County recount that climaxed his close reelection fight against none other than Ensign.

But that was all about to end. Heller, who was running for election in 2012 to the seat he had been appointed to, would not sign the blue slip. Reid asserted later that Heller blindsided him, that he only found out from his staff, and that "nobody had ever done that to me."

Heller would not say why he declined to sign the blue slip, but Washington reporters soon ferreted out the ostensible reason. Republicans on the Senate Judiciary Committee had found a questionnaire that Cadish had filled out in 2008 for Citizens for Responsible Government, a formerly Mormon-dominated organization that Reid had butted heads with before because it was so socially and culturally conservative. When asked whether she believed there was a constitutional right for an individual to bear arms, Cadish answered: "I do not believe there is this constitutional right. Thus, I believe that reasonable restrictions may be imposed on gun ownership in the interest of public safety. Of course, I will enforce the laws as they exist as a judge."

Technically, Cadish was correct, and it was shortly after she filled out the questionnaire that the US Supreme Court would decide the landmark and now ironically named Heller case (named for a police officer) that would cement a person's right to bear arms outside of a militia, as the constitutional language states. When she was being vetted by the White House, Cadish was told the issue would not be relevant because she gave her answer before *Heller.*

Nevertheless, the damage had been done, and Reid scrambled to contain it. By March 22, his office released a letter from Cadish to him saying she was not giving her "personal opinion," just reciting "my understanding of the state of federal law at the time." If she were asked today, she told Reid in the obviously choreographed letter, "I would say I believe there is a constitutional right for individuals to keep and bear arms, and I would make clear that I would faithfully apply the binding precedent on this issue."

Heller met with Cadish, but he refused to budge, saying publicly he could not support her because of her supposed waffling on the Second Amendment. Reid, as Cadish recalled, "was frustrated and agitated. Within a short time, he told me that it appeared the nomination would not be able to proceed."

Reid floated the idea of persuading Judiciary Chairman Patrick Leahy of Vermont to abandon precedent and hold a hearing without two blue slips, but that did not fly. Leahy was as much of an institutionalist, or more so, than Reid.

Whether or not the maneuver helped Heller in his Senate race is impossible to tell, but he won by under twelve thousand votes, or about 1 percent, over Democratic congresswoman Shelley Berkley. Reid, whose staff contacted Cadish, immediately said he would nominate her again. Reid hoped with the election out of the way, Heller would relent. He would not.

Even after his staff suggested it might not be fair to Cadish to renominate her, Reid plowed ahead, and Obama renominated the judge in early 2013. But the nomination remained doomed, Cadish withdrew, and she would decline Reid's offer later that year to secure her an appointment to the Court of International Trade in New York City.

Reid called the judge with another offer in November 2015. She was on her honeymoon in Mexico with Howard Beckerman, a Democratic activist. Reid asked Cadish to run for Congress in District 3, which was vacant because the incumbent, Republican Joe Heck, was taking on Democrat Catherine Cortez Masto in the Senate race. Cadish told Reid she preferred to be a judge, but she agreed to meet with Reid's right hand, Rebecca Lambe. Again, she demurred but told Lambe she would try to think of someone. Her husband suggested her bridesmaid, Jacky Rosen, a synagogue president. Cadish passed along Rosen's contact information.

Rosen agreed to run, defeated the perennial candidate Danny Tarkanian, and then agreed to take on Heller, at Team Reid's prodding, two years later. On Election Night 2018, the revenge was served cold: Cadish's bridesmaid defeated Sen. Dean Heller, and Cadish was elected to the state supreme court, where she still serves.

HARRY REID LOVED repeating rumors, as if they were fact, to almost anyone. Colleagues, friends, staffers—it did not matter. He was, in many ways, the TMZ of Capitol Hill, repeating everything from what he heard about DC-related gossip to the latest Nevada political scuttlebutt. As with most everything else, he had no filter.

That explains some—although not all—of what happened in the middle of 2012 amid a tightening presidential race. By the end of May, when

Mitt Romney became the presumptive Republican nominee by passing the required delegate threshold, Reid believed the former Massachusetts governor and fellow Mormon would be a formidable candidate against Barack Obama. As a partisan warrior, Reid wanted to be involved. So when he got a call from a person he originally described as someone who had done business with Romney when he was at Bain Capital, telling him the Republican candidate had not paid his fair share of taxes, Reid wasted no time. "They never told me he didn't pay taxes," Reid said. "They just said he didn't pay his fair share."

In their book about the 2012 presidential campaign, *Game Change*, Mark Halperin and John Heilemann asserted that Utah businessman Jon Huntsman Sr. was Reid's source. Huntsman, who was known to dislike Romney and with whom Reid had a relationship, denied the claim.

Reid approached the Democratic National Committee, the Democratic Senatorial Committee, and the White House. No one was willing to use allegations Reid could not prove.

"I thought it was a great issue," Reid said. "I gave everyone the opportunity to carry the ball over the finish line, but they weren't willing to do that. So I did it on my own."

Several times, as his staff prepared him for interviews, Reid told them he was going to bring up Romney and the tax issue. His aides pleaded with him not to, saying reporters would ask him for evidence and he would not be able to produce any. He listened, reluctantly, until . . . he didn't.

In late July, the Huffington Post writers Sam Stein and Ryan Grim interviewed Reid in his Capitol office. He had wanted to bring up the Romney/tax stuff, and his staff was relieved he had not as Grim and Stein got up to leave.

The two reporters were almost out of the office when Reid said, "Hey, guys, I've got something good for you." The reporters stopped and turned to face Reid and he said, with a glint in his eye, "Do you know that Mitt Romney has not paid taxes in 10 years?"

The story that Reid recounted to Stein and Grim was slightly different from the one he told in late 2021. He informed the Huffington Post duo

Romney had not paid any taxes in ten years, while he said before he died that Huntsman told him Romney did not pay his fair share, not that he did not pay them at all.

Reid knew that Romney had only agreed to release a couple of years' worth of tax returns, and the story, when it posted on July 27, noted that the information could not be verified and that even Reid conceded he didn't know whether it was accurate.

House Speaker Nancy Pelosi was about to go into an interview when a staffer pulled her aside, having seen the alert on the Huffington Post story. He relayed what Reid had said, and she replied, "That's my guy!"

Now that the allegations were public, Reid burst forth with the story everywhere he could, even on the Senate floor, which some considered a breach of protocol, especially for such a committed institutionalist.

"The word's out that he [Romney] hasn't paid any taxes for ten years," said the man who put that word out. "Let him prove that he has paid taxes because he hasn't."

Reid believed that average voters would be repelled by the revelation because, as he said on the floor that day, "Mitt Romney makes more money in a single day than the average voter makes in two years."

The story went from being the kindling Reid had ignited with Stein and Grim to a wildfire and then a full-on conflagration threatening to incinerate Romney's candidacy. Reid relished bringing the heat, and even some of Romney's Republican allies hoped their nominee would release more tax returns to douse it. But Romney refused, hoping the issue would be defused with a letter from his accountant saying he had paid an effective tax rate of 14 percent.

The Washington Post's fact-checker, Glenn Kessler, gave Reid his most egregious rating for the claim, four Pinocchios, concluding: "Reid holds a position of great authority in the U.S. Congress. He should hold himself to a high standard of accuracy when making claims about political opponents." PolitiFact was similarly lacerating, giving Reid a "Pants on Fire" rating and ending: "Reid has made an extreme claim with nothing solid to back it up."

Reid did not care.

His staff did, though. In early August, aides were worried after media inquiries that Reid, a multimillionaire, might have to release his tax returns and that would open a discussion of his wealth and effective tax rate. On August 6, his spokesman, Adam Jentleson, said Reid was not running for president and would not release his tax returns. But they were not taking any chances.

Reid's research director, Simon Sargent, took a deep dive into the senator's finances and raised several red flags, including that Reid's effective tax rate was not much lower than Romney's, in the mid to high teens for a person making enough money to warrant a 28 percent rate. "Is anyone concerned that Senator Reid's tax rate is as low as it is? The rate seems normal and easily justifiable to me but the public perception may be that it is much lower than some would expect," Sargent wrote to other staffers on August 9.

Sargent also raised issues that he considered potentially problematic if Reid released his returns, including a resurrection of controversy over his proceeds in a land deal with his close friend Jay Brown, his large donations to the LDS Church, a $3,750 contribution to a charity founded by Harvey Whittemore's wife shortly after his fundraising scandal, and the fact that Reid started claiming Social Security benefits when he turned sixty-six. ("I'm not sure if this is public knowledge. Does anyone have a concern with sharing this info?")

Jentleson expressed some concern over what Sargent found in an email to Chief of Staff Krone that same day:

> The rates make me nervous, especially since they are so far below his brackets. There is a real risk of the story being about reid not romney, with an emphasis on reid being hypocritical for hammering romney for "not paying his fair share" while using accounting tricks himself to avoid paying his own fair share. And in the future, every time reid talks about people not paying their fair share Rs will point out that he's not paying his, either.

Krone was not that concerned, emailing Jentleson:

> Bottom line is this does open HMR bare but it sure does put it back on Romney. HMR says I'm willing to lay myself open, why isn't a guy who wants to be president?

Then, an hour later, Jentleson pinged Krone:

> Fyi, HMR just called for a news update. He asked how the taxes were going and if we knew his rate. I told him it was an average of 17, ranging from 14 to 19. He said "oh I'm not going to release those." I said we have a call tomorrow to discuss and are still working through them. He said ok you guys make the decision.

As the criticism of Reid grew more widespread and more intense, he brought up Romney's supposed tax-dodging everywhere he went, including in early September at the Democratic National Convention in Charlotte, North Carolina. In national and local newspapers, Reid was savaged for what some called McCarthy-like tactics. His friend and publisher/owner of the *Las Vegas Sun,* Brian Greenspun, killed a column that was scathingly critical of Reid for the unsubstantiated attack.

After Romney lost, Reid believed he had been most responsible for his defeat. In an unrepentant interview in 2015 with CNN's Dana Bash, when challenged on the fact that his allegation was untrue, Reid said, matter-of-factly, with a slight smile, "Romney didn't win, did he?"

He was still boasting about it shortly before he died, seemingly with no regrets. "But for me, I'm pretty sure he [Romney] would have been elected," Reid said.

IN MID-JUNE 2012, Reid agreed to do a joint interview with Mitch McConnell, the Republican leader, to kick off the fall season for *60 Minutes.*

It was widely considered a disaster, with neither leader saying much or even looking at each other. The correspondent Steve Kroft said he was "exasperated" by the interview. Despite the rote addressing of each other as "my good friend," an echo of the Senate floor phoniness, the appearance was a microcosm of the relationship between the two men. Before he died Reid said the perceived public chilliness was real. Things had started warmly enough when they were the respective whips of their parties, with Reid describing their relationship as "close." Reid said he admired McConnell for surmounting polio, but he added, "Mitch McConnell is a very cold, calculating person. Now does that mean I don't like him? The answer is no. I just understand him. He is someone who never shows his cards."

Reid said unlike other Republican leaders, with whom he would have regular meetings, McConnell "didn't do that. He didn't want to do that. Every Tuesday the Republicans would have a lunch and we would have a lunch. And he never wanted to do one together." Reid said McConnell never gave him a reason.

One Reid insider said the two were very similar. "McConnell's a killer, but so is Reid." Reid said to a staffer at one point, as he longed for Bill Frist's tenure as leader to end, "McConnell's a killer, but at least he cares about the institution."

But Reid would come to believe that was not true once McConnell assembled sixty votes in the chamber. When Reid saw that his counterpart's primary goal was to defeat President Obama, he simply did not believe McConnell was an honest broker anymore on legislation. And once anyone lost trust with Reid, it was nearly impossible to regain it, so the relationship deteriorated. One ex-staffer thought Reid overestimated the friendship with McConnell that developed early in their careers, believing that the personal connection could overcome any political considerations. When it became clear that was not true, Reid became increasingly embittered.

The senators also were at odds over the confirmation of justices. Reid was growing increasingly frustrated and internal memos suggest he wanted more Democrats to speak out about what he called "this mindless Republican obstructionism of bipartisan, consensus district court nominees."

As the year ended, Reid had had enough and was prepared to make arguably the most dramatic legislative move of his career, one that would be controversial at the time and eventually echo through history as a Republican talking point for changing the rules of the Senate and the direction of the US Supreme Court.

CHAPTER TWENTY-TWO

GOING NUCLEAR

When he was a kid, Harry Reid did not leave Searchlight very often without his parents. But one summer, after his brother Dale had graduated from high school, he invited young Harry to join him in Ash Fork, a tiny dot in Arizona along Highway 40. Dale had found work at a gas station in the railroad town near an Indian reservation. There wasn't much memorable about the town or the railroad or the Native Americans he met, but what the young Harry Reid remembered was a lesson he learned there.

Dale's girlfriend had a younger brother about a year older than Harry and they spent the summer playing games together. Here's how Reid remembered it in 1986:

> Well, I could beat him in all the games. I don't remember the games he played, but I was better than him in all of them, but I never won a game because as we got into the games he would keep changing the rules. And so I could never win a game because the rules were changed during the game. I have always been since that time aware that I will never change the rules during a ball game. But I will try to understand the rules, I will try to stick to them. That is what I think life is all about. Don't change the rules during the game.

Those are resonant words from a forty-six-year-old looking back on an experience he had when he was about eight years old, words from a man who would decide a few decades later to change the rules of the Senate, a historic move that would change the course of history. Never change the rules. Never.

Never would find its endpoint soon after the end of 2012, a year that did not end well for Reid.

The negotiations on the so-called fiscal cliff were very trying and they were multilateral—between the House and Senate and between the Senate and the White House.

Reid had developed a good relationship with Republican House Speaker John Boehner, who would later call Reid the most "straight-up" leader he dealt with, much more transparent than McConnell. They both had jobs to do, including negotiating a fiscal deal at the end of 2012, and they had a mutual respect. Boehner had an obstreperous caucus and had been unable to get any of his plans through. So the Speaker returned to Ohio for Christmas, his family left the day after the holiday, and he was alone in the house and flipped on the television. There, on C-SPAN, was Reid on the Senate floor fulminating about how Boehner was running the House "like a dictatorship" and insisting the Speaker would not bring a bill to the floor. "I'm thinking, 'What a little fucker,'" Boehner recalled. "I mean, nobody on my staff has ever seen me angry. I don't do anger, it is not my thing. But that little son of a bitch made me, I mean, I was pissed."

Boehner was still fuming a few days later when he returned to Capitol Hill for a meeting with the principals at the White House. What happened next became a legendary tale in the capital. In Boehner's words:

> I walked up the steps from the first floor of the White House West Wing up to the West Wing lobby, and I walk into the rooms, twenty feet wide, forty feet long, big lobby. And Harry's on the other end of the lobby right next to the door, where you go back to the Oval, talking to Mitch McConnell. And I walked in my door on the other end, I locked eyes on that little bastard all

the way across that room. I mean, I'm glaring at him. Mitch is trying to say something to him. And by the time I got in front of Harry, Harry knew his ass was in trouble. That's when I told him he should go fuck himself.

Reid stammered that his staff had written it, but his chief of staff, David Krone, was sitting there, too, and reminded the senator in front of Boehner that he had extemporized. McConnell, meanwhile, was stunned or, as Boehner put it, "looked like he was about to have a heart attack." It was a turning point in the Speaker–majority leader relationship cemented by a note Reid sent a few days after the compromise bill passed on New Year's Eve. In a handwritten note marked "Personal and Confidential," Reid wrote to Boehner on January 3:

Dear John,

Congratulations on your new term as speaker. I was surprised with your greeting to me in the White House. But, a greeting I have had directed at me on other occasions. With all the pressure you have had it was probably disconcerting to you to have me pecking at you. So I was not offended. I really believe you reacted because "how could someone I respect be so negative to me." In short, I have a tough job—you have a tough job and we need to work together. As ever, I remain,

Sincerely, Harry.

Boehner decided they had to meet face-to-face to get past it once and for all, so he invited Reid to his office. They always met in the Speaker's office, so Boehner could smoke. Seconds after Reid arrived, they looked at each other, both burst out laughing, and the relationship was sealed. They would remain friends until Reid's death, and Reid even arranged for Boehner to be his partner when MGM Resorts started a think tank.

That year also had a jarring end because of the fiscal cliff negotiations—

federally mandated spending cuts and tax increases occurring simultaneously—that temporarily fractured his relationship with the White House. Reid was going back and forth with 1600 Pennsylvania on various proposals and the key issue was a $250,000 threshold for tax relief that Obama had campaigned on along with some of his senators. Toward the end of the year, Reid was sitting in his magisterial leadership office, a fire burning behind him in the sitting area near his desk, his chief, Krone, across from him, and other staffers arrayed on a plush velvet maroon couch. At one point, Krone handed Reid a piece of paper, telling him it was the Republicans' final offer and would avoid the cliff in a couple of days. President Obama had accepted the offer and wanted Reid to consummate the deal.

Reid looked at the paper, turned to Krone, and simply said, "No." He then turned around and threw the paper with the White House–proposed deal in the fire. No histrionics, no emotion. Just no.

As his then spokesman Adam Jentleson put it, "Reid was showing he was an independent operator from the president, that he had agency here, that he wasn't just going to accept it because the president had."

But Reid, the realist, also knew that if Obama wanted the deal, he couldn't get his caucus to reject it. So Reid told Krone to tell the White House that if Obama wanted an agreement, he would have to send someone to the Hill and sell it. For Reid, there were two things at play: he wanted to protect his senators who had made campaign promises on the tax relief, but he also approached every deal trying to extract the most he could. He did not think he was there yet, and, as usual, his risk tolerance was higher than anyone else's. Reid also was averse to giving ground at a time when Obama had just won reelection; he wanted to keep the momentum going.

However, Obama was not on the same page. So when McConnell publicly wondered whether there was anyone at the White House who could make a deal, Obama agreed to send Vice President Joe Biden to negotiate with McConnell, which the minority leader surely knew Biden would relish. The reality then became that Reid was—in a verb used repeatedly in the media—sidelined. Despite their closeness, Reid and Obama were really opposites. Obama wanted to be above the fray while Reid thrived by being in the tussle.

THE FISCAL CLIFF imbroglio was a historical footnote compared to what Reid would do by the end of 2013. The majority leader had been frustrated, then infuriated by what he saw as the tyranny of the minority, racking up filibuster after filibuster on Obama's judicial nominees.

In August 2012, Republican senators Roger Wicker and Lindsey Graham wrote a letter to the man who in 2005 had so fervently fought to block Bill Frist from considering the nuclear option to replace the filibuster with a majority requirement. It read in part:

> We are writing to express our concern regarding your recent remarks suggesting major changes to the rules of the Senate—changes that would severely compromise the rights of the minority. We fear that such statements threaten far-reaching consequences for the institution of the Senate and its current and future membership.

The Republicans reminded Reid of his 2005 stance and that he had previously agreed with McConnell not to invoke the so-called constitutional option to erase the filibuster, "a critical tool in keeping the majority in check."

Reid had no intention of going nuclear in 2012, but by February 2013, when the Republicans, for the first time in the country's history, filibustered a secretary of defense (Chuck Hagel), he had had enough. Those who knew his thinking at the time say Reid was already prepared to end the filibuster for lower-court nominations, at least, but that the Hagel episode catalyzed him to move forward.

"I think he basically came into 2013 ready to go there and just get the votes," Jentleson recalled. "So I think you can probably find some statements from him during the course of the year that there were no plans. But I think his own mind was made up, and there were a lot of squishy votes [in the Democratic caucus]."

It was more than the historic nature of the Hagel filibuster that catalyzed Reid to act, he said, as the Republicans blocked Obama sub-cabinet posts and judges for the DC Circuit Court of Appeals. The National Labor Relations Board, a critical body for unions, could not even get a quorum. Reid defended his action by saying rules had been changed plenty of times, but he was downplaying what a watershed this could be. He knew it, and the majority leader also firmly believed the future of the Obama presidency was at stake.

Reid chafed at any criticism that he was being hypocritical, denying the only difference between 2013 and 2005 was the party in power. He insisted that McConnell had made it his mission to thwart Obama at every turn and had changed the norms of the Senate. He also put his change of position in the context of his evolution on other issues, from abortion to immigration to gun control to gay rights. It was not situational, he argued; it was a sign of maturity.

Reid knew this was not a slam dunk, that corralling the votes inside the caucus might be difficult.

"There were half a dozen members that didn't want to vote," Reid's number two, Dick Durbin, said. "They felt it was the wrong decision. I think it was a terrible choice: either keep with the McConnell way of stopping these judges through the filibuster or changing the rules of the Senate in a way that would have a profound impact."

Obama, for his part, did not actively engage with senators. But he understood where Reid was coming from.

"I think that Harry was an institutionalist and had great respect for the Senate traditions," Obama said in 2022. "By that point, he had witnessed, we had all witnessed, a level of obstruction when it came to judicial nominations that we had never seen before. What had begun as selected instances of highly controversial Supreme Court justices being blocked was now a circumstance in which just routinely, [Republicans] were just going to prevent a Democratic administration from filling vacancies and on the federal bench. And McConnell was very explicit about the strategy. He didn't need a rationale; it no longer required that somehow."

Reid, and others, would argue that this *was* him being an institutionalist, that he was fighting to save the norms of the Senate, that he didn't wreck it, that it was already broken. What was paramount to him was the functioning of the Senate, or it was at that time in history.

Reid knew he didn't have the votes in the caucus, that he had to, in the words of one of his staffers, "lead them all to water on it." He slowly and methodically built the case that Obama's judges would never be confirmed if a supermajority vote was required. "I had to be talked into it," said Patty Murray, a member of his leadership team. "I had to really think about what the process was and what it would mean. And he'd reached his conclusion long before he talked me into it."

Murray said Reid was able to talk her and others into the change "by sharing his frustration. And he was passionate about this, and the need to fill the courts and fulfill our responsibilities."

As Reid lobbied his reluctant caucus members, he occasionally would seek counsel from the man he replaced, Tom Daschle: "I can't tell you the number of times he lamented how broken the Senate had become and would say to me what he said to me on countless occasions, 'Tom, it's nothing like when you were here, when we were there together.'"

Ironically, a few years earlier, after the 2008 release of Reid's autobiography, *The Good Fight*, in which he railed against the Republicans talking about invoking the nuclear option three years earlier, Reid sat down with Daschle for a conversation on C-SPAN.

"What the Republicans came up with was a way to change our country forever," Reid told Daschle. "They made a decision that if they didn't get every judge they wanted, then they were going to make the Senate just like the House of Representatives."

While it was true that filibusters geometrically increased since that time, Reid's Senate-is-the-cooling-saucer argument—that is, the House heated by the passions of the people would see its legislation tamped down by the more deliberate Senate—that he made with Daschle was timeless. He concluded that section of the C-SPAN conversation with his friend by saying he believed that invoking the nuclear option "would ruin the country."

Yet here he was, five years later, with California's Barbara Boxer and Dianne Feinstein the last holdouts, ready to do what he had said five years earlier would be the ruination of America. On November 21, knowing he had the votes, Reid invoked the nuclear option for all presidential nominees except prospective Supreme Court justices, and it passed 52–48. Three Democrats voted against the rules change—Carl Levin of Michigan, Joe Manchin of West Virginia, and Mark Pryor of Arkansas—but Reid had wiggle room.

Republicans, led by McConnell and Boehner, railed about the Democrats trying to distract from the poor rollout and tanking numbers of Obamacare and hoped and promised it would come home to roost in a year at the ballot box. But after the vote, Reid was elated, while another member of his leadership team, Chuck Schumer, seemed saddened. Schumer and Reid had talked for hours about the scheme, but Schumer was a reluctant yes vote—or so he would say later.

After the vote and unbeknownst to Reid, Faiz Shakir, a top aide and his bridge to the left, had gathered dozens of progressives into a room in the Capitol to celebrate. Many of those were special interests Reid and his team had harnessed to pressure his colleagues: union activists upset that the NLRB had been stymied, Common Cause members, MoveOn.org folks. They were all there. And when Reid entered the room, it thundered with applause. (Several Reid staffers believed if he could have rounded up the votes to end the filibuster for legislation, the majority leader would have done that, too.)

Reid, who rarely second-guessed himself, did not look back on his decision, even knowing McConnell as he did and realizing the partisan winds could shift. "I didn't look that far ahead," he remembered. "I knew that I wanted to get this done at this time, it was something that was important for the body. I'd worry about the future at a later time."

Shakir says Reid considered what might happen in a different scenario, but the discussions generally didn't last long for one reason: "Let's not be naive. I think he felt that Hillary Clinton would likely be the next president of the United States."

But that, of course, did not occur and in April 2017, after Donald Trump was elected, McConnell invoked the nuclear option on Supreme Court justices, which allowed Neil Gorsuch, Amy Coney Barrett, and Brett Kavanaugh to be approved on majority votes. Many on the left blamed Reid for enabling the change; many on the right gleefully thanked him as Trump was able to appoint three high court members. Reid said none of that trolling bothered him, and others said McConnell did not need a precedent to do what he did, that he was just waiting for a Republican Senate and White House occupant.

Reid continued until shortly before his death to insist he had no regrets for the move in 2013. Almost exactly two years after McConnell changed the rule to include high court justices, Reid wrote an op-ed in the *New York Times*, saying the filibuster had become an anachronism and needed to be abolished because the Senate had "become an unworkable legislative graveyard."

Reid seemed to truly believe, despite the partisanship that suffused the column, that the Senate had been badly damaged. But he was alternately bemused and furious as Democratic senators, some of whom voted for the 2013 change, went public with their buyer's remorse. "A couple of Democratic senators today have very short memories because they have stated publicly on the record that they wish that we had not changed the rules," Reid said before he died. "That's the dumbest damn thing. They were there. They voted for it. Now to come back and try to rewrite history is impossible."

Alabama Republican Richard Shelby, a onetime Democrat and one of Reid's closest friends in Congress, chuckled about Reid being in high dudgeon. Shelby said he believes Reid, if similarly situated, would have done just what McConnell did to enhance the prospects of remaking the US Supreme Court. "If you've already broken the glass, why not?" Shelby said wryly.

Schumer, Reid's close friend and ally, had an I-told-you-so moment shortly before Reid's death about the 2013 maneuver. "I told him, I thought it was a bad idea, but he was just so fed up and so pissed off," Schumer said. "I did get him to make sure that we didn't go nuclear on Supreme Court judges. And look what happened . . . McConnell came in and got rid of the role right away. But yes, I thought going nuclear would have bad consequences for us. And on that one, I may have been right."

ABOUT A MONTH before the nuclear option vote, Reid had to deal with another internal crisis as he was negotiating an end to a government shutdown engineered by conservative Republicans to defund Obamacare. The maneuver turned out disastrously for the Republicans, who had to capitulate and reopen the government after only a couple of weeks. But during that time, in an evening phone call on October 10, 2013, that would not be revealed until a year later, President Obama called Reid to complain about his chief, Krone, whom he suspected of leaking to the media. Krone's antipathy to Obama and the White House was already well-known, but on the call, not knowing Krone was listening in, Obama pressed Reid about his chief of staff's behavior. Krone spoke up and challenged the president.

Reid did not defend Krone, which almost destroyed their close relationship and ended Krone's employment. Krone was furious that his boss had not stood up for him, and Reid exhibited something he was rarely known for, if ever—panic, or a reasonable facsimile thereof.

After the call Reid sent a series of plaintive emails to his chief of staff:

> I am so sad—words cannot explain. Will u let me talk tu tonite? Otherwise I will not rest and will do something wrong. So please give me a chance to explain, remember I knew u were on the line

> How can I handle my life with all I have going—so let's talk—be mad, but give me a chance to explain other things going in my life other than govt
>
> If not for me could u for Landra talk to me—she knows my life won't work without u

Krone ignored his boss until the next day when he wrote back to Reid to essentially tender his resignation:

> The president questioned my character and you were silent. You did not stand up for me and did not tell him he was wrong. Worse, you agreed with him . . . Five years ago I upended my life in order to help you in a time of need. I am proud of what we have accomplished. Unfortunately, I do not know how I can continue in the role I played in your life. My hurt is too deep.

Reid pleaded with Krone to stay, and on October 12, he wrote to him:

> No matter the outcome of the last few hours always know that even tho I disappointed u, always and forever u have been my fifth son—and I hope u know I love u and will always

Krone eventually agreed to stay, but his vitriol toward Obama and the White House was unabated during the election cycle. Both men were upset as the 2014 election approached that the White House, in their view, had not made good on commitments to help fund the Senate Majority PAC, which had been started by Reid's lieutenants Susan McCue and Rebecca Lambe. Krone's tenor did not change as he wrote to Reid in May: "The President should be ashamed of himself for his pathetic White House." As it became clear in late summer that the Senate would probably fall into Republican hands, Krone emailed the senator:

> This will and should make you furious but I have it on good word the White House is starting to spin that losing the Senate will not be the worst thing in

> the world because it will free up the president to cut deals with Republicans and work around you. The WH is spinning that on things like trade deals and tax reform the president wants to work with republicans . . . I wonder who's [*sic*] side the White House is really on.

Reid's response:

> Pardon me as I need to get out of the car to vomit.

THE 2014 ELECTION indeed was cataclysmic for Reid, at home and in Washington.

In Nevada, his vaunted machine sputtered after he failed to persuade anyone credible to take on Brian Sandoval, the governor who had beaten his son four years earlier and was seen as a possible and formidable foe for Reid in 2016. Reid had persuaded an up-and-coming assemblywoman, Lucy Flores, whom he called a "perfect candidate," to run for lieutenant governor. She would be a backstop to Sandoval running against him because she would become governor if he won.

But without a candidate at the top of the ticket, the quirky Nevada choice "None of these candidates" won the Democratic primary, leaving the second-place finisher, an unknown septuagenarian named Bob Goodman, at the helm. A broad and deep red wave washed over the state. Republicans took every statewide office, captured both House swing seats, and took both the assembly and state senate away from the Democrats. It was an unmitigated disaster and without Flores in the number two slot, there was a real possibility that Sandoval, whom polls showed crushing the senator, would end his career in two years.

In the US Senate, Republicans picked up nine seats, thus putting the Democrats in the minority and changing Reid's title if he could retain the job, which was far from guaranteed.

It was clear a couple of days before the vote that he would have to finesse the cataclysmic election results to hold on to his leadership role. Reid assembled his senior staff for a meeting two days before the vote. Reid planned to call Minnesota's Amy Klobuchar and Massachusetts' Elizabeth Warren—he had been instrumental in bringing the latter to Washington in 2008 to help oversee the bank bailouts—both future presidential candidates, to inform them they would be elevated into leadership, a nod to a younger and more female caucus.

The staffers agreed that they needed to revamp the floor operations, which members had complained about, many having been spoiled by Reid's attentiveness to their needs and egos. One staffer suggested that Durbin retain the title of "whip" but that Schumer be given the title of "assistant leader" that usually went along with that job, to assuage egos and streamline the floor operations. Reid interjected that someone had to take direct responsibility for running the floor. The idea fell apart when another staffer pointed out that taking away a title from a current leader was untenable.

All agreed that Reid should use phrases such as "significant leadership positions" and "bringing in new blood" in his speech to the caucus to talk about Klobuchar and Warren. The plan was for Hawaii's Brian Schatz to counter if someone rose to speak against Reid.

By the time of the meeting November 13, word had reached Reid that West Virginia's Joe Manchin and others wanted to delay the vote. (One person close to Reid said Manchin was a constant thorn in the senator's side—"Manchin drove him crazy"—and some who followed him might understand that feeling.) That was a clear sign that his foes believed he had the votes, so any delay could be problematic for him.

"Are those asking for a delay motivated because they want to discuss my leadership or because they believe a delay will cause a different outcome?" Reid asked at the caucus meeting's outset, according to his prepared remarks. "If it is the former, then I am fully prepared to discuss my role as leader. I will not back down from that discussion. Frankly, I welcome it. If it is the latter, and you believe a delay is in the best interests of the caucus, then I respectfully disagree. We as a caucus cannot afford to walk out of this room today without resolving our leadership structure. We need to show unity and set the tone for the next Congress."

And then Reid's prepared remarks hit the button he knew would take a delay off the table:

> Let's be absolutely clear about what a delay would mean. It would be a nuclear explosion in the press. It would make Democratic divisions the top political story for weeks and probably months. Every senator in this room would spend the next week/or more being chased down the halls by reporters asking you to pick a side . . . It would get ugly, and Democrats would enter the next Congress divided when what we need more than anything is to be united.

Reid then told the caucus members he shared their frustration at the election results, but he used historical trends to argue that Obama's numbers should have cost them even more seats. In "the sixth year of an increasingly unpopular president . . . based on where the President's approval ratings were, we should have lost a minimum of twelve seats [not nine]." He put most of it on Obama, saying the Democrats had raised an unprecedented amount of money and defied historical trends. It was quite a magnificent bit of self-preservation spin.

Reid then went through a thorough trashing of the Republicans, reminding his colleagues of negotiations on deficit reduction and amendments that went nowhere and concluding, "The Republican leadership had a premeditated plan to prevent us from doing anything. And they worked that plan."

The meeting lasted four hours. No one spoke against Reid, but at least a half dozen members voted against him, as *Politico*'s Manu Raju and Burgess Everett reported: Claire McCaskill of Missouri, Heidi Heitkamp of North Dakota, Manchin, Tim Kaine of Virginia, Mary Landrieu of Louisiana, and Mark Warner of Virginia.

Reid held on despite the electoral disaster. He was the leader again, diminished in a diminished caucus. Now it was time to focus on reelection.

CHAPTER TWENTY-THREE

AN EXERCISE BAND SLIPS AND A CAREER FADES AWAY

On the morning of New Year's Day 2015, Harry Reid was doing his usual workout routine. He had set up an elastic band in the bathroom of his home in Henderson, attached to a sturdy brass handle on the shower. Reid would do repetitions with the band for each arm. Landra, as was her wont, was observing Reid, who had turned seventy-five a month earlier.

Suddenly the band slipped out of Reid's hand and he flew backward across the room, spun around, and smacked his head into a corner of a cabinet with a quartz countertop. Blood was spattering, coming from his right eye. He tried to get up but Landra told him not to move. She ran out to get his protective detail, and they found some blood-clotting medicine, which Landra always had handy since the senator had begun taking blood thinners after his ministroke a decade earlier.

Landra then called Dr. Ike Khan, the longtime family friend who was always their first call in a medical emergency. Landra told him what had happened and that they could not stop the bleeding. Khan told her to get him to the hospital right away, so they drove to St. Rose Dominican in Henderson, about a fifteen-minute drive from their home. The emergency room staff immediately performed an MRI on Reid, which showed he had fractured the orbit around the eye and there were bone chips, too. He also had broken ribs, but they seemed almost an afterthought compared to the danger posed by the eye injury.

Khan decided they had to get Reid to University Medical Center, the county hospital that had a trauma center and an ophthalmologist on call. Khan called Mason Van Houweling, the hospital's CEO, to alert him that Reid was on the way. Once the St. Rose team had stopped the bleeding, they drove Reid to Las Vegas, about a half hour away. He was in a lot of pain.

When they arrived at the county hospital, Reid was seen by an ophthalmologist, who immediately recognized the severity of the injury. There was bleeding in the eye, going back to the retina. Reid would need major surgery and his sight likely would be compromised or lost.

The visceral reaction of Team Reid, not surprisingly, was to downplay to the public what had happened. The first communications came from Chief of Staff David Krone, who was receiving updates (with a few other high-level staffers copied) from the special agent of the Capitol Police Eric Bridges, on the ground in Nevada. Internal emails illuminate the chain of events and show a mixture of shock and concern, and questions about how to deal with the media:

At 10:52 a.m., Pacific Standard Time, Bridges to Krone and others:

> HMR is at St. Rose Hospital in Henderson NV. He is suffering from a cut on his face after a resistance band broke and hit him in the face. He may also have injuries resulting from his fall afterwards.

At 11:00 a.m., Krone to communications team members Adam Jentleson and Kristen Orthman:

> Spoke with Eric. They are doing X-rays now. HMR is talking and seems to [be] sane of mind.

> They rushed him to the ER under HMR's name and not an alias. Not sure if anything will leak.
>
> Landra and Key are with him.

Shortly thereafter Krone spoke to Bridges, and he relayed the contents of the call to his deputy, Drew Willison, who *tried* to lighten the mood:

> Is this a good time to mention that I earmarked a TON of money to UMC in the bad old days?!?

Krone:

> Oh, I think they know that!!!!!!!
>
> When he shows up they see one thing . . . their meal ticket!!!!!

By that evening, Krone had talked to Dr. Khan, and he gave the team the download at 8:55 p.m.:

> HMR has three broken ribs and the right orbital bone is broken but no signs of internal bleeding. The right side of his face is black and blue and his eye is swollen shut.
>
> They had eye specialists in to examine him and they recommend he will need surgery or follow up which can be done at Walter Reed.
>
> They will do a CT scan in the morning and if all is fine they will release him.
>
> He is insisting he fly back to DC on Sunday so I am working on a plane.
>
> The only Senator who knows is Schumer who I called.

Reid's communications aide Kristen Orthman was on an early morning flight to Las Vegas to deal with the media. The first statement was not, as time would prove, wholly accurate:

> On Thursday, Senator Reid received treatment at University Medical Center

> in Las Vegas for injuries sustained in an accident he suffered while exercising at home in Henderson.
>
> A piece of equipment Senator Reid was using to exercise broke, causing him to fall and break a number of ribs and bones in his face.
>
> Senator Reid will return to Washington this weekend and be in the office Tuesday as the Senate prepares to reconvene. His doctors expect a full recovery.

When Reid arrived at home early on January 2 and declined to take all of the pain medications he was given, his staff saw a chance to burnish his image. Jentleson emailed:

> I agree with that concern for things he is taking but if he's not taking anything which it sounds like he's not, it's the kind of detail that sticks with people and makes him sound very tough.
>
> Then this: So he did take some morphine after they stopped the loden[s]. Now he's just on tylenol.
>
> I'll skip this detail for now, if all goes well when he's back tuesday he can say something off the cuff to reporters like, I popped a couple tylenol or something like that.

(Reid had a remarkably high tolerance for pain. Once, during a trip to raise money, his fundraiser Paul DiNino accidentally slammed the car door on Reid's fingers. Instead of screaming in pain, Reid looked calmly at DiNino and said, "My hand is in the door. Could you open the door?")

Krone was scrambling to find a plane to fly Reid back to DC, and he mentioned that Sheldon Adelson's right hand, Andy Abboud, had offered one. Krone also chatted with Reid the day after the accident and then filled in Myrick and Jentleson:

> I just spoke with him and next week is not going to be pretty. He will need a cane to walk and has zero vision out of his right eye. The worst is the doctors

> cannot tell him if/when vision will be restored . . . The articles are good in that they downplay his injury but people may be surprised when they see him.

Reid and Landra flew back to Washington on Sunday. "He looked terrible," Landra recalled. "And that's where we saw the doctors and realized that they wanted to do probably three surgeries and that they wouldn't know about his sight until they got rid of the blood."

On January 3, fielding a note from a well-wisher who said she was relieved the injuries were not serious (based on the media statement), Krone emailed back:

> Oh, he's seriously injured. We just aren't saying it.
>
> 3 broken ribs, a concussion, and a broken orbital bone of his right eye.
>
> His face is black and blue and his eye is swollen shut. No vision at all and doctors can't say if/when it will return.
>
> He will need surgery on his eye in about two weeks.
>
> He needs a cane to move and from what I can tell his speech is a bit slurred.
>
> What a freaking mess.

The next day, Krone said Reid's doctors had insisted that he use a cane, especially because of his balance issues, and that, of course, the senator did not want to use one.

On January 5, to give off an aura of normalcy that was very dissonant with reality, Reid announced in a news release the construction of a new VA hospital in Nevada. On January 10, he called into the local NPR affiliate to sound upbeat about his health and his reelection.

Reid was up early, working the phones, pacing around the Ritz-Carlton to get some exercise. His team made sure the media knew he was active and running, figuratively if not yet literally.

Reid made his first appearance at the Capitol on January 21 and then held his first media appearance the next day, three weeks after the accident, in an attempt to show the world he was still sharp despite being one-eyed. He looked bruised and battered, but he seemed sharp as ever, albeit noncommittal about his reelection, using conditional verbs such as "plan" and "intend."

Reid would have to undergo several surgeries. Krone visited him after the first one and reported what he saw to colleagues:

> I just left him. Overall, he looks okay. He's swollen and his voice is really different—probably from the tube they put down his throat. He's lying in a recliner with his eyes closed and a blanket over him. He will have to go back to the doctor all week.
>
> The doctors are pleased but no word yet on vision, and he will need further surgery to get to the back of the eye.
>
> On a funny note, he was asking about the cloture vote tonight. The guy never stops.

Reid had to sleep at his desk, putting his head down on a special pillow and getting painful eye drops periodically. He was not in good shape, but his palace guard had been activated and they were going to make sure everything seemed normal, even though he was out of his Capitol office for a couple of weeks. Some on his team felt the vultures who were exposed during the leadership vote were circling, and he also had to show no vulnerability, despite the injury, because he was running for a fifth term this cycle.

Two weeks after the first surgery, on February 12, Reid had a second, even more grueling operation. Krone's assessment in an email to his higher-level staff:

> Longer than expected, about 7-8 hours.
>
> They repaired what they could on the retina and did the cornea transplant. He's home now and had to lie face down on this special pillow/bed but he didn't sleep a wink. The doctors let him get in his recliner so he is at an angle and I think he's sleeping now.
>
> No verdict on his eyesight. It will take some time before they know.

The operation did not restore his vision, but his staff was still putting out the word that he was running for reelection. Rebecca Lambe was interviewing campaign staffers and was looking for a day-to-day campaign manager. Reid was raising money; he only needed one eye for that task.

It is only in hindsight that most or all of this turned out to be playacting, some by thespians who knew they were part of the performance and others who were simply reading lines they had been given. Reid had made his choice, informing some key staffers a week or two before an announcement. It was amazing that no word leaked, especially because of Reid's penchant for gossip—"Reid is the weak link but going to be a hard process keeping this under wraps," his top aide Gary Myrick wrote on March 16 to Krone.

Early in the morning hours of March 27, 2015, in a video and a *New York Times* story, Reid announced he would not seek reelection. He had informed very few people about his decision, only telling close associates such as Schumer hours before the video was uploaded to YouTube in the middle of the night.

In the video, Reid had bruises on the right side of his face, his bad eye obscured by a fogged-up lens on his glasses. About a minute into the three-and-a-half-minute video, he made the stunning announcement starting with a picture of him embracing Landra:

"This accident has caused us for the first time to have a little downtime. I have had the time to ponder and to think. We've got to be more concerned about the country, the Senate, the state of Nevada . . . And as a result of that, I am not going to run for reelection."

Reid went on to say it would be "inappropriate for me to soak up all those resources on me when I could be devoting them to the [Democratic] caucus" to try to recapture control of the Senate. And then this, which he said calmly but disingenuously: "The decision I have made has absolutely nothing to do with my injury."

Reid also claimed his "path to reelection is much easier than any time that I have run for reelection" and was not a factor. Indeed, the Republicans had no obvious top-tier candidates yet. It's almost impossible to pinpoint exactly when he made the decision. In a journal he kept mostly to write about family matters, Reid had mused as far back as 2007 that he might not run again, that he was worried about staying too long, as some of his colleagues had.

The truth is, according to Reid and his wife, while he believed he could win, the devastating injury combined with his chronic balance issues made it unlikely he could endure the travails of a campaign. The strain of being the Democratic leader and campaigning for a sixth term would just be too much. Reid, as he had demonstrated throughout his career and even at the age of seventy-five, knew only one speed.

"He was thinking about it before the accident," Landra said. "He said, 'You know, I might surprise them, I could decide not to run.' But when the accident happened, and he realized he had three surgeries ahead of him, there was no question about what he was going to do . . . the choice was that he wanted to be able to finish out his time as the leader."

Within days of the announcement, the conspiracy theorists unleashed on blogs and even Rush Limbaugh on his show suggested the real story was that Reid had been beaten up by the mob. Others suggested his brother Larry, who had recently been arrested for DUI, had pummeled his brother in a drunken rage. There was no evidence to support either claim, but this was the state of play in a polarized country where Reid evoked strong feelings on the right.

Ultimately, Reid's physical incapacitation was greater than the public or even his staff could see. He had trouble walking up and down stairs, he had little peripheral vision, and his chronic balance problems only exacerbated his condition. Reid also told his close friend Jay Brown that he had been advised that if he put too much strain on his left eye reading all the documents he needed to devour, he could lose sight in that eye, too, rendering him blind.

His chief political lieutenant, Lambe, quietly alerted Catherine Cortez Masto, who as attorney general had indicted a prospective Reid foe and badly wanted to be a senator, to be ready. She was. She announced her candidacy on April 8, less than two weeks after Reid's video was released, as if it had been choreographed.

FROM THE MOMENT he announced his retirement, Reid hardly gave his decision a second thought. He prided himself on not looking back after he made a decision, and this was no different. If anything, Reid was more unplugged than ever, focused on tasks at hand and unafraid to open his mouth. Reid—and his staff—may have been thinking about his legacy, but the senator also was intent on not slowing down. High on his to-do list was ensuring Nevada's successful role in the early-state matrix, that his eponymous machine elected a Democratic successor, and that the party's presidential nominee win Nevada.

To that latter end, Reid inserted himself—and decisively—into the state legislature, controlled after the 2014 debacle by Republicans, to ensure Nevada did not lose its early-state status. When the Republicans appeared to have the votes for a supermajority to pass a bill switching to a primary, which would have jeopardized Reid's agreement with the Democratic National Committee for early-state status, he called the key vote, a Democratic lawmaker named Harvey Munford. Munford was an African American assemblyman, and Reid told him that the country's first African American president needed his vote on this issue. Munford came out against the plan; the bill died.

Reid also was firming up the foundation of his legacy in notable areas. He persuaded President Obama to attend two of his signature events that year that would endure after he was gone—a Las Vegas Clean Energy Summit and a Lake Tahoe Summit. He would later express confidence that the president would designate an area near the Arizona border known as Gold Butte as a national monument (he would), a capstone to three decades of his work to protect pristine lands in his state that made him a hero to environmentalists and a villain to many rural Nevadans.

Reid's lips, though, were as loose as ever. He accused Justice Antonin

Scalia of endorsing racist tropes during an affirmative action case. PolitiFact gave him a "Pants on Fire" rating for ludicrously claiming 30 percent of American women get their only health care from Planned Parenthood. When asked in April by CNBC's John Harwood about the Republican presidential field, which included three of his colleagues, Reid retorted, "I don't really care. I think they're all losers."

Reid also had decided that he was going to sue the manufacturer of the exercise bands, Hygenic Intangible Property Holding Company, the Hygenic Corporation, and Performance Health LLC. The lawsuit filed in early October alleged the companies "combined to create, manufacture and market a defective product called TheraBand or Thera-Band exercise band."

This was the kind of product liability case that Harry Reid the trial lawyer was quite familiar with. It also was a Harry Reid special, the kind of case with little hope of winning that Reid the trial lawyer might have taken on. Reid had been using the band three times a week for years without a mishap and the senator initially said the band broke, but the remnants of the band had been tossed in the trash, so there was no evidence. Four years later, a jury would take only an hour to reject the claims.

REID'S FINAL YEAR as a US senator was eventful, including one maneuver that had a potentially deciding effect on the presidential race.

Nevada was once again the third state to vote in the Democratic presidential nominating caucus, and with two of his senators running, Bernie Sanders and Hillary Clinton, Reid was publicly neutral. However, Reid never believed Sanders could defeat Clinton, and he was certain the Vermont senator would lose the general election to whomever the Republicans nominated. But when Sanders and Clinton essentially tied in Iowa (she won by a quarter of a percentage point) and Sanders then won by a landslide in New Hampshire, Nevada's importance only became greater. Sanders had an organization in the state, and the powerful Culinary Union, like Reid, was publicly neutral, even though its heavily Hispanic members were generally thought to favor Clinton. Union leaders claimed it had no time to organize a campaign because of contract negotiations with the casinos. Clinton had a huge lead in Nevada, but it slowly evaporated, and the race seemed as if it could go either way. If Sanders won, he might have enough momentum to pose a serious threat to win the nomination.

That's when Reid telephoned the head of the Culinary Union, D. Taylor, and told him to start mobilizing his members to vote. Reid also called casino bosses, urging them to let their workers vote at caucus sites set up on the Strip. Reid knew this would help Clinton. She won by five percentage points, blunting Sanders's momentum, and went on to win South Carolina and the nomination.

"He [Reid] shared my opinion of Senator Sanders," Clinton recalled in an interview. "And he understood that he was a destructive force, not a constructive one, and that he didn't know how to get things done. But he could be a very effective demagogue. And I think Harry played it exactly right. He was always for me, his organization was always for me. We were always working together. And he waited until it was critical."

Later in the year, Reid's machine had to squelch a Sanders campaign attempt to overturn the results at the state convention, which ended in a near-riot at the Paris Hotel on the Strip. There would be bad blood between the Sanders forces and Team Reid that would fester for years in Nevada Democratic politics. But in the short run, Reid had done what he had to do to help Clinton become the nominee.

(Despite assisting Clinton and despite what she said about Reid sharing her view of Sanders, the Vermont and Nevada senators had a personal friendship they maintained before and after. They had bonded over Massachusetts senator John Kerry talking too much in caucus meetings, advocating for a time limit; Reid had once called the postmaster general in Sanders's presence to stop a post office from being shut down; they both had wives they implicitly trusted and were their closest counselors. When Sanders fell ill in Las Vegas during the 2020 election, Reid quietly went to visit him in the hospital. Reid was the consummate insider, Sanders the ultimate outsider.

But they found common ground, except when Reid felt his friend would hurt the party.)

Reid then became hyperfocused on November, hoping to ensure Clinton won Nevada and that his handpicked successor, Cortez Masto, was elected against a very difficult challenger, Rep. Joe Heck, a doctor and war vet. When Donald Trump became the Republican nominee that summer, Reid became an eager attack dog, just as he had been with Mitt Romney four years earlier. Trump and Reid had once been friendly. Reid now had no compunction calling the Trump campaign "fat, ugly, and dirty," and just as he had raised unsubstantiated claims about Romney, Reid publicly raised the specter of Trump's supposed ties to Russia. In a letter he wrote in August to the FBI director, James Comey, and that he later released, Reid wrote, in part:

> In my communications with you and other top officials in the national security community, it has become clear that you possess explosive information about close ties and coordination between Donald Trump, his top advisors, and the Russian government—a foreign interest openly hostile to the United States, which Trump praises at every opportunity. The public has a right to know this information. I wrote to you months ago calling for this information to be released to the public. There is no danger to American interests from releasing it. And yet, you continue to resist calls to inform the public of this critical information.

This was an incendiary charge, one Reid could not back up, but one he knew would make headlines. Reid would not stop, even though the *New York Times* reported in October that the FBI had found no clear nexus between Russia and the Trump campaign. But, he hoped, the damage had been done, and that he would soon be saying, as he did about Romney, that Trump lost so it was worth it. (After the election, Clinton said, Reid called her several times to apologize for not getting the Russia story more traction.)

When Election Night came, Clinton won Nevada, which would have mattered if the Midwest wall of states had not fallen, thus electing Trump. Reid's political organization, though, helped elect his successor, Cortez Masto, flipped control of the state senate to Democrats, and, acting on behalf of the man who once had an A rating from the NRA before it abandoned him in 2010, pushed a gun control ballot question over the top.

THE ELECTION WAS a fitting send-off for the senator, who took to the floor on December 8 to give a valedictory. He was introduced by his longtime nemesis, Mitch McConnell, who delivered a short and unusually sweet ode to his rival, mentioning their mutual love of baseball and Reid's adoration for Landra.

"It's clear that Harry and I have two very different worldviews, two different ways of doing things, and two different sets of legislative priorities," McConnell said. "But through the years, we've come to understand some things about one another. And we've endeavored to keep our disagreements professional rather than personal. We've also found some common ground through baseball. I hardly know what it's like to serve here without Harry."

Reid, uncharacteristically, spoke for more than an hour, with two of the most important women in his professional life, Patty Murray and Barbara Mikulski, sitting behind him. He prefaced his speech by responding to McConnell's words, saying that beyond their political differences, his colleague had been there for him when Landra got hurt or sick and after his eye accident.

Much of the rest of the speech was touting what he saw as his greatest accomplishments, from passing his early-career Taxpayer Bill of Rights to saving MGM Resorts by leaning on bankers during the recession, enacting the stimulus package and the Affordable Care Act, and helping downwinders, those Nevadans affected by aboveground nuclear tests. He peppered the speech with names of senators who had aided him in passing legislation. He also mentioned a few notable failures that stuck in his craw:

"McCarran Airport [in Las Vegas]. I've tried for years to get the name taken off that. He was a Democratic senator from Nevada, who was an awful man. I tried to get his name off; that didn't work. I tried to get J. Edgar Hoover's name off the FBI building; that didn't work."

Reid also mentioned some measures he pushed that didn't get as much attention, including funding for suicide prevention, a tribute to his father, and his little-known advocacy for stopping female genital mutilation (he spent twenty years working on the issue without any fanfare, even raising the issue with Mormon Church elders during a November 2016 visit), for which he gave a reliably graphic Harry Reid description during his valedictory.

He, of course, talked about squelching Yucca Mountain, his advocacy for clean energy, his passage of Nevada's first national park, his negotiations to pass a landmark water deal in northern Nevada. He mentioned the rainbow judiciary he had helped establish in the state.

He wrapped by gushing about his children and nineteen grandchildren and then, knowing he would not be able to maintain his usual stoicism, said, "Okay, here goes:

"Whatever success I had in my educational life, my life as a lawyer, my life as a politician, including my time in Congress, is directly attributable to Landra, my wife," Reid said, choking up a few times. "We met when Landra was a sophomore in high school and I was a junior. That was more than six decades ago. We married at age nineteen . . . She's been the being of my existence, in my personal life and my public life. Disraeli, the great [British] prime minister, said in 1837 . . . 'The magic of first love is that it never ends.' I believe that. She's my first love. It will never end."

A standing ovation followed. Durbin was the first to get to him, then Murray, then the parade of hand-shaking and well-wishes. It was over.

HARRY REID SLIPPED into life after politics—well, life after being an elected official, to be more accurate—effortlessly. MGM Resorts, which Reid had saved by putting the arm on banks almost a decade earlier, gave him an office and a consultant's job. He was able to open doors for the company in other jurisdictions with his bulging Rolodex, and he provided invaluable counsel to CEO Jim Murren. And for a while, just down the hall from him was another MGM consultant: Brian Sandoval. As big as Reid had gotten, the world of Nevada politics was still small.

The ex-senator also kept his hand in politics, talking to former colleagues and Reid Machine cogs, relishing more than when he had been in the Senate taking interviews and expounding on the issues of the day, ranging from his old "friend" Mitch McConnell going nuclear for Supreme Court justices to calling Donald Trump all manner of names, including "the worst president we've ever had."

One subject Reid felt much freer to talk about than he had when he had an elected title was UFOs, which his staff had persuaded him not to mention while he was in office. Unbeknownst to almost anyone, going back three decades, Reid had developed relationships on the subject with the Las Vegas television investigative reporter George Knapp, who had done a lot of reporting on UFOs, and Robert Bigelow, an entrepreneur who was fascinated by the topic. Reid had aided Knapp when he sought documents from government agencies and had secretly, as majority leader in 2007, directed, with the help of Daniel Inouye and Ted Stevens, the Pentagon to spend millions on what was known as the Advanced Aerospace Threat Identification Program.

Reid's staff was aware of his contacts with Knapp during this time, and they tried to thwart them as best they could. But one night, conscripted to go to a meeting with Knapp, his spokesman, Craig Varoga, had come along. They met in the parking lot of a school after Reid attended the opening, and the first thing the senator said was: "George, I know that Craig has been dodging you, but this is what I'm going to say. In Craig's defense, talking about UFOs is probably something that would give most press secretaries hemorrhoids. So understand, from his point of view, he's just doing his job and is trying to protect me." He then instructed Varoga not to evade Knapp's calls anymore.

The UFO program remained clandestine until the end of 2017, when the *New York Times* wrote about it and interviewed Reid. "I'm not embarrassed or ashamed or sorry I got this thing going," Reid told the *Times*. "I think it's one of the good things I did in my congressional service. I've done something that no one has done before."

The *Times* story exploded, nationally and internationally; *60 Minutes* did a piece. Reid refused to back away from the issue. About six months before he died, he wrote an op-ed for the *Times* on the subject that read in part:

> What have I personally learned from official investigations into unidentified aerial phenomena so far? The truth, disappointing as it may be, is that there's still a great deal we don't understand. It's unclear whether the U.F.O.s we have encountered could have been built by foreign adversaries, whether our pilots' visual perception during some encounters was somehow distorted, or whether we truly have credible evidence of extraterrestrial visitations. There may be other, as yet unknown explanations for some of these strange sightings.

Some close to him say they think Reid believed in aliens by the time he passed away. Illinois senator Dick Durbin said Reid called him at one point to tell him about the secret Pentagon program, and he was floored. "And he says, 'I hope you make sure that they're funded.' Well, you could have knocked me over with a feather. UFOs. I left and I went back to my office, and I thought, 'What has he got me into here? You know, how am I ever going to explain this? If they asked me back in Illinois, what are you doing to put money into this thing?' So I did it for the first year."

Durbin certainly thought it was peculiar, but he did not think Reid was crazy. He thought it illuminated a seminal part of Reid's makeup. "What it reflects is not that there's anything wrong with him, but it reflects in my mind, just the breadth of this man's curiosity, interest, intellect," he said a few months before Reid died. "We used to challenge one another to find a new book that the other one hadn't read. And he was always ahead of me. Two steps ahead of me. It was always the most obscure things. He had one about spelunking and exploring caverns. He wanted me to read the Koran."

In an interview about UFOs a few months before he died, Reid said, "I'm willing to accept the science and what it comes up with in the years to come, say these are from some different civilization, accept what you know, but I'm not going to be in some kind of conspiracy. It's got to be based on science. And I'm not a scientist, but I know science when I see it. And I am terribly interested in this phenomenon."

IN THE SPRING of 2018, Reid had a routine colonoscopy. But his doctor, Frank Nemec, encountered some resistance toward the end of the procedure and rather than risk perforating Reid's colon, he recommended that Reid finish with a virtual scan. This turned out to be a very fortunate occurrence for Reid because the virtual colonoscopy found a small spot on his pancreas that would have gone undetected had the regular procedure been completed.

Fearing it was cancerous, his friend Dr. Ike Khan determined that no one in Las Vegas did the volume of this kind of surgery for him to feel comfortable. He found a doctor at Johns Hopkins who had done hundreds of these surgeries, so he arranged for Reid to see him. The surgery took place in mid-May and the tumor was localized and caught early. Reid was lucky, but with pancreatic cancer, it usually is only a matter of time.

Reid's doctors at Johns Hopkins recommended twelve chemotherapy treatments, but Reid could probably only tolerate half that many. Soon, though, other complications arose in the form of a pair of successive compression fractures in his back, which caused him severe pain and eventually confined him to a wheelchair intermittently for the last couple of years of his life. Friends say the man who once could get up in the morning and run ten miles hated the wheelchair, abhorred being seen as disabled, but he still went out in public.

By early 2019, Reid was beginning to decline. On January 2, the *New York Times* essentially published a pre-obituary of the ex-senator, with the reporter Mark Leibovich declaring, "Reid, who is 79, does not have long to live."

Reid's family, friends, and staff were furious, but Leibovich was only reporting what he had found. Leibovich mentioned that lifetime honors were being bestowed by various groups and a plan to rename the Las Vegas airport after Reid was being resurrected. These were the signs of a slow-motion funeral. Pancreatic cancer was a killer, usually within a year, maybe two.

Later that year, Reid's condition had declined so much that he took the recommendation of a friend and was put in contact with Dr. Patrick Soon-Shiong in Los Angeles. The doctor was conducting a clinical trial with three other patients that eschewed bursts of radiation for what he called his compassionate use program for patients who had all but lost hope.

"The cancer has a way to hide and put your natural killer cell to sleep," Soon-Shiong told *People* magazine about the treatment. "What we do is 'find me, expose me, kill me, and then remember me,' meaning taking over the cancer's ability to invade the immune system and then activate your own immune system with our cells."

By mid-2020, after six months of traveling to LA once a week, Reid was, miraculously, cancer-free. That lasted several months, but by early 2021, he was going down to LA every week for more treatments and radiation, Landra said, and he was in a lot of pain. Reid was still relatively sharp mentally, but his memory had begun to fade and he began to repeat stories. His allies began to push the idea of renaming the airport for Reid. Pat McCarran had been arguably the most powerful senator in Nevada history until Reid. A tremendously influential Washington figure, he also turned out to be a nativist and anti-Semite who joined Joe McCarthy's red baiting.

By February 2021, over the objections of those who argued the airport should not be named for such a polarizing figure, the all-Democrat Clark County Commission voted unanimously to rename the facility after Reid. It would be expensive to go through all the bureaucratic hoops—perhaps as much as $5 million—but Stephen Cloobeck, a huge Democratic donor who was close to the senator, promised to raise the money. Eventually, others would contribute, including the convicted felon Billy Walters. Walters, a well-known gambler convicted of insider trading and whose sentence would be commuted by President Trump, had been represented by Reid's confidant Jay Brown, and Reid had written a letter supporting his pardon.

Reid's health began to wane as the year wore on, and shortly after his eighty-second birthday on December 2, he disappeared from public view. A ceremony to unveil the new airport signage and officially consecrate Harry Reid International was hastily put together on December 14. It was a small ceremony, but his eldest son, Rory, attended and Gov. Steve Sisolak spoke. Reid was not well enough to attend or Zoom into the ceremony.

But the senator was proud of the renaming, even if he wouldn't ever say so, and he privately thanked the commissioners, some with handwritten notes. As weak as he was, he called Sisolak to tell him how much he appreciated the governor pushing for the name change.

That day, Wayne Newton sent Reid a text: "Who would have thought when we were just kids that Harry Reid airport would be on Wayne Newton Boulevard [the name of the road running through the airport]." Reid responded: "Thank you. I love you, my forever friend."

Two weeks later, after a lifetime of doing what no one else would do, after surviving the FBI and the mob, after passing seminal legislation and insulting presidents, after being loyal to a fault to family and friends, after being uncommonly acerbic in public and uncommonly kind in private, after bringing billions back to a small state he put on the national political map, after leaving his indelible mark on Nevada's judiciary and the nation's, after changing the dynamic on energy and environmental policy, and after cementing his place as Nevada's most influential elected official and a man who changed the country, for good or ill, Harry Reid finally succumbed on December 28, 2021.

EPILOGUE

When Harry Reid's funeral was held in Las Vegas on January 8, 2022, it was perfectly fitting for Marcus Faust to preside.

Faust, a Mormon and close friend of Reid's, was also a lawyer/lobbyist on Capitol Hill. But just as there was a transactional element to their relationship, so, too, was there a real bond. Faust loved Reid, and it was obvious.

The ceremony lasted almost two and a half hours and featured moving valedictories from the senator's five children as well as President Joe Biden and Reid's legislative partners Chuck Schumer and Nancy Pelosi. Reid had asked Barack Obama to deliver his eulogy when he realized he was dying, and it was the one that would have meant the most to him. But he also would have been touched by the other speakers, including M. Russell Ballard, a Mormon elder, who talked of Reid's abiding faith, rarely seen by the outside world.

Obama, who came to have an extraordinary bond with a man who couldn't have been more different from him, came the closest to capturing Reid in his remarks.

"He didn't believe in highfalutin theories, or rigid ideologies," Obama told the two thousand people assembled at the Smith Center for the Performing Arts in downtown Las Vegas. "He thought most people make decisions based on their life experience, based on the immediate needs of their families, based on their own self-interest, no matter what they may tell themselves. And as a result, Harry met people where they were, not where he wanted them to be. And he was willing to cut deals, even with folks he didn't agree with, or particularly like."

Later, Obama gave this distillation of Reid's qualities: "Pragmatism, adaptability, premium on getting things done, lack of pretension, abiding loyalty."

Funerals are by their nature hagiographic ceremonies, unlikely to capture the true picture of anyone but saints. Harry Reid, as he would be the first to tell you, was no saint. His actual legacy, in the forever changed and polarized world he inhabited, may be distinct from how he is remembered, which may be refracted through a partisan prism.

Jeff Silver, who jousted with Reid and was deeply suspicious of him as a fellow gaming regulator in the 1970s, came to respect Reid and became his friend. "He orchestrated political elections in this state. He protected the gaming industry. He was a national figure. To me, I can't think of anybody else in Nevada that had that much input, had as much impact on the environment we have today."

Former Interior secretary Bruce Babbitt, who admired Reid's commitment to public lands but fought him on mining and Indian gaming policies, understood him well, too. "The first thing that always strikes you is he is entirely devoid of and totally uninterested in all of the razzmatazz that goes with, and all the BS that goes with politics," Babbitt said in 2022. "It's just as if it had never occurred to him . . . And he had a wonderful instinct for the jugular in the best sense of the word."

Babbitt's solicitor at the Interior Department, John Leshy, who also fought with Reid over mining, was otherwise impressed with his environmental legacy and told him so in a 2019 letter after Reid had retired.

"Your record on protecting public lands and the environment in general is practically unmatched in the annals of Congress," Leshy wrote. "Future generations owe you plenty and will justly honor your legacy."

Some will remember his little-known and numerous forays into helping people—a refusenik couple who had escaped to Jerusalem but needed money so he sent them some, a divorced Croatian couple in a child care dispute who motivated Reid to work for a rule that two parents had to sign for a child to get a passport, the amount of money he raised for Nevada's fledgling law school, and the anti-Semitism program he helped create there.

Others will remember the money he sent back to Nevada—don't call it pork! He found funding for projects big and small, even in rural Nevada, where there was little gratitude and much enmity as time went on, including one farmer who topped a fifteen-foot haystack with fluorescent letters: FUCK HARRY REID. He found a million dollars in a budget to give rural Bunkerville a secondary water system; when the airport that would one day bear his name needed money for a new terminal, Reid found a way to ensure officials could sell the bonds; solar projects across the country, and in Nevada, benefited from his insistence on renewable tax credits.

There are hundreds—nay thousands—of stories like those. Reid reveled in getting dinged by antipork groups for his prowess.

Some will recall Reid's work ethic, his plainspokenness, the laconic Westerner. Some will remember the political machine he built, a model for all others and one that lives on after his death, pushing his handpicked successor to a second term in 2022 and saving three Democratic House seats. Others on both sides of the aisle will recall that in a town where someone's word often was worthless, Reid's was gold.

"Well, he was one tough son of a bitch, there's no other way to say it," said the former Speaker John Boehner. "He had a good handle on his members, frankly good control over his members. And he knew what he wanted to get done. And he probably had a pretty good idea of how he wanted to get it done."

Others, though, will never forgive Reid for what he did to Romney, for his ad hominem attacks on George W. Bush, for his Machiavellian streak that might have made Machiavelli blush. For all his private acts of generosity and kindness, Reid also had plenty of political knifings that drew a lot of blood. He relished political combat like no one else, evidenced by the loyalty of his colleagues and the fear of his foes. Democrats loved how Reid fought for them and their issues, in a way they have not seen since he left the Senate.

Reid certainly could be nasty, brutish, and short with people, but he also was very loyal to his staff, who almost to a person adored him. Once, when a lobbyist for the city of Reno yelled at a scheduler in his office, he called the city's delegation into his office and lambasted them. He rarely punched down, and if someone did to anyone in his orbit, he had a long memory.

Reid also never forgot his high school pals, occasionally meeting them for lunch, regularly chatting with them on the phone. They truly loved one another and stayed close for nearly seven decades. His friend J. J. Balk wrote a poem about his Basic High classmate, a long string of verses that began:

Son of a Searchlight hard rock miner,
Harry Reid, he'll run for anything, yes indeed.
All knew early that Harry was a born fool,
When he chose to run for student body president of Basic High School,
He won that race with flying colors,
And we knew then and there, there would be numerous others

All politicians compartmentalize as a survival technique, but no one has ever done it as Reid did. For instance, he developed a sincere friendship with a Republican state senator named Warren Hardy, a fellow Mormon, but when election time came, Reid was out recruiting a candidate against him. Reid called Hardy when he left the state senate to offer condolences after his father died. But come campaign season, Hardy said, "I didn't realize how aggressively Harry Reid was trying to whack his good buddy. But it was just politics. It wasn't personal."

Reid also had a quality that separated him from most politicians, who were cocooned with enablers: he was remarkably self-aware. It helped that he had strong people he trusted who were willing to push back on him—Mike O'Callaghan, Susan McCue, David Krone, Rebecca Lambe, and, of course, Landra.

Nothing captured the two sides of Harry Reid better than his legacy of promoting and nurturing women in his orbit, including McCue, Lambe, and many others. He was clearly proud of that, but he suggested it was self-serving, too.

"First of all, if they're married, I told them that if they have a problem at home with their husband, don't come to work, work things out," Reid said before he died. "If you have a child or two, or something you need to do with them, stay home or take care of that. That's number one. I did that. As I said, people thought well, that's so nice. But it wasn't. It was very selfish on my part, because I know that helped me."

Reid's overall view of life was that he kept his word to people, and that was the quality he respected most. That's why he did not hesitate—although I am sure his staff cringed—to write character letters for a convicted murderer (Benny Binion), an impeached federal judge (Harry Claiborne), and a convicted inside trader (Billy Walters). It's also why he felt just as at home in the Old Nevada, dealing with mobsters or mob-adjacent types who ran the casinos—"There was no bullshit; they were people who live by their word," as he put it—as he was with the silk-suited corporate executives who succeeded them.

Reid respected successful people, but he despised those who he perceived had become rich not through hard work, acting as if they hit a home run when they were born on third base. That explains his disdain for Mitt Romney, for George W. Bush, for the Kochs. Reid was a self-made man, who came from nothing and made something of himself.

Reid also knew how to bond with people, through music—he had dozens of hours on his iPod but was partial to Woody Guthrie and Joan Baez, whose guitar he had hanging on a wall in his home. (Once, when he met U2's lead singer, Bono, Reid told him he was good, "but you're no Joan Baez.") He also connected through books—he exchanged them with friends and colleagues, especially biographies, and thanks to Evelyn Wood, he could read at lightning speed; and even movies—Reid was a film buff and even made a cameo in Steven Soderbergh's *Traffic*.

Reid's political legacy is indisputable. He changed Nevada into a reliably blue state, one that turned red only in the first cycle after he died, and his organization made and broke careers, helped decimate the Republican bench, and created an infrastructure that still exists after his death. The Reid Machine may live on, but it is like a car that has gone from having a Formula One racer at the wheel to one that is self-driving. Indeed, in the first presidential cycle after his death, the Reid Machine could not deliver Nevada for Kamala Harris. It is missing . . . something.

Reid, the man of so many contradictions, forever changed Nevada with his don't-call-it-pork billions, forever changed public policy by pushing through Obamacare and the economic stimulus package, and forever changed Washington with his ruthless, cutthroat style that led to spectacular victories and perpetual dysfunction.

While he would chafe at the comparison, he was LBJ without the profanity, a master of the Senate who didn't much care about what people thought of him so long as he accomplished what he wanted, no matter what he left in his wake.

Schumer and Pelosi pointed out during a ceremony as Reid lay in state at the Capitol that he would have hated all the pomp and circumstance that attended his death.

"His humility made him, some would say, unique in the political arena," Pelosi said. "It also made him truly beloved."

"Certainly Harry would have been deeply embarrassed, and probably a little annoyed at our holding not one, but multiple ceremonies in his honor," said Schumer.

Reid, after his final hang-up on the world, probably would have preferred Baez's simple lyric:

"When I'm dead and buried, don't you weep after me."

ACKNOWLEDGMENTS

This book would not have been possible without Harry Reid's cooperation, which was not easy to obtain. I had tried for years to get him to agree to a biography, but he consistently waved me off. Our relationship was not exactly smooth; as a lifelong Nevada journalist, I had often been quite scathing about him while also recognizing his prowess, and he tried to get me fired multiple times from the TV station owned by his good friend Jim Rogers. He finally achieved that goal after he met with Sinclair Broadcast Group executives, who were negotiating to purchase Rogers's NBC affiliates in Nevada after his death. When my program was canceled, Reid and his chief of staff, David Krone, celebrated in an email exchange I discovered while researching this book. Reid had asked David Smith, Sinclair's executive chairman, to fire me while the company was awaiting final approval on the purchase.

Smith emailed Krone shortly before the program was taken off the air at the end of 2014:

> When I met with the Senator in Vegas a while back, he mentioned to me that there was a program on Jim Rogers['s] station that was a rather large thorn in his side and that the show had it out for the Senator. Please let the Senator know that we have taken over the station and that biased individual will be leaving us shortly.

When Krone relayed the news to Reid, the senator's response was:

> U cannot believe the smile on my face! Convey to the new owners my deep, deep appreciation.

I knew firsthand what Reid was like—I had been writing about him since 1986 when he won his first Senate race—and I was not surprised. And yet: I still wanted to write the definitive biography of the most interesting and powerful man I had covered in my nearly forty-year career. Reid finally agreed to cooperate with me in the spring of 2021, despite the entreaties of Krone and others for him not to do so. Reid told me that we had something in common: we were both survivors, and while the retired senator knew he wouldn't like everything I wrote, he wanted to move forward. I am ever thankful for that and for the time he gave me before he died.

Reid and I began a series of Zoom interviews in late April 2021. We did a couple of dozen before he was too ill to continue, and I regret we did not have more time because I would have liked to have asked him about new information I uncovered during my reporting. He was more unguarded than he had ever been, even for him, and he provided me with some important insight into his behavior and motivations. Nearly every interview was memorable.

Reid also opened the door to a treasure trove of documents he donated to the University of Nevada, Reno Special Collections, a cache of emails, articles, and internal memos that illuminated so much and broadened my understanding of him and his career. Without the assistance of the peerless staff there led by Kim Anderson, and especially Jessica Maddox and Ian McGlory, I never would have found so many gems amid the hundreds of boxes and millions of digital files. The archive is not scheduled to be open to the public until later this year, so Reid's permission was essential.

I also want to thank Landra Reid, who granted me three sit-down interviews and made me understand even more why these two were together for six decades. She generously shared her unique understanding of her husband, and she helped clarify some of his blurry memories. (Thanks, also, to Key Reid, who facilitated and sat in on those interviews.)

This book also would not have been published without my agents at Javelin, Keith Urbahn and Matt Latimer, who believed in this project early on and who secured a contract with Simon & Schuster. My editor there, Mindy Marques, was both gentle and tough; without her, this book would have been bloated and unwieldy for everyone except me. She made this better, made me better.

Others who deserve special thanks:

Katie Rozner, a longtime Reid aide who was on most of the Zooms and helped guide him and me into productive discussions. She also helped me contact invaluable sources and access important documents. She is remarkable, and Reid was lucky to have her.

Reid's friends, including his high school classmates, were essential in helping me understand how Reid grew up, literally and figuratively.

Numerous Reid staffers and campaign workers took the time to tell stories and give insight that makes this book infinitely richer than it would have been. Extra-special thanks to Chris Brown and Valerie Wiener, who shared their old files. Brown was especially helpful—thank goodness he is such a pack rat.

So many of Reid's former colleagues granted me interviews, including every member of his leadership team and former Speaker Nancy Pelosi. President Obama and Hillary Clinton also were immensely helpful and, I believe, candid.

My friends Billy Vassiliadis, Bob Stoldal, and Elizabeth Thompson believed in this idea from a long time ago—their feedback and counsel were invaluable.

I am saddened that some of those close to Reid, especially Mike O'Callaghan, were not around to interview. I also regret that Mitch McConnell, John Ensign, and Dean Heller declined to be interviewed. I am very thankful that members of Ensign's 1998 campaign were willing to amplify what happened during the year that Reid's career almost ended, perhaps should have ended.

Finally, I cannot ever properly convey my gratitude for my wife's role in this process. Sara has not only patiently put up with four years of my obsession with this project, but she has been as supportive, with words of encouragement, and as helpful, as a sounding board, editor and researcher, as I could have wanted. Her embrace of this project and her unconditional love always surrounding me have meant everything.

NOTES

This book took years of research and interviews. I have tried to keep the endnotes to a reasonable length by not providing citations for well-known or widely covered historical events. Some of the material for this book was collected from two dozen interviews with Harry Reid in the spring and summer of 2021, shortly before he died in December. Unless otherwise noted, all Harry Reid quotes emanate from those conversations. I also conducted interviews with dozens of others, including family, friends, former staffers, and Capitol Hill colleagues, as well as searched through thousands of documents, including memos, handwritten notes, and newspaper clippings, many found in Reid's archive at the University of Nevada, Reno (referred to as "RA" in the notes), as well as reams of Gaming Control Board transcripts from Reid's 1977–81 tenure. Most of the Reid staffers went on the record for the quotes cited in this book, but in a few cases, they insisted they not be attributed. I also used stories from various newspapers and online publications to help contextualize the events of his life. Where convenient, I have aggregated newspaper citations into one note; where necessary, I cite individual articles. Contextual events generally were culled from contemporaneous news sources and not individually cited. All Landra Reid quotes come from three interviews in 2022 and 2023. Reid also obtained FBI files relating to him, most of them redacted but encased in his UNR archive. Of course, I also relied on my thirty years of reporting on and interacting with

Reid to frame the narrative where possible, and many of those contextual sections are not noted here.

PROLOGUE

1 *"out on a table"*: "Police Guarding H. Reid Family," *Las Vegas Review-Journal,* June 22, 1979.

3 *"tough as nails"*: Chuck Schumer at Reid remembrance in DC, January 12, 2022.

5 *"vengeance is in my soul"*: Reid staffer interview, July 14, 2022.

6 *"very insecure people"*: Kristen Orthman interview, November 4, 2022.

6 *"didn't worry about what people thought"*: Kai Anderson interview, November 1, 2022.

6 *"two people I hate"*: Jordan Gehrke interview, February 4, 2023.

CHAPTER 1: THE BOY WHO WOULDN'T FAIL

9 *origin of the town's name*: Searchlight history culled from Harry Reid, *Searchlight: The Camp That Didn't Fail* (Reno: University of Nevada Press, 2007), 49–50, and Harry Reid with Mark Warren, *The Good Fight: Hard Lessons from Searchlight to Washington* (New York: G. P. Putnam's Sons, 2008), 25.

11 *A stick of dynamite exploded*: Various contemporaneous articles, RA.

12 *making only $432*: Reid Sr. tax return, 1939, RA.

12 *Harry Reid Sr. was extraordinarily strong*: Interviews with Harry and Key Reid.

13 *Inez Orena Reid was gregarious*: Reid interviews.

14 *The school in Searchlight*: Reid interviews.

18 *even taking a C-SPAN crew*: "Searchlight: The Camp That Didn't Fail," C-SPAN, July 1, 1998, https://www.c-span.org/program/book-tv/searchlight-the-camp-that-didnt-fail/81593.

18 *"unfortunate characterization"*: AP letter, May 20, 1986, RA.

18 *"it serves as a reminder"*: Senate floor speech, July 21, 2008.

NOTES

CHAPTER 2: THE ONES WHO MATTERED

20 *"the missionary teachings of the church"*: Marlan Walker interview, March 25, 2022.

21 *"fell in love with being smart"*: Richie Vincent interview, January 20, 2022.

21 *"No one's gonna go check the yearbook"*: Left guard picture, Basic High School yearbook, 1957.

23 *He took her to a movie*: Landra Reid interview, April 7, 2022.

23 *"purest love"*: Rebecca Kirszner Katz interview, October 29, 2021.

25 *"There was always something different"*: Mike O'Callaghan, foreword to *Searchlight: The Camp That Didn't Fail*, by Harry Reid (Reno: University of Nevada Press, 2007).

26 *"he knew he was going to get hurt"*: J. J. Balk interview, January 7, 2022.

26 *had quite the list of accomplishments*: Basic High School yearbook, 1957.

26 *Doc Gould put his foot down*: Landra Reid interview, April 7, 2022.

28 *"We bought a case of Regal Pale beer"*: Vincent interview, January 20, 2022.

29 *"'So I gave it my best shot'"*: Walker interview, March 25, 2022.

30 *"I've never had anything like that"*: Don Wilson interview, January 21, 2022.

33 *"admitted at a later date"*: Bar exam order from Nevada Supreme Court, RA.

33 *admitted to the Nevada bar*: RA.

CHAPTER 3: LIFE BEFORE THE ARENA BECKONED

35 *"Harry Reid specials"*: Bruce Alverson interview, March 2, 2022.

36 *"Harry got him off"*: Richard Bryan interview, August 3, 2021.

36 *about $100,000 in today's dollars*: Reid tax return, 1964, RA.

36 *"Harry took that case"*: Mike O'Callaghan, foreword to *Searchlight: The Camp That Didn't Fail*, by Harry Reid (Reno: University of Nevada Press, 2007).

37 *"John Wayne, Wyatt Earp, and Dirty Harry"*: Rep. Dina Titus on the House floor, July 3, 2015.

37 *"Nobody took on Ralph in those days"*: Bill Marion interview, January 19, 2022.

37 *"He really felt sorry for people"*: Alverson interview, March 2, 2022.

37 *"Harry joined none"*: Bryan interview, August 3, 2021.

37 *by a unanimous vote*: Henderson council meeting minutes, August 25, 1965, RA.

37 *"inside track"*: *Las Vegas Review-Journal* editorial, August 25, 1965.

38 *Reid showed respectably*: Hospital trustee primary election results, Clark County government records, 1966.

39 *The ads emphasized*: Reid hospital trustee ads, 1966, RA.

39 *"it is essential that a new face come on the board"*: *Las Vegas Sun* endorsement, November 1, 1966, RA.

39 *it wasn't close*: Hospital trustee general election results, Clark County government records, 1966.

40 *Reid would get $28,000*: Law firm partnership agreement, March 13, 1967, RA.

41 *criticizing Staggs every chance he could*: Hospital board clips, 1966, RA.

CHAPTER 4: A CAPITAL IDEA

43 *one of nineteen candidates*: *Las Vegas Review-Journal*, July 17, 1968, RA.

43 *Reid also came forward with a proposal*: Reid campaign positions, 1968 assembly race, RA.

44 *his largest donor*: Reid legal pad contribution amounts, RA.

44 *"Harry Reid Is Qualified"*: Reid assembly ads, RA.

45 *he finished first*: Assembly primary election results, Clark County government records, 1968.

45 *The money kept coming in*: Assembly donations, Reid legal pads, 1968, RA.

45 *Reid's assault on the utility*: Reid vs. phone company, various newspaper clips, 1968, RA.

46 *propelling him to a first-place finish*: Assembly general election results, Clark County government records, 1968.

47 *"To Whom it May Concern"*: Reid memo, 1968, RA.

47 *"He dropped the nickel on us"*: Richard Bryan interview, August 3, 2021.

49 *"If my wife"*: Assembly journals, 1969 Nevada legislative session.

51 *the bill lost in a landslide*: Henderson dog track saga, various news clips, 1969, RA; assembly journals, 1969 Nevada legislative session.

52 *"They liked me better"*: Bryan interview, August 3, 2021.

52 *"He has qualifications"*: Paul Price clip, 1969, RA.

53 *Reid said he was committed to fight*: Lieutenant governor announcement speech, May 12, 1970, RA.

53 "*one-dollar hot dog cookout*": Bob List interview, September 23, 2021.

55 "*a fine young man*": Bob Broadbent announcement speech, 1970, RA.

55 "*uninformed, manufactured candidate*": Reid rebuttal to Broadbent speech, 1970, RA.

55 "*Agreement with O'Callaghan*": 1970, RA.

55 "*probably knows more*": *Review-Journal* endorsement for lieutenant governor, October 29, 1970, RA.

55 "*prominent Nevadans*": Reid family ad, 1970, RA.

56 *Reid won by nearly fourteen thousand votes*: General election results, Clark County government records, 1970, RA.

56 "*exceeded their most imaginative dreams*": Hank Greenspun column, *Las Vegas Sun,* November 8, 1970, RA.

CHAPTER 5: CHASING HUGHES AND CLIMBING THE NEXT RUNG

59 "*first saw Howard Hughes*": Memos written by Reid after series of meetings with Hughes intimates, RA.

62 *He received four separate payments*: Lawsuit deposition, December 10, 1973, RA.

64 "*The public will not identify*": Clark County Democratic convention remarks, 1972, RA.

64 "*So he didn't forget when payback time came*": J. J. Balk interview, January 7, 2022.

65 "*scene out of a cowboy movie*": Balk interview, January 7, 2022.

66 "*image and campaign approaches*": Gubernatorial campaign budget memo, October 1973, RA.

67 *O'Callaghan announced his decision*: "No Place Like Home Says Mike," *Las Vegas Sun*, April 7, 1974, RA.

CHAPTER 6: TWO STRIKES AND YOU'RE NOT QUITE OUT

69 *79,000 statewide Democratic voter registration edge*: Clark County government records, 1974.

70 *"The public is entitled to know"*: Dianne Trahan, "Reid Fires First Salvo," *Las Vegas Sun*, April 9, 1974.

70 *some welcome news*: Don Digilio, "Reid's First Campaign Break," *Las Vegas Review-Journal*, May 23, 1974.

71 *took issue with* Roe v. Wade: "Abortion Controls Needed—Reid," *Las Vegas Sun*, August 8, 1974.

71 *both Reid and Laxalt won handily*: "Laxalt and Reid Gain Finals in Race for the U.S. Senate," *Las Vegas Review-Journal*, September 4, 1974.

71 *"Income Projection"*: Legal pad memo, 1974, RA.

73 *a televised confrontation*: Ken Langbell, "Hughes Connection Debate Accepted," *Las Vegas Sun*, September 28, 1974.

74 *"possible grounds for a perjury case"*: Debates coverage, various clips from the *Sun* and *Review-Journal*, 1974, RA.

74 *"Laxalt's people cleverly turned that issue"*: Richard Bryan interview, August 3, 2021.

75 *"bold leadership"*: Various editorials on Reid vs. Laxalt, 1974, RA.

75 *"Northern Nevada newspapers treated me unfairly"*: "Reid Says Northern Press Cause of Loss," *Las Vegas Review-Journal*, November 8, 1974.

76 *Reid was acting Nixonian*: UPI, November 8, 1974.

76 *refused to pay bills*: Pat Caddell correspondence, July 17, 1975, RA.

76 *Reid's lawyers demanding a hand count*: Recount maneuvers, various newspaper clips, 1974, RA.

76 *he would have won*: Jon Ralston, "Paul Laxalt: The Man, the Myth, the Legend," *Nevada Independent*, August 12, 2018.

76 *"think about all the fun"*: Reid note to Laxalt, 2000, RA.

77 *"a staggering financial burden"*: Washoe Democratic Party speech, January 23, 1975, RA.

78 *"We didn't need another loss"*: J. J. Balk interview, January 7, 2022.

80 *"did not take it with grace and dignity"*: Various newspaper editorials, May–June, 1975.

CHAPTER 7: A NEW JOB, A BRIBE, AND A MOB ASSOCIATE

82 *The case would drag on for years*: Greenspun lawsuit, RA.

82 *"Your column, I have enjoyed"*: Reid note to Frank Rosenthal, June 1, 1976, RA.

82 *a notorious figure in Nevada*: Scott Roeben, "12 WTF Facts About Vegas Mobster Frank 'Lefty' Rosenthal," *Vital Vegas* (blog), November 5, 2014.

84 *"I don't intend to be tough"*: Harold Hyman, "Chairman Reid Vows Fairness," *Las Vegas Sun*, April 28, 1977.

84 *rare positive mention*: *Las Vegas Review-Journal* editorial, April 25, 1977.

84 *"a new era with Harry Reid"*: Rosenthal column, 1977, RA.

84 *"wouldn't hold water"*: Gaming Control Board transcript, July 24, 1977.

85 *"engineered by Harry Reid"*: Jeff Silver interview, March 4, 2022.

85 *"Reid came on strong"*: *Las Vegas Review-Journal* editorial, July 27, 1977.

86 *"I was concerned about it"*: Jeff Silver interview, March 24, 2022.

86 *"limping along for a long while"*: Gaming Control Board transcript, September 15, 1977.

87 *more appropriate for carnivals*: Gaming Control Board transcript, July 20, 1978.

88 *"'Jeff, you got to help me'"*: Silver interview, March 4, 2022.

88 *"Well, I guess we're all set to go"*: FBI internal documents, RA.

88 *"rattling of the doorknob"*: Bruce Alverson interview, March 2, 2022.

90 *"kangaroo court"*: Video of Rosenthal confronting Reid, *Mob on the Run*, 1978.

90 *Reid delivered a lengthy speech*: Gaming Control Board transcript, December 19, 1978.

91 *"Rosenthal was the perfect test case"*: Silver interview, March 4, 2022.

91 *he never considered booting the Democrat*: Bob List interview, September 23, 2021.

CHAPTER 8: CLEANFACE, MR. LAS VEGAS, AND OL' BLUE EYES

93 *the FBI began investigating Harry Reid*: FBI internal documents, various newspaper accounts, May/June 1979.

96 *"He said, 'Harry if you did something wrong'"*: Jay Brown interview, August 31, 2021.

98 *"There were no improprieties"*: "Mr. Clean Clean as a Whistle—Top Gamer Reid Totally Cleared," *Las Vegas Sun*, February 26, 1980.

99 *"I personally commend Wayne Newton"*: Gaming Control Board transcript, September 18, 1980.

100 *"He called Penosi"*: *Wayne Newton vs. NBC*, Reid deposition, March 4, 1982.

100 *"Life has no blessing like a prudent friend"*: Reid note to Newton, March 3, 2002, RA.

100 *Dorgan gave Reid a simple message*: Byron Dorgan interview, November 9, 2021.

101 *"I'm now a Frank Sinatra fan"*: Gaming Control Board transcript, September 18, 1980.

102 *"dignity, good grace, integrity and common sense"*: Various newspapers on Reid farewell, RA.

CHAPTER 9: MR. REID GOES TO WASHINGTON

103 *"The car was just missing"*: Harry Reid and Landra Reid interviews.

105 *He asserted he was a moderate*: Chris Broderick, "Reid Announces Bid for Congressional Seat," *Las Vegas Review-Journal*, October 6, 1981.

105 *"Nevada know-how"*: Campaign strategy memo, polling, 1982, RA.

107 *Reid insisted*: Jane Ann Morrison, "Names of 183 Spilotro's Callers Unsealed," *Las Vegas Review-Journal*, March 5, 1982.

107 *"I would have put two and two together"*: Stan Hunterton interview, January 22, 2022.

107 *pointing out the error*: Chris Broderick, "Reid Never Called Spilotro," *Las Vegas Review-Journal*, March 6, 1982.

107 *"This is not the time"*: Reid announcement speech, spring 1982, RA.

108 *"Government is good"*: Reid speech to Democratic convention, 1982, RA.

108 *"former lawman"*: TV ads, 1982, RA.

109 *"furnishing false information"*: FBI internal documents, 1982, RA.

111 *Reid began criticizing Yablonsky*: Letters to FBI with Barbara Vucanovich, October 4, 1983, RA.

112 *was even elected secretary-treasurer*: California delegation letterhead, "Ne-

vada Legislator Named Secretary-Treasurer of California Delegation," *Reno Gazette-Journal*, January 29, 1985.

113 *"one of only six people chosen"*: Jim Wright letter, 1985, RA.

113 *"my vote was made resolute"*: Reid note to President Reagan, March 1985, RA.

114 *"If I can ever be of any help"*: Reid note to *Review-Journal* executives, 1983, RA.

114 *one of the House's twenty millionaires*: Congressional financial disclosure, 1983, RA.

114 *"If you or any of your staff have further questions"*: UNLV resolution on nuclear waste, Reid note to Reagan, February 15, 1984, RA.

116 *"Nevada, Las Vegas is not clean"*: *60 Minutes* transcript, 1984, RA.

118 *All of Reid's media alliances*: Reid newspaper, TV endorsements, 1984, RA.

CHAPTER 10: A SECOND CHANCE

121 *"'Congratulations, Senator Reid'"*: Valerie Wiener interview, January 6, 2022.

121 *"orderly transfer"*: Tarrance poll, September 10, 1984, RA.

123 *"Reid may have intervened for mob figures"*: Associated Press, November 12, 1985.

123 *"Round 2 of the Mr. Clean battle"*: Larry Werner memo, November 14, 1985, RA.

124 *"the question of whether or not he took payoffs"*: Ned Day, "Specter of 'Mr. Cleanface' Still Haunts Harry Reid," *Las Vegas Review-Journal*, November 18, 1985.

124 *"Harry Reid and I had many differences"*: George Swarts, "Rep. Harry Reid's Record Defended," *Las Vegas Review-Journal*, November 24, 1985.

124 *a popular news anchor*: Sue Lowden fundraiser, 1985, RA.

126 *"all-time high"*: Chris Brown plan, 1985, RA.

127 *"We learned early on that Santini was a sweater"*: Reid interview.

128 *36–31 lead statewide*: Reid poll, February 1986, RA.

128 *"SINE QUA NON OF OUR ENTIRE STRATEGY"*: "Victory Vote Model," Spring 1986, RA.

129 *"I'm generally opposed to the regulation of guns"*: David Koenig, "Reid, Vucanovich Nix Interstate Ban on Gun Sales," *Las Vegas Review-Journal*, April 10, 1986.

129 *"They will be giving both of you an A rating"*: John Dingell note, October 1986, RA.

130 *"I could not, in good conscience"*: Pro-Family Coalition documents, October 1986, RA.

131 *"Harry Reid the man"*: Sandra Jolley interview, September 14, 2021.

131 *"I would do a better job"*: Steve Wynn note, March 21, 1986, RA.

132 "*donated huge amounts of money to my campaign*": Fertitta/Martinez note, 1986, RA.

133 "'*a Las Vegas politician who has done little or nothing*'": Rural Nevada Report, June 11, 1986, RA.

133 *"It was hard because they hated him"*: Rory Reid interview, July 25, 2022.

133 *"Goodness, lighten up"*: Santini note, spring 1986, RA.

134 *persuade the House Ways and Means chairman*: Dan Rostenkowski notes, Kennecott Bingham Copper Mine Modernization Project document, July 1986, RA.

134 *56 percent to 24 percent lead*: UNLV poll, September 12, 1986, RA.

134 *"The race goes well"*: Gary Hart note, September 22, 1986, RA.

135 *lacerating editorial*: *Las Vegas Review-Journal*, October 19, 1986.

135 *Two October debates were essentially nonevents*: Jon Ralston, "Reid, Santini Rehash Issues in Debate," *Las Vegas Review-Journal*, October 14, 1986.

136 "'*May your moccasins make many happy tracks*'": Claiborne note, November 11, 1986, RA.

CHAPTER 11: A BYRD IN THE HAND

137 *"your campaign has the organization"*: Bennett Johnston note, June 16, 1986, RA.

138 *Reid pivoted quickly*: Robert Byrd notes, November 1986, RA.

138 *Reid wasn't done lobbying*: Letters on Appropriations slot, November 1986, RA.

139 *his ability to funnel money and jobs*: Appropriations accomplishments memo, 1987, RA.

139 *"He watched the masters"*: Barbara Mikulski interview, March 9, 2022.

139 *"friend and mentor"*: Byrd notes, 1987, RA.

141 *"ambushed"*: Jim Santini, "Reid and Bilbray Ambushed at Conference Committee Pass," *Las Vegas Review-Journal*, December 21, 1987.

143 *long, handwritten thank-you note*: Souter letter, 2000, RA.

144 *"I wanted a conservative justice"*: Reid Bork speech, October 3, 1987, RA.

145 *nineteen-page memo*: Trippi "Nevada Plan," July 2, 1988, RA.

146 *"quiet, almost mousy man"*: Michael Barone, *The Almanac of American Politics* (Washington, DC: National Journal, 1987).

CHAPTER 12: FRIEND OF ENVIRONMENTALISTS AND MINERS

148 *This was still a tiny fraction*: Jon Ralston, "Wilderness Proposals Divide State Lawmakers, Challengers," *Las Vegas Review-Journal*, September 4, 1988.

148 *"it all worked out well"*: Dick Cheney note, November 11, 1989, RA.

149 *"You are a tough adversary!"*: Malcolm Wallop note, November 21, 1989, RA.

149 *"'We're not signing that'"*: Rogich interview, November 9, 2021.

150 *"They won't be able to quote me now!"*: President Bush thank-you note, December 6, 1989, RA.

150 *"They can continue to live in poverty"*: Mineral/Esmeralda note, 2008, RA.

151 *"'Why would I want to pick this up'"*: Marcus Faust interview, January 20, 2022.

152 *"'don't come out'"*: Sue Oldham, "A Look Back at the Truckee River Operating Agreement," December 10, 2015.

152 *"insurmountable odds"*: "Reid Water Bill a Monumental Achievement," *Reno Gazette-Journal*, November 21, 1990.

153 *the company eventually was able to fight him off*: T. Boone Pickens and Reid, various clips, RA.

154 *"these incredibly eloquent speeches"*: Michael Brown interview, February 9, 2022.

154 *"'People need to understand'"*: Jimmy Ryan interview, November 5, 2021.

156 *"may be of help"*: Reid note to ethics committee, October 24, 1990, RA.

157 *"we feel it is an embarrassment"*: Centel letters, mid-1989, RA.

CHAPTER 13: DOUBTING THOMAS

159 *"grossly insensitive to women"*: Shaun McKinnon, "Reid Aide: Nevadans 'Split' on Thomas," *Las Vegas Review-Journal*, October 11, 1991.

160 *"Judge Thomas is on trial before us"*: Reid speech on Clarence Thomas, October 15, 1991, RA.

161 *"every political bone in my body"*: Shaun McKinnon, "Nevadans Switch to Oppose Thomas," *Las Vegas Review-Journal*, October 11, 1991.

161 *"an embarrassment to the court"*: Michael A. Fletcher, "Reid Says He Could Back Scalia for Chief Justice," *Washington Post*, December 6, 2004.

161 *"five white men"*: "Harry Reid Apparently Thinks Clarence Thomas Is White," Fox News, July 9, 2014.

162 *guns . . . and abortion*: NEA questionnaire, February 1, 1992, RA.

163 *"mild-mannered but proven that he can be tough"*: Michael Barone, *The Almanac of American Politics* (Washington, DC: National Journal, 1993).

164 *"integrity and guts"*: Personality Parade, 1994, RA.

166 *"an adversarial tone"*: Del Webb memos, October 2, 1994, RA.

167 *"You are a great friend"*: Tom Daschle to Reid note, April 18, 1994, RA.

167 *"we've been friends too long"*: Chris Dodd to Reid note, December 7, 1994, RA.

168 *"if you don't mind"*: Dodd interview, December 10, 2021.

168 *"opposition from Nevada's senior senator"*: Frank Murkowski letter, September 26, 1996, RA.

169 *"the best orator"*: Senate notes, spring 1997, RA.

170 *"He's made some tremendous mistakes": Mining World* magazine, May 1995, RA.

170 *"hurt feelings"*: Notes to Bruce Babbitt, 1995, RA.

171 *"tragic mistake"*: "Senate Confirms Greenspan Despite a Few Demo Protests," Associated Press, June 21, 1996.

171 *Safire's political dictionary*: David Nir, "Reid: Greenspan 'One of the Biggest Political Hacks' in DC!" Daily Kos, March 3, 2005.

171 *"talk of the luncheon"*: Daschle email to Reid, March 2, 2004, RA.

171 *Reid led Ensign*: Senate poll, 1998, RA.

172 *"grants immigration preferences"*: Jon Ralston, "An Immigration Push Reid Regrets," *Las Vegas Sun*, July 21, 2010.

172 *"for which I am so apologetic"*: Senate floor speech, August 5, 2006, RA.

173 *"Hispanics are expanding their presence"*: Hispanic Leadership Summit brochure, 1997, RA.

CHAPTER 14: A NEAR-DEATH EXPERIENCE

178 *This is who Harry Reid was*: Reid record document, 1998, RA.

179 *"you could feel it"*: Mike Slanker interview, July 27, 2022.

179 *showed him well ahead*: Reid internal polling, late 1997, RA.

179 *"there had been very few candidates"*: Jack Finn interview, July 26, 2022.

179 *Reid with a robust advantage*: Jane Ann Morrison, "Reid Leads Ensign in Senate Race; District 1 House Candidates Close," *Las Vegas Review-Journal*, February 26, 1998.

180 *The rest of the high-level fundraising commitments*: Yellow legal pad fundraising numbers, 1998, RA.

180 *"like it was a hundred thousand dollars"*: Paul DiNino interview, January 11, 2022.

181 *"I can only attribute your frustration"*: Molasky letter, August 3, 1998, RA.

182 *"Nobody treated him worse than the Mormons"*: Rory Reid interview, July 25, 2022.

182 *"They decorated with his [Reid's] face"*: Megan Jones interview, August 31, 2021.

183 *"For Nevadans angry at Clinton"*: "Presidential Scandal Responses," September 1998, RA.

184 *the issue of Reid's seniority*: Various campaign materials, 1998, RA.

184 *a state Democratic Party poll*: Various polls, 1998, RA.

185 *"The high-level nuclear waste dump will be on its way"*: Brian Greenspun, "Clinton: I Need Reid," *Las Vegas Sun*, October 29, 1998.

185 *"three or four larger"*: Slanker interview, July 27, 2022.

186 *Reid's lead had completely evaporated*: Various interviews of Reid/Ensign aides about Election Night 1998.

187 *"a ballot not counted"*: Election hearing document, November 7, 1998, RA.

187 *victory would stand*: Martin Griffith, "Nevada Senate Race in Doubt After Judge's OK of Recount," *Las Vegas Sun*, November 8, 1998.

187 *Ensign had picked up 58 votes*: Various stories from Nevada newspapers in election aftermath, 1998, RA.

188 *"we are working a free media strategy"*: Internal Reid campaign documents, November 13, 1998, RA.

189 *"Possible Legal Issues Facing Senator Reid"*: Internal Reid recount documents/news stories, late 1998, RA.

190 *"Skip Recount This Time"*: News accounts/commentary culled from clips, late 1998, RA.

192 *"There was a box in the corner"*: Slanker interview, July 27, 2022.

193 *"they were all Jews"*: Joe Lieberman interview, January 18, 2022.

CHAPTER 15: BUILDING A MACHINE

196 *"a thorough analysis"*: Susan McCue memo, RA.

197 *"Reid saw that as an opportunity"*: Jimmy Ryan interview, November 5, 2021.

197 *"'we've got to get this bill done'"*: Eddie Ayoob interview, January 21, 2022.

198 *"get to know everybody's problems"*: Gary Myrick interview, November 2, 2021.

199 *"It was invaluable"*: Tom Daschle interview, November 3, 2021.

199 *"There are so many rules"*: Mikulski interview, March 8, 2022.

199 *"'You've got to do what I did'"*: Durbin interview, October 26, 2021.

200 *"the future of mining law reform remains uncertain"*: Bill Clinton mining letter, March 16, 1995, RA.

200 *"It's not going anywhere"*: Christine Dorsey, "Mining Fee Proposal Criticized," *Las Vegas Review-Journal*, November 17, 1999.

201 *Nevada's Hispanic population was projected to grow*: Hispanic outreach document, 1999, RA.

201 *"he has committed grievous wrongs"*: Floor speech on Clinton/Lewinsky, January 25, 1999, RA.

202 *pushed Reid to do meetings*: McCue meeting memos, 1999, RA.

205 *"Jim doesn't care if God is running"*: McCue leader matrix document, 1999, RA.

206 *"worst foreign policy mistake"*: "Reid: Iraq War 'Worst Foreign Policy Mistake' in U.S. History," CNN, February 18, 2007.

CHAPTER 16: A LEADER IS BORN

208 *"change in policy"*: McCue memos on ethics, October 22, 2002, RA.

209 *"the Name to Know Is Reid"*: Chuck Neubauer and Richard T. Cooper, "In Nevada, the Name to Know Is Reid," *Los Angeles Times*, June 23, 2003.

210 *"The article is slanted"*: Kai Anderson note, June 23, 2003, RA.

210 *"highly misleading parts"*: Dean Baquet letter, June 2003, RA.

210 *"Irresponsible, inaccurate journalism"*: Harry Reid response packet, June 2003, RA.

211 *"Senator Downplays Family Ties"*: *Las Vegas Sun* and *Las Vegas Review-Journal* clips, June 2003, RA.

211 *"No family member of the Senator"*: McCue updated memo on lobbying, June 8, 2006, RA.

213 *"a bunch of broken-down desks"*: Rebecca Lambe interview, May 15, 2023.

213 *immediately notify the senator*: VIP list, Front Desk Manual, RA.

213 *"is clearly in trouble"*: Southwest Group poll memo, July 4, 2003, RA.

214 *"we want there to be a Republican primary"*: Leif Reid memo, October 14, 2003, RA.

215 *"I don't need to think it through"*: Interviews with Reid, McCue, and others present on Election Night 2004.

216 *"Harry would work the phones"*: Durbin interview, October 26, 2021.

216 *"We are faced with a wartime President"*: Reid remarks to caucus, November 13, 2004, RA.

CHAPTER 17: CREATING A WAR ROOM AND DEFENDING THE FILIBUSTER

219 *"war room"*: Susan McCue postelection memos, November 2004, RA.

220 *"Harry Reid was way behind"*: McCue interview, November 4, 2021.

220 *"never been done before"*: Rebecca Katz interview, October 29, 2021.

221 *"serious political universe"*: Ari Rabin-Havt interview, February 1, 2022.

222 *"it was an easy answer"*: Patty Murray interview, January 20, 2022.

222 *"he really meant it"*: Durbin interview, October 26, 2021.

222 *"I earned capital"*: Marc Sandalow, "Bush Claims Mandate, Sets 2nd-Term Goals," *SF Gate*, November 5, 2004.

223 *"We had to bring his numbers down"*: Nancy Pelosi interview, November 2, 2021.

223 *"Reid had a significant problem"*: Rabin-Havt interview, February 1, 2022.

225 *"A few students chuckled"*: Erin Neff, "DEL SOL HIGH SCHOOL APPEARANCE: Reid Calls Bush 'a Loser,'" *Las Vegas Review-Journal*, May 7, 2005.

225 *"'this guy is a loser'"*: Tessa Hafen interview, January 31, 2022.

226 *"You've called Bush a loser"*: Eric Bates, "Harry Reid: The Gunslinger," *Rolling Stone*, June 16, 2005.

226 *"We were on equal footing"*: Katz interview, October 29, 2001.

226 *a group the war room created*: Latinos for a Secure Retirement, February 25, 2005, RA.

227 *"target list"*: Filibuster target list/strategy memo, 2005, RA.

228 *"just an extension of the House"*: *Face the Nation* transcript, April 10, 2005, RA.

229 *"spotty record of verbal gaffes"*: David Broder, "Nuclear Cloud over the Senate," *Washington Post*, May 18, 2005.

229 *"The nuclear option is gone"*: Carl Hulse, "Many Republicans Are Already Eager to Challenge Agreement on Filibusters," *New York Times*, May 25, 2005.

230 *"he was slurring and he was incoherent"*: Brian McGinty interview, August 2, 2021.

231 *looked and sounded fine*: Staff/Landra interviews.

CHAPTER 18: MEDDLING AT HOME AND IN A PRESIDENTIAL RACE

234 *"You have to really stretch things . . ."*: Matthew Continetti, "The Friends of Jack Abramoff," *Washington Examiner*, January 16, 2006.

234 *"a few verbal bombs"*: McCue poll reaction email, May 22, 2006, RA.

234 *his national role and his Nevada role*: Lambe response email, May 24, 2006, RA.

234 *pre–political obituary*: Sherman Frederick, "When Harry Met Nancy," *Las Vegas Review-Journal*, May 21, 2006.

235 *"'Why can't Tessa do it?'"*: Megan Jones interview, August 31, 2021.

236 *"Senator Reid was a chess player"*: Tessa Hafen interview, January 31, 2022.

237 *the man from Searchlight*: Daniela Deane, "Reid Elected as New Senate Majority Leader," *Washington Post*, November 13, 2006.

237 *"Harry is not a romantic"*: Barack Obama interview, March 22, 2022.

238 *"didn't know what to believe"*: Hillary Clinton interview, May 16, 2022.

238 *"I briefed him"*: Rebecca Lambe interview, May 15, 2023.

240 *"war is lost"*: Jeff Zeleny, "Leading Democrat in Senate Tells Reporters, 'This War Is Lost,'" *New York Times*, April 20, 2007.

240 *"a continuing embarrassment"*: David Broder, "The Democrats' Gonzales," *Washington Post*, April 25, 2007.

240 *"In this age of scripted politicians"*: Chuck Schumer response to Broder, RA.

241 *changing demographics*: Sasha Abramsky, "How the West Might Be Won," *Mother Jones*, September 2007.

241 *"I do not subscribe to Mother Jones"*: Reid to Durbin on *Mother Jones*, RA.

243 *"lead to Harry Reid"*: "Krolicki Blames Reid for Inquiry," *Las Vegas Review-Journal*, November 25, 2008.

244 *four felonies*: Steve Friess, "No. 2 Official in Nevada Is Indicted for Fraud," *New York Times*, December 3, 2008.

244 *"Harry was very, very supportive"*: Clinton interview, May 16, 2022.

CHAPTER 19: THE YEAR OF LIVING DANGEROUSLY

245 *"you know people are upset with you"*: Joe Lieberman interview, January 18, 2022.

245 *The vote was overwhelming*: "Senate Democrats Vote: Lieberman Keeps Chairmanship," ABC News, November 18, 2008.

246 *spending like drunken sailors*: Private Obamacare strategy sessions, notes from participant.

247 *"get to the bottom line"*: Rahm Emanuel interview, November 12, 2021.

248 *the Senate did so*: David Rogers, "Senate Passes $787 Billion Stimulus Bill," *Politico*, February 13, 2009.

248 *"I went to Senator Reid"*: Jim Murren interview, August 3, 2022.

250 *"this is going to be a permanent scar"*: Jimmy Ryan interview, November 5, 2021.

250 *"Harry said health care"*: Chuck Schumer interview, December 8, 2021.

250 *"I wanted to do financial reform first"*: Emanuel interview, November 12, 2021.

251 *"maybe too patiently"*: Durbin interview, October 26, 2021.

252 *"thought in fairly transactional terms"*: Barack Obama interview, March 22, 2022.

253 *"support a public plan"*: AARP meeting, 2009, RA.

254 *With too many voters*: Committee votes timeline, various news clips, 2009, RA.

254 *"I know Senator Schumer is your close friend"*: David Krone-Reid emails, October 15, 2009, RA.

255 *"When we fail to get 60 votes"*: Durbin interview, October 26, 2021.

255 *"'you got to get ready'"*: Barbara Mikulski interview, March 9, 2022.

256 *"I'm not gonna vote for the bill"*: Lieberman interview, January 18, 2022.

258 *"negotiate a deal with that"*: Patty Murray interview, January 20, 2022.

259 *"I don't know what would have happened"*: Barbara Boxer interview, August 3, 2022.

260 *"this monumental result"*: Chris Dodd note, December 24, 2009, RA.

260 *"transactional morality"*: David Broder, "Health Reform's Stench of Victory," *Washington Post*, December 24, 2009.

260 *"The bill was terrible"*: Nancy Pelosi interview, November 2, 2021.

262 *"The end's a-comin', Harry"*: Sherman Frederick, "Might Harry Call It a Day?" *Las Vegas Review-Journal*, January 10, 2010.

CHAPTER 20: THE RIGHT ANGLE

263 *They were most worried about Dean Heller*: Brandon Hall interview, February 9, 2023.

264 *"I hope you go out of business"*: Sherman Frederick, "Enough Is Enough, Harry," *Las Vegas Review-Journal*, August 30, 2009.

264 *Team Reid was going to be prepared*: Reid conclave notes, RA.

266 *released the police report*: Lisa Mascaro, "Reid, Lowden Spar over Car Bomb Story, Gibbons Joins Mix," *Las Vegas Sun*, October 28, 2009.

266 *"no Negro dialect"*: Jeff Zeleny, "Reid Apologizes for Remarks on Obama's Color and 'Dialect,'" *New York Times*, January 9, 2010.

267 *"don't worry about it"*: Barack Obama interview, March 22, 2022.

267 *"'It's a 9-1-1'"*: Megan Jones interview, August 31, 2021.

268 *"I deeply regret"*: Reid statement on Obama remarks, January 9, 2010, RA.

269 *"The general election starts today"*: Matt Fuehrmeyer interview, February 16, 2022.

269 *published a poll*: Steve Tetreault, "Lowden leads GOP Senate field," *Las Vegas Review-Journal*, February 28, 2010

269 *"The only time I ever saw Harry cry"*: Chuck Schumer interview, December 8, 2021.

270 *"Nutty NV Sen clip"*: Email from Kelly Steele to Eric Kleefeld, April 12, 2010.

270 *Kleefeld published the video*: Eric Kleefeld, "NV-SEN Candidate Sue Lowden (R): 'Barter with Your Doctor' (VIDEO)," Talking Points Memo, April 12, 2010.

271 *"they would bring a chicken to the doctor"*: "Nevada Newsmakers," April 19, 2010.

271 *"[We] were just dumbfounded"*: Paul Smith interview, September 6, 2022.

271 *"Has Sue Lowden Lost Her Mind?"*: Reid release on bartering, April 20, 2010, RA.

272 *knife, piercing her torso*: Brandon Hall cartoon, mid-2010, RA.

272 *Lowden coming back to the field*: Alexander Burns, "Poll: Angle Closes on Lowden," *Politico*, May 13, 2010.

272 *"I had a tap on my shoulder"*: Marlene Lockard interview, January 30, 2023.

272 *Angle had taken the lead*: "Angle Takes Lead in GOP Primary," *Las Vegas Review-Journal*, June 5, 2010.

273 *"He didn't believe it"*: Brandon Hall interview, February 9, 2023.

273 *"We all prayed and hoped"*: Fuehrmeyer interview, February 16, 2022.

275 *"Second Amendment remedies"*: Sam Stein, "Sharron Angle Floated '2nd Amendment Remedies' as 'Cure' for 'the Harry Reid Problems,'" HuffPost, June 16, 2010.

275 *"a lemon situation"*: Sam Stein, "Sharron Angle's Advice For Rape Victims Considering Abortion: Turn Lemons into Lemonade," HuffPost, July 8, 2010.

276 *"There was never a moment"*: Hall interview, February 9, 2023.

276 *"Reid Stands Up"*: NRA letter/Reid internal NRA document, 2009, RA.

277 *"The NRA will not be endorsing"*: Jim Geraghty, "No NRA Endorsement for Harry Reid," *National Review*, August 27, 2010.

277 *"We are going to win"*: Hall interview, February 9, 2023.

278 *"taking Sherm to the woodshed"*: Jon Summers memo, July 4, 2010, RA.

278 *The coordination was unmistakable*: Brian Greenspun, "The Motive Behind a Despicable Dig at Reid," *Las Vegas Sun*, July 11, 2010.

278 *the editor hung up on him*: James Rainey, "On the Media: Las Vegas Papers Take Sides in Reid-Angle Race," *Los Angeles Times*, July 16, 2010.

278 *"not here in Nevada"*: Scott Wong, "Critics Slam Reid Immigration Remark," *Politico*, July 14, 2010.

279 *"growing increasingly frustrated"*: David M. Drucker, "Finger-Pointing Begins as Reid Challenger Sags," Roll Call, July 23, 2010.

279 *"this could cause some problems"*: Justin Barasky email, August 10, 2010, RA.

280 *could have cost him the election*: Mellman polling, 2010, RA.

280 *"the 'hottest' member"*: Maggie Haberman, "Reid Calls Gillibrand the 'Hottest' Member at Fundraiser," *Politico*, September 20, 2010.

281 *"politically disconnected"*: Endorsement, *Las Vegas Review-Journal*, October 2, 2010.

281 *"what questions they will ask"*: Steven Montoya email, October 7, 2010, RA.

281 *had the race at 44–40*: Mellman polling, October 14, 2010, RA.

282 *detailed his wealth*: Reid wealth document, October 2010, RA.

283 *"he doesn't have the best cell service"*: David Krone email, October 15, 2010, RA.

283 *"Some of you look a little more Asian"*: Susan Saulny, "Video from Angle Event Reopens Subject of Race," *New York Times*, October 19, 2010.

283 *"get me out of this mess"*: Jordan Gehrke/Jarrod Agen interview, February 5, 2023.

284 *Gilbert wrote to the campaign*: Campaign internal emails on early voting/Election Day numbers, 2010, RA.

284 *"mining needs Reid"*: Tim Crowley email, November 2, 2010, RA.

285 *"craziest shit I've ever seen"*: Jordan Gehrke/Jarrod Agen interview, February 5, 2023.

286 *"do you think I'll get a holiday card"*: Sherman Frederick, "The High Price of Saving Reid," *Las Vegas Review-Journal*, November 6, 2010.

CHAPTER 21: DOING WHAT NO ONE ELSE WOULD DO

288 *"All of them got done"*: Barack Obama interview, March 22, 2022.

288 *"you just gotta roll the dice"*: Ryan Grim, "Harry Reid Had the Courage of Obama's Convictions," Intercept, January 11, 2022.

290 *"You can tell them to go to hell"*: Various David Krone emails, 2011, RA.

291 *"Let's talk to boss"*: Anderson/McCue emails, February 25, 2004, RA.

292 *"you are a man of your word"*: Reid note to Whittemore, late 2007, RA.

292 *"unknowingly filed a false report"*: Department of Justice release, May 29, 2013.

293 *"I wanted to put a Jew on the federal bench"*: Elissa Cadish nomination, letters, releases, various clips, Cadish/Reid interviews, late 2012, RA.

296 *"not paid taxes in 10 years"*: Sam Stein and Ryan Grim, "Harry Reid: Bain Investor Told Me That Mitt Romney 'Didn't Pay Any Taxes for 10 Years,'" HuffPost, July 31, 2012.

297 *"The word's out"*: Reid on Senate floor, August 2, 2012.

297 *"should hold himself to a high standard"*: Glenn Kessler, "4 Pinocchios for Harry Reid's Claim About Mitt Romney's Taxes," *Washington Post*, August 7, 2012.

298 *"reid being hypocritical"*: Reid tax return controversy, emails, Reid office documents, late 2012, RA.

299 *"Romney didn't win, did he?"*: Ashley Codianni, "Harry Reid Doesn't Regret Accusing Mitt Romney of Not Paying Taxes," CNN, March 31, 2015.

300 *"my good friend"*: *60 Minutes* staff, "An Exasperating Interview with Senate Leaders," CBS News, November 4, 2012.

CHAPTER 22: GOING NUCLEAR

304 *Never change the rules*: Ash Fork remembrance, 1986, RA.

304 *"I walked up the steps"*: John Boehner interview, December 7, 2021.

305 *"you have a tough job"*: Reid note to Boehner, January 3, 2013, RA.

306 *"Reid was showing he was an independent operator"*: Adam Jentleson interview, November 3, 2021.

307 *"major changes to the rules of the Senate"*: Graham-Wicker letter, August 2012, RA.

308 *"his own mind was made up"*: Jentleson interview, November 3, 2021.

308 *"felt it was the wrong decision"*: Durbin interview, October 26, 2021.

308 *"Harry was an institutionalist"*: Barack Obama interview, March 22, 2022.

309 *"sharing his frustration"*: Patty Murray interview, January 20, 2022.

309 *"lamented how broken the Senate had become"*: Tom Daschle interview, November 3, 2021.

309 *"They made a decision"*: 2008 C-SPAN transcript, November 5, 2008, RA.

310 *it passed 52–48*: Burgess Everett, "'Senate Goes for 'Nuclear Option,'" *Politico*, November 21, 2013.

310 *thundered with applause*: Faiz Shakir interview, January 14, 2022.

311 *"become an unworkable legislative graveyard"*: Harry Reid, "Harry Reid: The Filibuster Is Suffocating the Will of the American People," *New York Times*, August 12, 2019.

312 *"If you've already broken the glass"*: Richard Shelby interview, November 2, 2021.

312 *"I may have been right"*: Chuck Schumer interview, December 8, 2021.

312 *"I am so sad"*: Reid-Krone emails, October 10, 2013, RA.

315 *"Manchin drove him crazy"*: Internal communications on saving leadership slot, late 2014, RA.

316 *The meeting lasted four hours*: Manu Raju and Burgess Everett, "Reid's Red-State Defectors," *Politico*, November 13, 2014.

CHAPTER 23: AN EXERCISE BAND SLIPS AND A CAREER FADES AWAY

317 *band slipped out of Reid's hand*: Landra Reid interview, April 25, 2022.

318 *Khan told her to get him to the hospital:* Ike Khan interview, December 11, 2021.

318 *illuminate the chain of events*: Internal emails after Reid exercise band accident, early 2015, RA.

320 *"My hand is in the door"*: Paul DiNino interview, January 11, 2022.

321 *first media appearance*: Steve Tetreault, "Reid to Undergo Eye Surgery," *Las Vegas Review-Journal*, January 21, 2015.

322 *"just left him"*: Krone emails, early 2015, RA.

323 *"Reid is the weak link"*: Myrick email, March 16, 2015, RA.

323 New York Times *story*: Carl Hulse, "Harry Reid to Retire from Senate in 2016," *New York Times*, March 27, 2015.

323 *"I am not going to run for reelection"*: Reid retirement video, March 27, 2015.

325 *as if it had been choreographed*: Jose A. DelReal, "Catherine Cortez Masto Announces Bid to Succeed Harry Reid in the Senate, Gets DSCC Backing," *Washington Post*, April 8, 2015.

325 *he called the key vote*: Jon Ralston, "How Nevada Lost a Presidential Primary and, Perhaps, Its White House Race Clout," *Ralston Reports*, June 3, 2015.

326 *endorsing racist tropes*: Mike DeBonis, "Harry Reid Rips Antonin Scalia, Says He Endorsed 'Racist Ideas' from Bench," *Washington Post*, December 10, 2015.

326 *ludicrously claiming*: Louis Jacobson, "Harry Reid Is Way Off on Claim that 30% of Women Rely Only on Planned Parenthood for Health Care," PolitiFact, July 31, 2015.

326 *"I think they're all losers"*: John Harwood, "CNBC Digital Video Exclusive: Senate Democratic Leader Harry Reid Sits Down with CNBC's Chief Washington Correspondent John Harwood," CNBC, April 15, 2015.

326 *jury would take only an hour*: Exercise band lawsuit, RA.

327 *telephoned the head of the Culinary*: Jon Ralston, "Reid-Culinary Bond Won Nevada for Clinton," *Reno Gazette-Journal*, February 20, 2016.

327 *"He [Reid] shared my opinion"*: Hillary Clinton interview, May 16, 2022.

328 *had no compunction*: Niels Lesniewski, "Harry Reid Calls Trump Campaign 'Fat, Ugly and Dirty,'" Roll Call, October 18, 2016.

328 *"Trump, his top advisors, and the Russian government"*: Comey letter, August 27, 2016, RA.

329 *spoke for more than an hour*: Reid farewell speech, YouTube.

331 *all manner of names*: Devan Cole, "Harry Reid: Trump Is 'Amoral' and 'the Worst President We've Ever Had,'" CNN, January 2, 2019.

331 *"I'm not embarrassed or ashamed"*: Helene Cooper, Ralph Blumenthal, and Leslie Kean, "Glowing Auras and 'Black Money': The Pentagon's Mysterious U.F.O. Program," *New York Times*, December 16, 2017.

332 *"there's still a great deal we don't understand"*: Harry Reid, "What We Believe About U.F.O.s," *New York Times*, May 21, 2021.

332 *"'What has he got me into here?'"*: Durbin interview, October 26, 2021.

333 *"does not have long to live"*: Mark Leibovich, "Harry Reid Has a Few Words for Washington," *New York Times*, January 2, 2019.

334 *cancer-free*: Sean Neumann, "Former Sen. Harry Reid Says He's in 'Complete Remission' After Pancreatic Cancer Treatment," *People*, June 25, 2020.

335 *the senator was proud of the renaming*: Howard Stutz, "Tributes Pour In as Las Vegas' McCarran Airport Renamed After Harry Reid," *Nevada Independent*, December 14, 2021.

335 *"I love you, my forever friend"*: Wayne Newton interview, September 7, 2022.

EPILOGUE

337 *"He didn't believe in highfalutin theories"*: Reid funeral video, YouTube, January 8, 2022.

338 *"He protected the gaming industry"*: Jeff Silver interview, March 4, 2022.

338 *"totally uninterested in all of the razzmatazz"*: Bruce Babbitt interview, January 9, 2023.

338 *"practically unmatched"*: Leshy letter, via Leshy interview, January 13, 2023.

339 *"tough son of a bitch"*: Boehner interview, December 27, 2021.

340 *"Son of a Searchlight hard rock miner"*: Poem via J. J. Balk.

342 *"made him truly beloved"*: Nancy Pelosi interview, November 2, 2021.

342 *"deeply embarrassed"*: Chuck Schumer interview, December 8, 2021.

INDEX

INDEX

INDEX

INDEX